ESSENTIAL
GCSE ENGLISH FOR
MATURE STUDENTS

Also in the HarperCollins Essential Series

Essential Psychology
G.C. Davenport

Essential Government and Politics
Jim Cordell

Essential Marketing
Tony Proctor

Essential Accountancy and Finance
Bijon Kar

Essential Business Studies
Stephen Barnes

Forthcoming Titles in the Essential Series

Essential Research Skills
Val Bailey et al.

Essential Information Technology
Tony Berk

Essential GCSE Business Studies
Renee Huggett

Essential Business Law
Paul Hilder

Series Editor: Roger Gomm

ESSENTIAL
GCSE ENGLISH FOR
MATURE STUDENTS

Diana Wallsgrove

Collins Educational
An imprint of HarperCollins*Publishers*

Published by Collins Educational
77–85 Fulham Palace Road
Hammersmith
London W6 8JB

0003223604

A catalogue record for this book is available from the British Library.

Design by Derek Lee.
Cover by Ridgeway Associates and David Jones.

Typeset by Create Publishing Services Ltd, Bath.
Printed and bound by Cambridge University Press, Cambridge.

Acknowledgements

Chapter 1   Describing

Unit 1
P.D. James, *Devices and Desires*, Penguin 1991

Unit 2
Henrik Ibsen, *Hedda Gabler*, Methuen 1980
James Joyce, 'Eveline', *The Dubliners*, Penguin 1992
A.S. Byatt, *Possession*, Vintage 1991
Ben Okri, *The Famished Road*, Vintage 1992
Elizabeth Taylor, *Angel*, Virago 1984
Mary Webb, *Precious Bane*, Duckworth 1978
H.G. Wells, 'The Country of the Blind', *Selected Short Stories*, Penguin 1989
Patricia Beer 'The Fifth Sense', *Collected Poems*, Carcanet Press, 1988

Unit 4
Amy Tan, *The Joy Luck Club*, Minerva (an imprint of Mandarin Paperbacks) 1990
E.M. Forster, *A Passage to India*, Penguin 1989

Unit 5
Dylan Thomas, 'One Warm Sunday', *Portrait of the Artist as a Young Dog*, Everyman
    Classics, Dent 1991
Mary Webb, *Precious Bane*, Duckworth 1978
Ben Okri, *The Famished Road*, Vintage 1992

Unit 6
Club Cantabrica Brochure 1992, Holiday House
Robin McKie, The *Observer*, 26 July 1992
John Collee, The *Observer*, 12 July 1992

Chapter 2   Narrating

Unit 2
William Shakespeare, *Romeo and Juliet*, The Alexander Text of the Complete Works of Shakespeare,
    HarperCollins

Unit 3
Wilkie Collins, *The Woman in White*, Penguin 1994
Don Taylor, *The Exorcism*, Samuel French 1981
Charlotte Bronte, *Jane Eyre*, Penguin 1994
P.D. James, *Devices and Desires*, Penguin 1991

Unit 4
Richard Harris, *Stepping Out*, Amber Lane 1985
Amy Tan, *The Joy Luck Club*, Minerva (an imprint of Mandarin Paperback) 1990
Alan Ayckbourn, *How the Other Half Loves*, Samuel French 1982
David Hare, *Racing Demon*, Faber and Faber 1991
Brian Clark, *Whose Life is it Anyway?* Heinemann Educational 1993

Unit 5
Anonymous, *Tam Lin*

Chapter 3   Responding to Literature

Unit 1
Isaac Asimov, 'Insert Knob A into Hole B', *Nightfall and Other Stories*

Unit 2
William Shakespeare, Sonnets, The Alexander Text of the Complete Works of Shakespeare, HarperCollins.
Adrian Henri, 'Love Is', *Penguin Modern Poets: The Mersey Sound*, Penguin 1974
James Joyce, 'Eveline', *The Dubliners*, Penguin 1992

Unit 3
Company Magazine
Independent on Sunday
John Naughton, The *Guardian*, 7 July 1994

Unit 4
Rupert Brooke, 'The Soldier', *Collected Poems, 4th Edition*, Sidgwick and Jackson 1987
Elizabeth Chandler, 'The Three Lads', *Scars Upon My Heart: Women's Poetry and Verse of the First World War*, edited by Catherine Reilly, Virago 1981
Wilfred Owen, 'Dulce et Decorum Est', *The Collected Poems of Wilfred Owen*, Chatto and Windus 1963
Wilfred Owen, 'Exposure', *The Collected Poems of Wilfred Owen*, Chatto and Windus 1963
Eva Dobell, 'Night Duty' *Scars Upon My Heart: Women's Poetry and Verse of the First World War*, edited by Catherine Reilly, Virago 1981

Unit 5
William Blake, 'Infant Joy', *Songs of Innocence and Experience*, Oxford University Press 1990
William Blake, 'Infant Sorrow', *Songs of Innocence and Experience*, Oxford University Press 1990
Spike Milligan, 'The New Rose', *Small Dreams of a Scorpion*, Michael Joseph Ltd 1972
Spike Milligan, 'Unto Us', *Small Dreams of a Scorpion*, Michael Joseph Ltd 1972
Thomas Hardy, 'To an Unborn Pauper Child', *Collected Poetry*
Louis MacNeice, 'Prayer Before Birth', *Poetry, 1900–75* edited by George MacBeth, Longman 1980

Chapter 4   Informing and Reporting

Unit 4
London–Crewe–Chester–North Wales–Liverpool British Rail Timetable, not current

Chapter 5   Arguing and Persuading

Unit 2
Anna Coote, *Equal at Work? Women in Men's Jobs*, Collins 1979
Selima Hill, 'The Ram', *New British Poetry*, Grafton 1988
Charlotte Bronte, *Jane Eyre*, Penguin 1994

Contents

Introduction

Starting Your Course

Welcome to *Essential GCSE English*! Before you start working towards your English qualification, there are probably a few questions that you'd like to ask. I'll try to provide the answers for you here.

What Equipment Do You Need?

You don't need very much equipment. These are the essential items:

- **Paper** – a supply of A4 paper is necessary, mainly it should be ruled but some plain might come in handy.
- **Pen** – you obviously need something to write with. You will find in some assignments that you can use more than one colour and may be writing large headlines. Some coloured felt tip pens and a pencil may be useful.
- **Dictionary** – you need to have a dictionary. *The Collins Paperback English Dictionary* is inexpensive and perfectly adequate for this course. Get into the habit from the start of checking the spelling or meaning of words whenever you are uncertain.

These items are optional:

- **A Notebook** – a notebook with an alphabetical index where you can keep a record of useful words and their meaning.
- **A Typewriter or Word Processor** – if you have access to a typewriter or word processor, you may wish to type some assignments. It is never compulsory to do so and syllabuses limit the percentage of coursework that can be typed (usually 30 per cent). If typing would improve the presentation of a piece of work this is made clear in the instructions given for that task.
- **A Tape Recorder** – a tape recorder on which you can record what you say may be useful. In a number of oral assignments you are allowed to make a tape rather than speaking directly to your tutor or group of students. If you have a suitable machine at home, fine, if not, and you have joined a class at a college, one will be provided when necessary by your tutor.

What Does the Course Involve?

Three main areas are assessed on your course:

1 **Speaking and listening** (20 per cent) – Attainment Target En 1.
2 **Reading** (40 per cent) – Attainment Target En 2.

3   **Writing** (40 per cent) – Attainment Target En 5.

Spelling, handwriting and presentation are also included in writing as Attainment Targets En 4 and 3.

Assessment is made in two ways:

1   **Coursework** (40 per cent of the total).
2   **Examination** (60 per cent of the total).

Speaking and listening is only assessed during the course; there is no exam.

Reading and writing are partly assessed through coursework and partly through examination. For each, 10 per cent is assessed through coursework and 30 per cent in the exam.

What Will You Be Doing?

During the course you will be producing work suitable for your coursework folder and practising for the examination.

What Speaking and Listening Coursework Will You Need to Do?

You will do a variety of activities. Some will involve conveying and understanding information, others expressing and responding to ideas and feelings. You are likely to do some assignments on you own and other work in a pair or group situation. You will keep a record of all the assessments you have done either on the Coursework Index Form in the Appendix at the back of this book or on one like it provided by your tutor. You will select you best pieces, with guidance from your teacher, to enter in your Coursework Record Form. This form will be provided by the examining board.

What Reading and Writing Coursework Will You Need to Do?

The requirements of individual syllabuses vary a little. Your tutor will tell you which syllabus you are following so that you can make sure that you do everything necessary.

You will certainly have to read and respond to a whole work of literature. This doesn't have to be as daunting as it sounds. A 'whole work' can mean a short story and the term 'literature' doesn't imply that it has to be heavy and serious. You have to study a work by Shakespeare but it doesn't have to be a play, it can be a short poem. You need to have one piece in your final folder 'in response to literature' but it doesn't have to be the piece on Shakespeare.

Most syllabuses ask for 'personal' writing. This is where you are expressing thoughts and feelings of your own or of the characters in a story or situation. You will find plenty of varied activities in Chapters 1 and 2 of this book that would be suitable.

One syllabus specifies that a piece about language should be included in the folder (consult the Activity List, page 309). Others merely ask for candidates to produce a variety of types of writing.

As with speaking and listening coursework, you will keep a record on your Index Form of all the pieces of coursework that you have submitted for assessment. Guided by your tutor, you will select your **best** pieces, making sure that you have covered everything that the syllabus requires. Your folder will probably contain four or five pieces with a total length of 1500 to 2000 words.

How Will You Prepare For the Exam?

Apart from speaking and listening, the skills assessed in the exam are the same as those assessed in the coursework. The only difference is that in coursework you have the opportunity for revising and redrafting as there is no specified time limit. By working on the coursework you will improve your English skills. In the exam you will be tested on the same skills.

The structure of the examination varies from one syllabus to another. Your centre will have chosen an examining group and a syllabus to meet the needs of its students. Your tutor will have told you which syllabus you are following and will probably give you some sample or past papers to practise on. If you wish to, you may obtain papers yourself by writing directly to the board. You should telephone before sending in an order to find out what is available and how much it will cost.

You do not need to learn pages of facts for your English exam. You will be presented with written material, and your understanding will be assessed through your answers to some questions. You are also likely to be asked to respond sensitively and appropriately to written material, including an extract from literature, perhaps writing a description, continuing a story, writing instructions or a factual article or producing a persuasive letter or leaflet. Again, many units have activities of this sort. The accuracy and presentation of you work is assessed – as it will be by your tutor.

How Can You Make Sure That You are Fully Prepared?

1   Look at the table on page 315. Here you will see a list of the activities that are similar to those which may appear in the examination and which should be done within a recommended time limit. Do as many of these as you feel to be necessary or useful.

2   Look carefully at Chapter 6. You will be consulting this chapter at various times during the course but shortly before the exam it would be sensible to work carefully through some of the units, depending on what your strengths and weaknesses are. You may wish to brush up on such aspects as speech punctuation and letter layouts. It would be a good idea to read and do the exercises in Unit 5, 'Choosing the Right Word'.

Now That You Know What's Involved, Where Should You Start?

This book is arranged into chapters that deal with the varieties of communication involved in English.

You should complete the **first** unit in **every** chapter. You should then, as a rule, select at least **one more** unit from each.

If you wish to find a task that covers a particular aspect of your course, consult the Activity List in the Appendix, page 309. The list indicates the following:

- speaking and listening coursework;
- reading coursework;
- writing coursework;
- response to literature coursework;
- study of language coursework;
- examination practice.

# **1** *Describing*

*I*N this chapter we'll be looking at one broad area of personal writing and we'll be trying out some speaking and listening activities. Most syllabuses say that personal writing should be included in a coursework folder so it's a good idea to tackle at least one unit from this chapter.

This is what we will be working on:

- giving a precise and accurate description of a person or a place;
- choosing words carefully both in speech and in writing;
- understanding the need to use different words in different situations;
- revising work so that it's both interesting and correct;
- reading closely to see what methods can be used and what their effects are.

Where Should You Begin?

Work through all the activities in Unit 1. You may then choose another unit from this chapter – it's advisable to do about two units from each – or you may prefer to turn to the first unit of another chapter, returning to this one later in the course.

At the end of Unit 1 you will find a summary of the Keystage 4 Attainment Targets that you have covered. Write down the assessed coursework, along with the relevant Attainment Targets on your Coursework Index Form. You will find this in the Appendix or you may have been issued with one by your tutor.

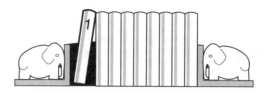

UNIT *Positive Identification*

How closely do we look at the people around us? How much can you remember about the appearance of a bank teller or shop assistant who served you recently? Can you describe clearly someone you saw earlier today? If you can, it's probably because of some distinctive feature which made that person stand out.

ACTIVITY

Preparatory Writing – Observation

Spend a few minutes looking closely at someone. Don't be embarrassed, really examine the face, trying to pinpoint the shape of each individual feature. Move on to the hair, body shape and clothes. What makes that person's physical appearance unique?

Write a paragraph describing the person carefully, starting with the face and moving on to other aspects. Don't guess or make assumptions. If the person is sitting down, can you estimate how tall he or she is? Could your description apply to anyone else? If it could, it's not precise enough.

When you have finished, read through what you have written. If that person moved away, leaving behind an important-looking bag, could someone else make a positive identification of him or her from your description? If you don't feel that would be possible, alter your descrip-tion until you're satisfied it would be.

Now read the two passages below. Each describes the same person. In terms of style, is your own description more like the first or the second extract?

Passage A

The girl sitting across the room from me looks quite young. Her face is medium sized and rather round. Her nose is quite small, her mouth is medium sized. Her hair is dark and quite long. You can't see her ears very well. She isn't wearing any make-up. She has hoop gold earrings and is wearing some rings. She is wearing jeans, a T-shirt and Reebok trainers. She is of medium height.

Passage B

The girl sitting across the room looks about eighteen but may be a little older. Her face is round and she has a dimple in her right cheek when she smiles. Her nose is very small and it's slightly tilted upwards at the end. It's like the little button noses young children have. She might find it difficult to wear spectacles! Her eyes are a very dark brown and her eyelashes are thick – she may use mascara. Her eyebrows form a regular curve and may have been plucked to get an even shape. They are quite thin but dark brown in colour. Her complexion is pale and fairly healthy. She does have a few small blemishes on her chin and her forehead and she has a mole above her right eyebrow. Her mouth is small with the lower lip fuller, suggesting a gentle and sensitive personality. Her hair just reaches her shoulders. It is brushed back from her forehead but covers her ears. She frequently runs her fingers through it to get it off her face. Her large gold hoop earrings can just be seen. On her right hand she is wearing a gold signet ring and on her left hand, two silver rings, one plain, one shaped like clasped hands. Her clothes are very casual. She is wearing a white T-shirt with a small logo embroidered in purple on the front. Her jeans are Levi 501s and she is wearing Reebok trainers. These are white with purple trimmings. The trainers look quite old as they are rather battered and a little muddy.

Would a reliable identification be possible from Passage A?

Compare the two descriptions carefully and look back at your own. What makes a description precise and vivid? From Passage A, pick out vague, meaningless phrases. From Passage B, pick out the more distinctive phrases that could apply only to this person.

Make a list of words that could be used to describe the shapes of people's features. You could do this in a group so that ideas are shared. Try using *Roget's Thesaurus* to broaden your vocabulary. Do check words in a dictionary, though, to make sure they're suited to the context in which you wish to use them.

ACTIVITY

1b

Preparatory Writing – Beauty or the Beast

In this activity, instead of using observation, use imagination. Write a paragraph describing either the most beautiful person you can picture **or** the most hideous and terrifying. Don't attempt to make up a story, just describe their appearance. Use precise meaningful words and avoid words like 'nice', 'pleasant', 'ugly', 'nasty'. Tell the reader **exactly** what you are visualising. Make sure you write in sentences rather than in note form.

When you feel that you have finished, read your work through carefully. Does it convey a vivid picture? Would we admire this person or cringe from him or her in terror? Is it accurate? Check your spelling using a dictionary (the *Collins Paperback Dictionary* would be a good one to use). Check your punctuation (you can consult Chapter 6 for help with this).

If possible, read your description aloud to someone. See if it provokes the response you were aiming at.

ACTIVITY

1c

Reading and Understanding

Read the following description. It is taken from the detective novel *Devices and Desires* by P.D. James. Check any words you are unfamiliar with in the dictionary.

> He rang and there was only a short delay before Alice Mair opened the door. He saw a tall, handsome woman dressed with careful and expensive informality in a black cashmere sweater with a silk scarf at the throat and fawn trousers. He would have recognised her from her strong resemblance to her brother, although she looked the elder by some years. She took it for granted that each knew who the other was. . . . It was a distinguished face with deep-set, widely spaced eyes beneath straight brows, a well-shaped, rather secretive mouth and strong greying hair swept upwards and curled into a chignon. In her publicity photographs she could, he recalled, look beautiful in a somewhat intimidating, intellectual and very English mould. But seen face to face, even in the informality of her own house, the absence of a spark of sexuality and, he sensed, a deep-seated reserve, made her seem less feminine and more formidable than he had expected, and she held herself stiffly as if repelling invaders of her personal space.

Devices and Desires, P.D. James

This passage occurs towards the beginning of the novel. The male character is Adam Dalgliesh, a high-ranking police officer from Scotland Yard. Dalgliesh is meeting Alice Mair for the first time, on a purely personal matter. Consider these questions:

a Is there anything in the description that might suggest that Dalgliesh is a detective?

b What impressions do we obtain of Alice Mair's personality from the description? How would the picture of her change if we replaced the words 'strong greying' with 'fluffy blond'?

c Clearly, at this stage, the author is not going to give away the fact that the woman is a killer. Does the writer drop any hints that she might be? Pick out particular words that could fit with this knowledge. Knowing that she is a murderer, do we interpret parts of this passage differently?

ACTIVITY

1d

Coursework – Writing

We often have the opportunity to observe people we don't know. Sometimes we draw conclusions about their lives and personalities from their appearances. Next time you're in a café or restaurant, look at the people at the next table and invent the relationships between them and speculate about their circumstances. You'll probably come to all the wrong conclusions but it's an entertaining game!

Choose one of the titles listed below for a piece of written work:

- In the Queue;
- The Waiting Room;
- On the Tube Train.

Planning

Whichever title you choose, invent two or three characters who are present and describe them vividly. Try to give suggestions, from your description, about their personalities and circumstances. Don't write about more than three people – you won't have time to go into enough detail.

You may wish, briefly, to describe the setting. That may be a good idea, but concentrate on the people. Don't include conversation – we'll come to speech later on. Speech punctuation is tricky so it's best to avoid it for the moment. Perhaps this is one of those situations in which no one speaks to anyone else.

If, for example, you choose to write about 'The Waiting Room', and you decide it is at the dentist's, you may wish to give an atmosphere of anxiety. Similarly, if you choose 'In the Queue', decide what sort of queue it is and how different people may react to a boring and uncomfortable wait.

Aim to write about 500 words – that's about two sides of A4 paper in average-sized handwriting. Don't worry too much about layout and neatness at this stage.

Drafting and Revising

When you feel that you've finished, carry out the checks listed below (you may wish to consult your tutor at this stage).

Content

Have you given a vivid and precise impression of each person described? If not, replace vague words with more meaningful ones. Would your piece be more effective if the characters were presented in a different order? Do you convey a sense of actually being there? Revise and adjust it accordingly.

Accuracy

Is the spelling correct? Check words you are unsure of in the dictionary. Is the punctuation accurate, especially the placing of full stops? Does it make perfect sense? (Consult Chapter 6.)

Try to look at your work as if it's someone else's. It's all too easy to see what you intended to write rather than what's actually there. Sometimes it helps if you can put your work aside for a day or two and then return to it.

Turn now to the advice in Chapter 6, Unit 6 about the presentation of written work.

When you are happy that you have checked this piece thoroughly, write it out neatly. Put the title, your name and the date of writing at the top. You can now hand it in to your tutor for assessment.

ACTIVITY

1e

Coursework – Speaking and Listening

This activity should be carried out in a group of three people. It's a bit like the game 'Chinese Whispers' which you may have played as a child.

Positive identification may sometimes be made from an oral rather than a written description. This is the situation: a message must be passed to a particular man in Room F109 of the Apex Building. You don't know his name but you have been given a description of his physical appearance. The message contains sensitive information concerning 'a matter of National Security' and so it is very important that the right man can be recognised from the description.

1   Work out in your own mind what the man looks like. He must be an ordinary-looking person (not like the character you wrote about in 'Beauty or the Beast'!). Think of about ten specific things to describe his appearance.

   A crisis arises and you are unable to pass the information to him yourself. Therefore you have to ask someone else (who is totally trustworthy, of course!) to pass the message on to him instead.

2   Tell your 'substitute' what he looks like. You may use brief notes to remind you but you may not read out a prepared statement. Your substitute may make brief written notes and may ask you questions.

3   Another crisis occurs and your substitute can't pass on the message. This time your substitute has to repeat (2) with the third member of your group, out of your hearing.

4   The message has supposedly been delivered. The third person describes the man to you as he has been described to him or her. Does it sound like the same person? How similar is the description to your original one? Has anything been added or left out? Do you think that positive identification would be possible?

ACTIVITY

1f

Optional Further Reading

Look out for detective novels in your local library. There are lots of popular authors including Agatha Christie, Dorothy Sayers, Ruth Rendell, and P.D. James, many of whose books have been filmed or serialised for television. Can you tell, from the early descriptions, 'who dunnit'?

Review of Unit 1

- Activity A was preparatory writing (En 3).
- Activity B was preparatory writing (En 3).
- Activity C was reading and understanding (En 2.1, 4).
- Activity D was written coursework (En 3).
- Activity E was speaking and listening coursework (En 1.1, 4).
- Activity F was optional further reading (En 2.1).

Making a Record

If you completed and were assessed for Activities D and E, this is what you should enter in your Coursework Index: in the first column headed 'number', write 1 and also 1, 1, D – this will remind you that the first assessed activity that you completed was Chapter 1, Unit 1, Activity D.

Put the date you wrote it in the second column and the title in the third. Put En 3 in the final column. In the box below put 2 and 1, 1, E in the first column (the second piece of assessed work – Chapter 1, Unit 1, Activity E). Put the date in the second column, group oral work in the third and En 1.1, D in the final column.

Turn to the Coursework Checklist on page 309. Put a tick by 1 and 4 of En 1. Put a tick by each aspect of En 3. Don't worry if you end up with ticks in all the available boxes. It is necessary, however, to have at least one tick in each box.

If you missed one of these activities, only complete a record of what you covered.

What Should You Do Now?

If you wish to try a different style of writing, turn to Unit 1 of another chapter. If you would like to do some more work on describing, here is some information about the other units in this chapter.

Unit 2 – A Room of My Own

This unit involves writing and speaking about a real and an ideal room. You will also read some descriptions by other writers.

Unit 3 – Five Senses

Instead of concentrating on sight, in this unit you are encouraged to use the other senses when writing description. You will also look at examples of this in a variety of material.

Unit 4 – A Traditional Celebration

In this unit there is an opportunity to describe various celebrations and festivals, from your own and other cultures.

Unit 5 – The Bustling Crowd

This unit concentrates on describing the atmosphere and impression of places and occasions where many people gather together – for example at the seaside or at a fairground.

Unit 6 – Far Away Places

This unit gives you the chance to read about places you might like to visit and to write descriptively about those you have been to already.

Choose the unit that sounds most interesting to you.

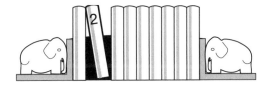

In Unit 1, people were the focus of your attention. In this unit, people are linked with specific places. As we have seen, careful observation is a very important aspect of descriptive writing. Let's start, therefore, by looking at a real room. We need to begin by collecting information about the room before going on to write in a way that conveys a precise and vivid picture of it.

ACTIVITY

(2a)

Preparation – Writing a Factual Description

Most people can identify a room that they might describe as 'theirs', even if they own a whole house. Decide which 'your' room is: it doesn't matter which it is; it could be a bedroom, sitting room, kitchen or workshop. If you have a choice, select the one in which you feel most at home. If you spend hours relaxing in the bath, then choose the bathroom! Find a plain piece of A4-size paper, a ruler and a pencil. Now draw a simple plan of the room you've chosen.

Once you've drawn the basic shape – don't worry too much about scale – put in the windows, doors, radiators and any fixed items like fitted cupboards.

Have you ever looked at the leaflets which estate agents produce to give their clients detailed information on properties? Their description of a bedroom might read something like the passage below.

BEDROOM NO. 2

10′6″ x 12′. South-facing window with blind. Fitted wardrobes with louvred doors. Integral dressing table with drawer. Avocado wash basin with vanity unit. Telephone point. Double plug socket. Radiator. Fitted carpet.

Look carefully at this description. Notice that it is written in note form. This gives an abrupt tone to the writing that may be appropriate for a list of facts.

Working from your plan, write a description of your room using the same approach. Add any relevant details that will not appear on the plan but which would be important for someone considering a purchase – for example fireplaces, plug sockets, wall lights. When you think you've finished, read it through. Have you included all the necessary features? If not, add them now.

Coursework – Writing

Ideally, while sitting in the room, write a new description. (This might be a bit tricky in the bathroom but do your best!) This time concentrate on colours, furniture, pictures and so on – all the features which don't appear on your plan. Keep it factual but write in sentences. You can allow enthusiasm (or disgust) to show in your tone. If the room is rather messy when you are writing about it, include references to dust, empty coffee cups, dog hairs or whatever. After all, we are talking about the facts.

Planning

First concentrate on planning your description. You may wish to start off by writing a list of the room's important features. You can organise these into how noticeable or important they are, placing the most significant one first. For example, if I were writing about my breakfast room, my list would be something like this:

- cream walls with poppy border at the top;
- huge piles of boxes and plastic aircraft kits belonging to my husband;
- chaotic desk with anglepoise lamp;
- bookcase with still more boxes half falling off it;
- ironing board with grubby floral cover;
- cork-tiled floor, faded in front of the patio doors;
- sunshine.

When you've done this, write a first draft.

Drafting and Revising

When you've finished this, read through what you've written. Is it interesting? Often in writing like this there is a tendency to use a rather repetitive style – 'Next to the settee . . . Next to this . . . Next to that . . . '. If you've done this you may want to rewrite it. Have you used precise words to describe the colours? If you just say that the carpet is green it doesn't really convey a vivid picture. Try to say what sort of green it is. Work through the checklist that follows.

Content

- Is your piece of writing well organised? Does each point follow on from the one before without being repetitive in its style? If not, rearrange it.
- Have you given clear and precise descriptions of the shapes and colours of the room's features? If you haven't, add more precise descriptive words.
- Have you conveyed the room's essential qualities – how it feels? If not, try to do so now.

Accuracy

- Are your sentences complete and correct? (Consult Chapter 6 if you are unsure of anything.)
- Is the spelling accurate? Look up words in a dictionary in order to check.

When you are happy that this piece is as well written as possible, write it out neatly, put the title 'My Room' and your name and the date of writing at the top. This is the first part of a longer piece of work, a sort of 'before' and 'after'. At present it is probably too short to stand as a piece of coursework on its own. Move on, therefore, to the next activity.

ACTIVITY

2c

Planning an Ideal Room

Congratulations! You have won first prize in the 'Fantasy Homescape Competition'. This means that experts will redecorate and refurnish your room, with no expense spared, according to your instructions.

Go back to your ground plan. Keeping the shape and size unaltered, decide what is possible in the way of additional features. If you wish, existing fitted items could be replaced by new more luxurious ones or, if there are none now, these could be added.

Put into your plan any items of furniture that you wish to keep. Add new pieces and place them where you wish them to be. Choose the colour scheme, floor covering, fabrics, lights, and so on.

In order to select the final design you may wish to consult various sources. You could buy magazines on interior design – (*Homes and Gardens* is a well-known one) or take a look at them next time you are in your doctor's or dentist's waiting room! You could also look at 'housekeeping' magazines which often include features on refurbishing rooms. You might want to look catalogues from companies like Laura Ashley, Habitat or Ikea or you could look at items in a more general mail order catalogue. This is your opportunity to indulge your wildest dreams – whether your taste is for primary colours and cool modern designs or the Victorian look that was fashionable in the late eighties, it's up to you. Assemble your ideas. You may wish to cut illustrations of furniture out of magazines or catalogues, to obtain snippets of material and wallpapers and samples of paint colours (the major firms produce colour charts).

ACTIVITY

2d

Coursework – Speaking and Listening

Ideally you should work with a partner who is also studying this unit. Alternatively, you could enlist a friend and, attempting only Task 1 (p. 16), tape your discussion.

Task 1

Explain to your partner exactly what you have planned for your room. Describe each feature as accurately and in as much detail as possible. Indicate, by referring to your plan, what will be placed where. Show your illustrations and explain exactly what your intentions are. Try to describe the overall effect you wish to create.

Your partner will ask questions as necessary for clarification. It may be that he or she has alternative suggestions about your choice or positioning of certain features. Perhaps he or she will make objections or offer suggestions for improvements. Listen to the points made and either justify your decisions or incorporate the other person's ideas.

Task 2

When you both feel that you have discussed your room as fully as possible, change over. You are now in the position of listener, advisor and critic. You should offer constructive comments and suggestions when you have heard your partner's plans.

ACTIVITY

2e

Coursework – Writing

Having made any adjustments that have occurred to you as a result of your discussion in Activity D, you can now write about your new and improved room.

It is probably a good idea to hand in your plan and any illustrations and samples that you have collected. You may wish either to draw your original plan again or paste it onto a larger sheet of paper. You might even wish to use graph paper in order to have an accurate scale. Any samples and illustrations can be pasted onto the sheet with explanatory labels. You can hand this in with your coursework as a supplementary reference sheet.

On a new sheet of paper, describe the room. You may refer to the supplementary sheet in order to clarify or illustrate points made. Try, as before, to plan the order in which you describe features both for clarity and also for interest. Show what effect you are trying to create.

Drafting and Revising

As always, when you think you have finished your piece of work, check it for content and accuracy. If you think you can improve it, write a second draft. Once you are satisfied, write it out neatly and add it to the first piece. You may wish to write a final paragraph comparing the two. It might say what you think will be better about the new room or perhaps what you'd miss from the original. If you really had the money available, would you carry out your plans? Read your two descriptions through in order to decide what to say in conclusion. You will almost certainly need to write this new part 'in rough' before adding it to the end of your neat work. Check that it is saying something useful and that it rounds the piece off. Once you are satisfied that it's finished, give the whole assignment to your tutor.

ACTIVITY

2f

Reading and Response – Examination Practice

So far we have been looking at your room, now let's look at other people's. It should be possible to learn about the owners or occupants from reading a description of their rooms or houses. Roger Hargreaves, the children's author, always makes sure there is a direct connection between his 'Mr Men' and the houses that they live in. Mr Silly, for example, lives in a crooked L-shaped house which is made extra silly by being wall-papered on the outside. Similarly, Mr Topsy-turvy, predictably, has an upside down front door and curtains that could be described as hanging from the windowsills except that, of course, the sills are at the top!

Read the following passages and answer the questions that follow them. Look up any unfamiliar words in your dictionary. This is good preparation for the written examination where you are likely to be reading extracts and responding to them in a variety of ways. Do not worry at this stage about setting yourself a time limit.

Extract A

This is the description of the stage set for the play *Hedda Gabler* by Henrik Ibsen. ('Upstage' means towards the back of the stage, 'downstage' means nearer the audience.)

A large drawing room, handsomely and tastefully furnished; decorated in dark colours. In the rear wall is a broad open doorway, with curtains drawn back to either side. It leads to a smaller room decorated in the same style as the drawing room. In the right-hand wall of the drawing room a folding door leads out to the hall. The opposite wall, on the left, contains French windows, also with curtains drawn back on either side. Through the glass we can see part of a veranda and trees in autumnal colours. Downstage stands an oval table, covered by a cloth and surrounded by chairs. Downstage right, against the wall, is a broad stove (for heating not cooking) tiled with dark porcelain; in front of it stand a high-backed armchair, a cushioned footrest and two footstools. Upstage right, in an alcove, is a corner sofa, with a small, round table. Downstage left, a little away from the wall, is another sofa. Upstage of the French windows is a piano. On either side of the open doorway in the rear wall stand whatnots holding ornaments of terracotta and majolica. Against the rear wall of the smaller room can be seen a sofa, a table and a couple of chairs. Above this sofa hangs the portrait of a handsome old man in general's uniform. Above the table a lamp hangs from the ceiling, with a shade of opalescent milky glass. All round the drawing room bunches of flowers stand in vases and glasses. More bunches lie on the tables. The floors of both rooms are covered in thick carpets. Morning light. The sun shines in through the French windows.

Hedda Gabler, Henrik Ibsen, translated by Michael Mayer

Answer the following questions about Extract A.

a   Do you think this is a play set in the present? Point out particular items mentioned to support your argument.

b   What can you deduce about the financial status and social class of the room's inhabitants?

c   Why might there be so many flowers?

d   There are very few clues here about the owners' identities. Suggest possibilities basing your answer on anything in the passage.

Extract B

This extract is taken from a short story by James Joyce.

> Home! She looked round the room, reviewing all its familiar objects which she had dusted once a week for so many years, wondering where on earth all the dust came from. Perhaps she would never see again those familiar objects from which she had never dreamed of being divided. And yet during all those years she had never found out the name of the priest whose yellowing photograph hung on the wall above the broken harmonium beside the coloured print of the promises made to Blessed Margaret Mary Alacoque.
>
> 'Eveline', from *The Dubliners*, James Joyce

Answer the following questions about Extract B.

a   What can you deduce about the age and circumstances of the female character here?

b   What do you think is going to happen to divide her from the room?

c   Do you get any impression of her mood?

Extract C

Extract C is taken from the novel *Possession* by A.S. Byatt.

> He moved gingerly inside the bathroom, which was not a place to sit and read or to lie and soak, but a chill green glassy place, glittering with cleanness, huge dark green stoppered jars on water-green thick glass shelves, a floor tiled in glass tiles into whose brief and illusory depths one might peer, a shimmering shower curtain like a glass waterfall, a blind to match, over the window, full of watery lights. Maud's great green-trellised towels were systematically folded on a towel-heater. Not a speck of talcum powder, not a smear of soap, on any surface. He saw his face in the glaucous basin as he cleaned his teeth. He thought of his home bathroom, full of old underwear, open pots of eyepaint, dangling shirts and stockings, sticky bottles of hair conditioner and tubes of shaving foam.
>
> *Possession*, A.S. Byatt

Answer the following questions about Extract C.

a What do you gather about the person called Maud whose bathroom this is?

b What do you learn about the male character's background and personality?

c Whose bathroom would you prefer to use and why?

Extract D

Extract D is taken from the novel *The Famished Road* by Ben Okri.

> The room was empty. A kerosene lamp burned steadily on the centre table. When I first opened my eyes on the new world of home everything was different. Large shadows everywhere made the spaces smaller. The floor was rough. Long columns of ants crawled alongside the walls. There were ant-mounds near the cupboard. An earthworm stretched itself past Dad's shoes. Wall-geckos and lizards scurried up and down the walls. At the far corner of the room a washing line was slack with the weight of too many clothes. Mum's objects of trade were all over the place. Her sacks were piled around the cupboard. Blackened pots and crockery and basins were scrambled everywhere. It was as if Mum and Dad had moved in, dumped their possessions wherever there was space, and had never found time to arrange anything. The more I took in the cracks in the walls, the holes in the zinc ceiling, the cobwebs, the smell of earth and gar, cigarette and mosquito coil smoke, the more it seemed as if we hadn't moved at all. Everything felt the same. The only difference was that I wasn't used to the sameness.

> *The Famished Road*, Ben Okri

Answer the following questions about Extract D.

a Where, geographically, do you think this is set?

b What do you gather about the character who is describing the room?

c What mood is conveyed?

Having read all the extracts and answered the questions, look at these final ones that follow. You may well meet this sort of activity in the examination.

1 What are the main differences between the passages? Which did you find most interesting? Say why.

2 Choose one passage and continue the description. You might wish to add further details to the room that is being written about or to describe another room of the same sort and in the same style.

3 Write a paragraph describing the room that you imagine belonging to two of the following: the prime minister; a fanatical supporter of a particular football team or pop group; a refugee; a king or queen; a monk; an animal rights campaigner; an astronaut (while in space).

Optional Further Reading

Find a copy of *The L-Shaped Room* by Lynne Reid Banks (it should be available in your local or college library). See how the central character's view of her room changes during the course of the novel.

Review of Unit 2

- Activity A was preparatory writing (En 3).
- Activity B was written coursework (En 3) (with Activity E).
- Activity C was preparatory reading and planning (En 2.3).
- Activity D was speaking and listening coursework (En 1.1, 2).
- Activity E was written coursework (En 3) (with Activity B).
- Activity F was examination practice – reading and response (En 2.1, 4; En 3).
- Activity G was optional further reading (En 2.1).

Making a Record

You should now write down the assessed coursework from this unit on your Coursework Index Form. The relevant Activities here are B and E which should be recorded together in one space but showing more than one date if necessary. You will also record Activity D which was an oral assignment carried out in a pair.

Once you have done this, tick the relevant boxes on the Coursework Checklist.

What Should You Do Now?

Choose another unit from this chapter or turn to Unit 1 in another chapter.

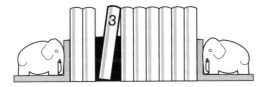

UNIT *Five Senses*

In the first two units of this chapter on describing you have been relying purely on sight and imagination to collect the information for your written work. This is only one aspect of description. The best writers use more than one sense when trying to convey the essence of a place or a character's feelings in a particular situation. What are the five senses? They are sight, hearing, smell, taste and touch.

ACTIVITY

3a

Preparatory Writing – Focusing on an Individual Sense

First, sit in absolute silence for two minutes. Write down every sound you can hear. It's surprising how many background noises are unnoticed because we are not really listening for them. If you listen, you'll find that your pen makes a surprisingly loud sound as you write!

Second, take each sense in turn, think of two delightful and two horrible examples of it, and write them down. Put the name of the sense on one side of your paper with your examples next to it like a table. For example, for your attractive things you might choose something like this:

SENSE	ATTRACTIVE
Sight	a child sleeping, a newly-opened flower
Hearing	bird song, a gurgling mountain stream
Smell	bacon frying, ground coffee
Taste	a ripe peach, a piece of hot buttered toast
Touch	velvet, a kitten's fur

These suggestions may, for you, be horrible rather than delightful. Try to put down examples that evoke a really strong response rather than ones that you vaguely like or dislike.

Third, let's expand it a bit. For each sense apart from sight (you probably use this a lot anyway) you are now going to write a few lines of description. Use either your attractive or repulsive examples as the basis for your writing but add in a place or character associated with them. Here's an example using the sense of smell:

> I woke up and stretched. A wonderful aroma wafted up from downstairs. Someone was frying bacon. The smell was savoury and enticing. I jumped out of bed and hastily flung on my dressing gown. When I reached the kitchen, mingling with the original smell there was the rich dark fragrance of freshly ground coffee. Suddenly I realised how hungry I was.

When you have written a few lines on each sense, four in all, check through to see if you really have concentrated on that specific sense. Notice that in the example given above various describing words (adjectives) were added to try to evoke the smells: 'savoury' and 'enticing' for the bacon, 'rich' and 'dark' for the coffee. Have you done this? The idea is to try to communicate precisely what you imagine, whether your reader is familiar with the image or not.

This happens, perhaps to excess, in writing about food and even more so, about wine. You might well find something like the passage below in one of the broadsheet newspapers. Here taste and smell are being combined: it is quite difficult to isolate taste from smell they are closely connected – when you have a cold you're all too aware of this!

> Now for the food. The fried aubergines and peppers with spicy sauce needed a wine with weight and acidity. A full-bodied Chardonnay from the South of France, full of oak, proved ideal. For variety there was also a Madeira – its sweet, raisiny flavour, strength and acid bite complementing the red peppers. The main course was an onion tart flavoured with nutmeg. It was rich and creamy, needing a fruity but still acidic wine. The lemony flavour of a New Zealand Reisling was perfect: just a hint of remaining sweetness enhanced the flavour of the onions. The dessert wine, from Germany, had a rich but balanced flavour, its sweetness restrained. There was a powerful combination of mango, honey and shortbread in its smoothness. This was excellent with the salad of citrus and exotic fruits that rounded off the meal.

Compared with some writing about food and wine, this is very restrained! I've heard wines described as containing wheelbarrows of fruit, marmalade, ginger, compost – everything, it seems, except grapes!

Fourth, find examples of this sort of writing and tune in to any programmes on food and drink on radio or television. Find your own examples of the range of weird and wonderful things that wines are compared to. When you've immersed yourself in enough of this, write your own. You could write a 'straight' version where you really try to describe a particular drink or meal in these terms; alternatively it might be more fun to choose a very ordinary meal: baked beans on toast with a cup of tea, for example, and write about it in this style. It doesn't need to be very long: a couple of hundred words is plenty. As always, when you think you've finished, check that it makes sense, is as vivid as possible – obviously you can afford to go 'over the top' a bit here – and that your spelling and punctuation are accurate.

ACTIVITY

3b

Reading and Response – Preparation for Writing

Read extracts A and B and answer the questions that follow. The first is from *Angel* by Elizabeth Taylor. Angel and Nora are two elderly women living with their cats in a big house. Marvell is the handyman. The second extract is from *Precious Bane* by Mary Webb.

Extract A

Winter

Snow muffled Paradise House. It went up in drifts to the lower window-sills. Each morning Marvell had to dig his way in to see to the fires. The cats could not or would not go out and Angel had ashes carried in for them to put in the empty grate in one of the unfurnished rooms.

'It smells like the tiger-house in the zoo,' Marvell grumbled.

Before dark he went back to his stuffy room to fry a bloater or dig into a jar of pickled onions. The two old women were alone in the house. The snow sealed them in. By morning the drifts had been renewed, Marvell's footprints across the yard covered over. On all the frosted windows, ferns delicately grew and icicles hung from the guttering.

As the snow continued, birds that had always been chary of the house with its swarming cats came nearer, for shelter and the hope of food. They printed their dagger-like footmarks across the terrace and scuffled the snow upon the windowsills. Against the whiteness of the garden, the stone walls of the house were as dark as lead. Smoke rose from the chimneys and discoloured the pale grey sky. The days seemed long, the evenings longer.

Angel, apparently unaware of the cold, shut herself up in the ice-cold drawing room, playing the piano and looking out at the buried garden, at the sad monochrome landscape. Weeds, roses, were all gone. Only thorned branches broke the snow, looped across the whiteness like barbed wire.

Angel, Elizabeth Taylor

Extract B

Summer

That was the best time of year for our lake, when in the still hot noons the water looked so kind, being of a calm, pale blue, that you would never think it could drown anybody. All round stood the tall trees, thick-leaved with rich summer green, unstirring, caught in a spell, sending down their coloured shadows into the mere, so the tree tops almost met in the middle. From either hand the notes of the small birds that had not yet given up singing went winging out across the water, and so quiet it was that though they were only such thin songs as those of willow wrens and robins, you could hear them all across the mere. Even on such a burning day as this, there was a sweet cool air from the water, very heady and full of life. All around the lake stood the tall bulrushes with their stout heads of brown plush. Within the ring of rushes was another ring of lilies, and at this time of the year they were the most beautiful thing at Sarn. The big bright leaves lay calm upon the water and calmer yet upon the leaves lay the lilies, white and yellow.

Precious Bane, Mary Webb

Answer the following questions on the two extracts.

a   How many senses are used in the descriptions in Extracts A and B? Find examples of each if possible and write them down clearly labelled. You can count sensation, feeling hot or cold, as touch.

b   Make two columns on your paper, heading one 'winter' and the other 'summer'. Put down the main differences between the passages – include weather, colours, mood and any other features you can spot. Are there any similarities?

c   Which piece of writing do you think best conveys the essence of the place described? Say why.

ACTIVITY
3c

Coursework – Writing

Choose a place outdoors that you know well. It could be your own garden, a local park, a place you visit for walking or fishing, a golf course, anything of this sort.

Write two pieces of description, one of this place in winter, one of it in summer. Use senses in addition to sight to make the descriptions as vivid as possible. It will probably be best to write in the first person (I) so that you can convey a strong impression of how you feel. Make the weather extreme: in winter very cold and in summer very hot and sunny. If you prefer cold weather to hot it's quite acceptable, though, to reverse what might be the expected idea of horrible winter and delightful summer. Whenever you write, originality is desirable. Include whatever people, activities and wildlife that you might expect to be there. You don't just have to confine yourself to landscape and weather. You could write up to three or four hundred words on each season.

Drafting and Revising

As always, when you have written a rough draft, check it for content and accuracy. Revise it as necessary. When you are satisfied, write it out neatly with your name at the top and the headings 'Summer' and 'Winter' appropriately placed. Hand it in to your tutor for assessment.

ACTIVITY
3d

Reading and Response – Examination Practice

This activity is designed to give you some practice with the type of question that you may meet in the written examination. Read the passages in extracts A and B and carry out the assignment. Spend no more than one and a half hours on this.

Extract A

This extract is from a story by H.G. Wells called 'The Country of the Blind'. Nunez, a traveller from Bogota accidentally comes across a country hidden in the mountains where the sense of sight is unknown. Because he possesses this sense he thinks he will be superior to the inhabitants. He has heard it said 'In the country of the blind the one-eyed man is king'. He has not reckoned on their adaptation of their environment.

He heard a voice calling to him from out of the village.

'Ya ho there, Bogota! Come hither!'

At that he stood up smiling. He would show these people once and for all what sight would do for a man. They would seek him but not find him.

'You move not, Bogota,' said the voice.

He laughed noiselessly, and made two stealthy steps aside from the path.

'Trample not on the grass, Bogota; that is not allowed.'

Nunez had hardly heard the sound he made himself. He stopped amazed.

The owner of the voice came running up the piebald path towards him.

He stepped back onto the pathway. 'Here I am,' he said.

'Why did you not come when I called you?' said the blind man. 'Must you be led like a child? Cannot you hear the path, as you walk?'

Nunez laughed. 'I can see it,' he said.

'There is no such word as "see",' said the blind man, after a pause. 'Cease this folly, and follow the sound of my feet.' He went athwart one of their meadows, leaving a track of trampled grass behind his feet and presently sat down by the side of one of their ways. Far away he saw a number of men carrying spades and sticks come out of the street of houses, and advance in a spreading line along the several paths towards him. They advanced slowly, speaking frequently to one another, and every now and again the whole cordon would halt and sniff the air and listen.

The first time they did this Nunez laughed. But afterwards he did not laugh.

One struck his trail in the meadow grass and came stooping and feeling his way along it.

'The Country of the Blind', *Selected Short Stories*, H.G. Wells

Extract B

The Fifth Sense

'A 65-year-old Cypriot Greek shepherd, Nicolis Loizou, was wounded by security forces early today. He was challenged twice; when he failed to answer, troops opened fire. A subsequent hospital examination showed that the man was deaf.' News item, December 30th, 1957.

Lamps burn all the night
Here, where people must be watched and seen,
And I, a shepherd, Nicolis Loizou,
Wish for the dark, for I have been
Sure-footed in the dark, but now my sight
Stumbles among these beds, scattered white boulders,

As I lean towards my far slumbering house
With the night lying upon my shoulders.
My sight was always good,
Better than others. I could taste wine and bread
And name the field they spattered when the harvest
Broke. I could coil in the red
Scent of the fox out of a maze of wood
And grass. I could touch mist, I could touch breath.
But of my sharp senses I had only four.
The fifth one pinned me to my death.
The soldiers must have called
The word they needed: Halt. Not hearing it,
I was their failure, relaxed against the winter
Sky, the flag of their defeat.
With their five senses they could not have told
That I lacked one, and so they had to shoot.
They would fire at a rainbow if it had
A colour less than they were taught.
Christ said that when one sheep
Was lost, the rest meant nothing any more.
Here in this hospital, where others' breathing
Swings like a lantern in the polished floor
And squeezes those who cannot sleep,
I see how precious each thing is, how dear,
For I may never touch, smell, taste or see
Again, because I could not hear.

'The Fifth Sense', *Patricia Beer*

Having read the passages, answer these questions:

a   Why, in Extract A, does Nunez fail in his attempts to evade the blind people?
b   According to what you have read here, if a person lacks one of their senses, what happens to the other senses?
c   In Extract B what attitude does the shepherd have towards the soldiers?
d   Describe a house as you would imagine it to be in 'The Country of the Blind'.
e   Write about an incident in which the lack of one of the senses is of critical importance.

ACTIVITY

3e

Coursework – Speaking and Listening – Performance Activities

Attempt one or more of the following activities:

1   Read the poem 'The Fifth Sense' aloud to a friend or class member. Discuss with him or her how effectively you think Patricia Beer communicates the ideas in the poem. This could be taped and assessed as oral coursework.

2 Obtain copies of the play *Children of a Lesser God* by Mark Medoff. Read this aloud in a group. Choose one or more scenes and work out expression, movements, and so forth. You will find that if you actually learn the words, gestures and actions become much easier as you are not hampered by holding the book. This can then be performed for your tutor as part of your coursework. It could also be filmed on videotape.

3 Write a script or improvise your own scene where one or more characters lacks one of the senses. It need not be hearing. As with (2), this can be performed or recorded for assessment.

ACTIVITY

3f

Optional Further Reading

Obtain a copy of *Selected Short Stories* by H.G. Wells (it should be available in your local or college library). Read the story 'The Country of the Blind'.

Review of Unit 3

- Activity A was preparatory writing (En 3).
- Activity B was reading and response (En 2.1, 4).
- Activity C was written coursework (En 3).
- Activity D was examination practice – reading and response (En 2.1, 4, En 3).
- Activity E was speaking and listening coursework (En 1).
- Activity F was optional further reading (En 2.1).

Making a Record

Write down the necessary information about the coursework in this unit on your Coursework Index Form. This will be the written work in Activity C and the individual oral work in Activity E. Tick all the aspects of En 1 and En 3 on your Coursework Checklist.

What Should You Do Now?

Choose another unit in this chapter or turn to Unit 1 in another chapter.

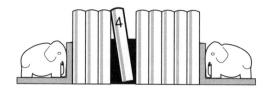

 A Traditional Celebration

In this unit, instead of looking at a person or a place or concentrating on the method of description, we are going to use particular events as a basis for writing.

ACTIVITY

Reading – Research and Information Retrieval

Using a piece of A4 paper, list down the side all the months of the year. Opposite the months put down any celebration, whether seasonal or religious, which takes place during that month. Try to find examples from as many different traditions and cultures as possible. You can probably put down Christmas Day easily enough but what about Eid, Yom Kippur or the Moon Festival? You may find that your diary gives the dates of some of these but try to glean information from as many sources as possible until you have a comprehensive picture of what is celebrated by the many different cultural groups that make up the UK today.

Having collected their names, how much do you actually know about these festivals? The main areas to think about are their origins or meanings, what is celebrated and what particular behaviour is associated with each. Are special clothes worn or foods prepared, for example?

Let's look at 5 November (known as Guy Fawkes or Bonfire Night) as an illustration. If you were brought up in the UK or have lived here for any length of time you will know that people light bonfires and let off fireworks – but why? This is a celebration of what probably seems to most of us to be a pretty obscure and irrelevant piece of history.

As an intended prelude to a Catholic uprising, barrels of gunpowder were placed in a vault under the House of Lords. A man called Guy Fawkes was the hapless individual whose job it was to light the gunpowder fuse. Unfortunately for him, Tresham, one of the plotters, warned his Catholic relative, Lord Monteagle, who revealed the plot to the authorities. The cellars were searched and Guy Fawkes was found. All this took place on 5 November 1605, and the vaults have been checked annually ever since in case anyone tries it again. In this particular celebration, then, we are celebrating the failure of a plot to blow up Parliament nearly four hundred years ago. Had the plot succeeded, some might say, there might have been more to celebrate!

In terms of the behaviour associated with this event, there is little apart from the actual bonfire and fireworks. Because of the time of year, it is necessary to dress in warm clothes and in recent years it has become traditional to eat hot dogs and burgers instead of the more old-fashioned jacket potatoes and 'parkin' which perhaps would have been associated with Guy Fawkes night earlier this century.

In terms of celebrations changing over the years, look at Halloween. All Hallows' Eve (31 October), to give it its older name, was the last day of the Celtic calendar. The night of 31 October was the last when witches and warlocks were able to be about. Christian All Saints Day follows immediately after it on 1 November. Earlier this century, apart from the odd Black Mass or churchyard vigil, probably nothing much was done by way of celebrating Halloween. There were some parties with a fancy dress theme but nothing very widespread. The American tradition of 'trick or treat' has become popular recently although there have been attempts to ban it because householders' and children's safety was thought to be at risk. In the USA, children in fancy dress roam the streets trying to persuade householders to give them something good to eat in order to avoid some unpleasant prank. Even in Britain, pumpkins adorn the shelves of the local supermarkets and soups and pies are made using recipes from the States.

Choose two of the festivals that you have put down on your chart, one from your own culture, one from another. Find out as much as you can about each of them. Ignore Christmas; we'll come to that later.

ACTIVITY

4b

Coursework – Writing a Magazine Article

When you have gathered together all the facts that you need about the festival you chose to write about in Activity A, write up your material in the form of an article for a magazine. You may well be able to find examples of this sort of piece in your newsagents. The idea is to make it informative, interesting and, of course, descriptive. Structure it by using the following as headings (in your mind if not actually in your writing):

- background;
- purpose;
- customs;
- dress;
- food and drink.

You may want to include recipes for the dishes traditionally consumed on this occasion.

Drafting and Revising

Once you feel you have written all you can about your two choices, read carefully through your work. Does it flow naturally from one point to another? Have you included enough detail about what is done, what is worn and so on? Add in anything which would make your writing more vivid. Now check the accuracy. Is your punctuation right? Check it by using Chapter 6. Have you spelt words correctly? Check in a dictionary. Once you are satisfied, write it out neatly. In order to make it really look like a magazine article, you might want to type it (preferably on a word processor for ease of revision). If you have illustrations which could accompany the written text – drawings or photographs – that would be an added bonus although the artwork won't actually be assessed.

ACTIVITY

4c

Reading and Response – Examination Practice

Read Extracts A and B which are descriptions of traditional celebrations then complete the assignment which follows. This is the sort of work that is likely to appear in the written examination. Spend no more than one and a half hours in total on this.

Extract A

This extract is from *The Joy Luck Club* by Amy Tan. It describes the Moon (or Mid-Autumn) Festival in pre-Communist China.

> Our entire family was already standing outside, chatting excitedly. Everybody was dressed in important-looking clothes. Baba was in a new brown-coloured gown, which while plain was of an obviously fine-quality silk weave and workmanship. Mama had on a jacket and skirt with colours that were the reverse of mine: black silk with yellow bands. My half-sisters wore rose-coloured tunics and so did their mothers, my father's concubines. My older brother had on a blue jacket embroidered with shapes resembling Buddha sceptres for long life. Even the old ladies had put on their best clothes to celebrate: Mama's aunt, Baba's mother and her cousin, and Great-uncle's fat wife, who still plucked her forehead bald and always walked as if she were crossing a slippery stream, two tiny steps and then a scared look.
>
> The servants had already packed and loaded a rickshaw with the day's basic provisions: a woven hamper filled with 'zong zi' – the sticky rice wrapped in lotus leaves, some filled with roasted ham, some with sweet lotus seeds; a small stove for boiling water for hot tea; another hamper containing cups and bowls and chopsticks; a cotton sack of apples, pomegranates, and pears; sweaty earthen jars of preserved meats and vegetables; stacks of red boxes lined with four mooncakes each; and of course, sleeping mats for our afternoon nap.
>
> Then everybody climbed into rickshaws, the younger children sitting next to their amahs. . . . When we arrived at the lake, . . . the old ladies and men started climbing aboard a large boat our family had rented. The boat looked like a floating teahouse, with an open-air pavilion larger than the one in our courtyard. It had many red columns and a peaked tile roof, and behind that what looked like a garden house with round windows. . . . Red lanterns hanging from the roof and railings swayed, as if pushed by a breeze.
>
> *The Joy Luck Club*, Amy Tan

Extract B

This extract is from *A Passage to India* by E.M. Forster. You may need to use a dictionary to look up some of the words used here.

In a land where all else was unpunctual, the hour of the Birth was chronometrically observed. Three minutes before it was due, a Brahman brought forth a model of the village of Gokul (the Bethlehem in that nebulous story) and placed it in front of an altar. The model was on a wooden tray about a yard square; it was of clay, and was gaily blue and white with streamers and paint. Here, upon a chair too small for him and with a head too large, sat King Kansa, who is Herod, directing the murder of some Innocents, and in a corner, similarly proportioned, stood the father and mother of the Lord, warned to depart in a dream. The model was not holy, but more than a decoration, for it diverted men from the actual image of the God, and increased their sacred bewilderment. The clock struck midnight, and simultaneously the rending note of the conch broke forth, followed by the trumpeting of elephants; all who had packets of powder threw them at the altar, and in the rosy dust and incense, and clanging and shouts, Infinite Love took upon itself the form of Shri Krishna, and saved the world. All sorrow was annihilated, not only for Indians, but for foreigners, birds, caves, railways, and the stars; all became joy, all laughter; there had never been disease nor doubt, misunderstanding, cruelty, fear. Some jumped in the air, others flung themselves prone; the women behind the purdah slapped and shrieked; the little girl slipped out and danced by herself, her black pigtails flying.

A Passage to India, E.M. Forster

Assignment

Answer these questions as fully as possible using evidence from the passages in Extracts A and B.

- a   What do you learn about the family in A?
- b   What do you learn about the geographical location in B?
- c   What differing aspect of the celebrations do you feel the writers concentrate on in the two passages?
- d   Look at the language used in the two passages. What observations can you make about the different styles? What effect do you think this has on the reader?
- e   Write about the religious or spiritual aspect of a traditional celebration with which you are familiar.
- f   Imagine that you are a child involved in a celebration or festival. Write a short description of what is taking place. Try to look at aspects other than those covered in your answer to (e), above.

ACTIVITY

4d

Reading – Research and Information Retrieval

Christmas in this country is celebrated on 25 December: gifts are exchanged; many people go to church; a traditional meal of roast turkey and plum pudding is usually served. In other countries, even those in Europe, things are rather different. Find out about Christmas customs in as many countries as possible.

Certain decorations and traditions are specifically associated with a British Christmas. Find out what you can about the origins and background of some of the following: Christmas trees; Christmas cards; the use of holly and mistletoe; the yule log; carol singing; mince pies; Christmas crackers; Advent calendars; Christmas stockings; Father Christmas; Twelfth Night.

ACTIVITY

4e

Coursework – Speaking and Listening

This activity offers you some options for preparing and giving a talk or speech. In each case you can record the talk on audio or videotape for assessment. For guidance on how to prepare a talk see Unit 6, Activity G in this chapter.

Choose one or more of the following options for oral coursework.

1 Using information you have collected in Activity D, prepare a talk on Christmas customs. Imagine that this would be broadcast on the radio. You can tape-record it to make it seem real.
2 Give a talk based on your own feelings about Christmas or another traditional celebration that you participate in. You could describe your best and worst memories associated with it, what feelings of anticipation you have beforehand and what it means to you. Instead of this being just a talk, if it's practical, this could be a discussion in a small group where feelings and ideas are shared and exchanged. This could be tape-recorded to make assessment easier.
3 The Queen broadcasts to the people of the UK and Commonwealth on Christmas Day. If you were to take her place, what would you say to the audience? If possible listen to or watch a recording of her most recent speech. Your own speech could either be tape-recorded or videoed.

ACTIVITY

4f

Coursework – Writing

So far in this unit you have been looking at seasonal or religious festivals where everyone celebrates together on the same date. There are, however, other occasions where individual families come together in a traditional way. These are sometimes called 'rites of passage': they are birth (or rather baptism), coming of age celebrations, marriage and death. The way in which these events are noted varies considerably from one culture or religion to another.

As with the previous celebrations, try to find out about customs which differ from those you are familiar with. For example, Christian brides wear white but Muslim brides wear red and gold, white being the Muslim colour of mourning.

Write a description of one, or if possible, two contrasting rites of passage. As before try to give a full and vivid picture. Imagine that you are writing for someone who is not familiar with what traditionally happens. You can use a real event, such as your own wedding or one you have attended, or you may prefer to invent one. Don't write a story. This is a description so it doesn't need a plot or background details. Start at an interesting point such as the bride being dressed in her finery.

Drafting and Revising

When you think you've written a full account, read it through. Check the content; check for accuracy. When you're satisfied, write it out neatly, give it an appropriate title and put your name and the date of writing at the top.

If the idea above does not appeal you might like to try and think of a humorous and eccentric variation on the traditional. For example, in an Irish play called *The Shadow of the Glen* by J.M. Synge the 'corpse' sits up during the wake and objects when he thinks his widow is about to arrange to marry a man he disapproves of. There are stories, usually from the United States, about couples designing their own ideal wedding and personalised vows. Write a description of something like this. As always, revise and correct your work once you have written a draft.

ACTIVITY

4g

Optional Further Reading

Perhaps the best-known story about Christmas is *A Christmas Carol* by Charles Dickens. This is usually published in a collection of his shorter stories entitled *Christmas Books*. Obtain a copy of this from a library or bookshop. You probably know the story anyway from the various television and film versions which exist. This is your opportunity to read the original version.

As part of your course, you are required to study literature written before 1900. *A Christmas Carol* is an example of this. Use this, if you wish, as the basis for a piece of written coursework, as in Activity H.

ACTIVITY

4h

Optional Coursework – Writing in Response to Literature (Pre-Twentieth Century)

Imagine that you are a member of the Crachit family and describe Christmas with them. Choose two different occasions, one with poor and meagre fare, the other with generous plenty provided by the reformed Scrooge.

Drafting and Revising

When you have finished, check and revise your work as necessary. If you have used speech, make sure you have punctuated it correctly by looking at Chapter 6, Unit 4.

Review of Unit 4

- Activity A was reading, research and information retrieval (En 2.3).
- Activity B was written coursework using researched information (En 2.3, En 3).
- Activity C was examination practice – reading and response (En 2.1, 4, En 3).
- Activity D was reading, research and information retrieval (En 2.3).
- Activity E was speaking and listening coursework (En 1, 2).
- Activity F was written coursework (En 3).
- Activity G was optional further reading (En 2.1).
- Activity H was optional written coursework in response to literature (En 2.1, En 3) (pre-twentieth century).

Making a Record

Write the necessary information about the coursework in this unit on your Coursework Index Form. This was the written work in Activity B which also involved reading, research and information retrieval, the individual oral assignment in Activity E, the written coursework in Activity F and also the optional work in response to literature in Activity H. Tick the relevant aspects of En 1, En 2 and En 3 on your Coursework Checklist.

What Should You Do Now?

Choose another unit in this chapter or turn to Unit 1 in another chapter.

UNIT (**5**)   *The Bustling Crowd*

In this unit we're going to concentrate on looking at people crowded together in various situations. It may be helpful to refer back to Activity A of Unit 1 of this chapter which offers guidance when describing people and to Activity A of Unit 3 of this chapter which is about using the five senses in description.

ACTIVITY

Preparation – Picturing the Scene

Make a list of five or six different places where a wide variety of people are likely to be grouped together, not necessarily by their own choice. You'll probably find you've included social events, places associated with travel and public institutions such as hospitals.

Choose two examples from your list and look at them more closely.

What sort of people would be there? How would they be dressed? What would their mood be? What would they be doing? What is the place like? What would the atmosphere be? What would the typical sounds and smells be?

You'll probably find that there's a close connection between the location, the reason people are there and their dress and behaviour.

ACTIVITY

Reading and Analysis – Knowledge about Language

Look carefully at the following description of a crowded beach written by Dylan Thomas, and then answer the questions that follow it.

Beach Scene

The young man in a sailor's jersey, sitting near the summer huts to see the brown and white women coming out and the groups of pretty-faced girls with pale eyes and scorched backs who picked their way delicately on ugly, red-toed feet over the sharp stones to the sea, drew on the sand a large, indented woman's figure; and a naked child, just out of the sea, ran over it and shook water, marking on the figure two wide wet eyes and a hole in the footprinted middle. He rubbed the woman away and drew a paunched man; the child ran over it, tossing her hair, and shook a row of buttons down its belly and a line of drops, like piddle in a child's drawing, between the long legs stuck with shells.

In a huddle of picnicking women and their children, stretched out limp and damp in the sweltering sun or fussing over paper carriers or building castles that were once destroyed by the tattered march of other picnickers to different pieces of the beach, among the ice-cream cries, the angrily happy shouts of boys playing ball, and the screams of girls as the sea rose to their waists, the young man sat alone with the shadows of his failure at his side. Some silent husbands with rolled up trousers and suspenders dangling, paddled slowly on the border of the sea, paddling women, in thick, black picnic dresses, laughed at their own legs, dogs chased stones, and one proud boy rode the water on a rubber seal. The young man, in his wilderness, saw the holiday Saturday set down before him, false and pretty, as a flat picture under the vulgar sun; the disporting families with paper bags, buckets and spades, parasols and bottles, the happy, hot, and aching girls with sunburn liniments in their bags, the bronzed young men with chests, and the envious white young men in waistcoats, the thin pale hairy, pathetic legs of the husbands silently walking through the water, the plump and curly, shaven-headed and bowed-backed children up to no sense with unrepeatable delight in the dirty sand, moved him, he thought dramatically in his isolation, to an old shame and pity; outside all holiday, like a young man doomed for ever to the company of his maggots, beyond the high and ordinary, sweating, sun-awakened power and stupidity of the summer flesh on a day and a world out, he caught the ball that a small boy had whacked into the air with a tin tray, and rose to throw it back.

'One Warm Sunday', *Portrait of the Artist as a Young Dog*, Dylan Thomas

Questions

a How many different types of people are there in this description? List them.

b Dylan Thomas uses language in an original way. Having looked back at the passage to find the context, explain what picture you think he is trying to create by the following phrases:
'ice-cream cries'; 'angrily happy shouts'; 'happy, hot, aching girls'; 'bronzed young men with chests'; 'bowed-backed children up to no sense'; 'doomed forever to the company of his maggots'.

c The young man is used by Dylan Thomas to provide a point of view for the scene. What is his attitude to it all? What difference does his attitude make to the impression gained by the reader?

d This extract contains very long sentences. With a pencil, mark each full stop in the passage. Suggest why the writer uses such long sentences and what effect you think this has when you read it.

Coursework – Writing

Bearing in mind the techniques used by Dylan Thomas, write a description of a crowd scene. Use one of the ideas that you worked on in Activity A or substitute a new idea if you like but go through the same process as before to decide who is there, what they're doing and what the setting looks, sounds and smells like.

Try to have a person whose eyes we're looking through as in the beach scene. You could write in the first person (I) if you like.

If you don't feel that you have thought of a really good idea yet, here are some suggestions:

- an airport departure lounge when there's a serious delay;
- a nightclub;
- a sports fixture such as a Grand Prix motor race or a football final;
- a fairground or theme park.

Try to give an impression of the mood, for example frustration and boredom in the airport scene, excitement and hilarity at the theme park. Include descriptions of smells and sounds. In some scenes these will be really important: burgers and onions cooking at the fair and the blaring music from the rides, the sound of the engines and smell of burnt oil at the motor race.

When you write, it is always best to use your own experience to make your work vivid and interesting. Your imagination is useful to supply details of people, but try to describe a place that you've actually been to. The result will be much more credible than if you're using imagination alone.

Drafting and Revising

Once you have written a first draft, read your work through. You should aim to write about 500 words in a piece like this. Make a rough calculation of the number of words and write some more if it's too short. Have you given a lively impression of the scene? Have you created a clear picture of the sorts of people who are there? Have you remembered to use senses other than just sight? Have you thought deliberately about using vivid phrases and longer or shorter sentences in order to achieve the right effect? Are punctuation and spelling accurate? If you are unsure about punctuation check with Unit 4 of Chapter 6.

If you feel your piece could be improved in any way, rewrite it until you are satisfied with it. Once you are happy, write it out neatly with an appropriate title; put your name and the date you wrote it at the top.

Reading and Response – Examination Practice

Read the descriptions of crowd scenes in Extract A and B and complete the assignment that follows. This activity is similar to the sort of thing you will find in the examination. Spend no more than one and a half hours on this in total.

Extract A

This extract is taken from *Precious Bane*, a novel set in rural Shropshire in the early nineteenth century. It was written in the 1920s. The scene is a hiring fair, the occasion when country people who wished to change their employment were able to offer their services to interested masters.

> The long row of young folks, and some not so young, who were there to be hired, began near our stall. Each one carried the sign of his trade or hers. A cook had a big wooden spoon, and if the young fellows were too gallus she'd smack them over the head with the flat of it. Men that went with the teams had whips, hedgers a brummock, gardeners a spade. Cowmen carried a bright tin milk pail, thatchers a bundle of straw. A blacksmith wore a horseshoe in his hat, and there were a tuthree of them, for a few big farms would club together and hire a blacksmith by year. Shepherds had a crook and bailiffs a lanthorn to show how late they'd be out and about after robbers. There were tailors and weavers, wool carders and cobblers too, for the farmers clubbed together for them also. The carder had a hank of coloured wool, and the tailors made great game running up and down the line of young women and threatening to cut their petticoats short.
>
> Jancis laughed with the rest, but I could see she'd been crying. She looked a real picture in her print gown and bonnet, with the dairymaid's milking stool. They were a tidy set of young women, the housemaids with broom on shoulder, the laundrymaids with dollies. It was no wonder that many a young farmer, who wanted neither cook nor dairymaid, should linger a bit, and that it should come into his mind that he wanted a wife.
>
> *Precious Bane*, Mary Webb

Extract B

This extract is from *The Famished Road* by Ben Okri. Azaro, the young boy who is the main character, is visiting a very strange bar that appears to be inhabited by some extraordinary, even supernatural, customers.

> I managed to make my way to my position near the earthenware pot. All the seats were taken, and two midgets shared a stool, drinking serenely. I did not recognise either of them but they both smiled at me. The toothless woman turned towards me, staring hard, and then, very slowly, pulled out something from beneath the table. I watched, fascinated by her magician's gesture. When she had pulled it out completely, I saw that it was a

sack. I screamed and tried to get out of the door, but every available space was packed. The crowd jostled me, blocking my way, as though they were deliberately trying to prevent my escape, while not seeming to do so. I shouted and a deep-throated laughter drowned my voice. I pushed and the harder I tried the more completely I was surrounded.

Then I realised that more people were pouring in from the doorway, materialising, it seemed, from the night air. The clientele kept multiplying, filling out the spaces. They stood over me, giant figures with hair that fell off in clumps on my face. Their multiplication frightened me. The woman with no teeth became two. The midgets became four. The two men with dark glasses and white hair became three. The man with a bulbous eye acquired a double and the double acquired a bulbous eye on the other side of his face. I calmed down. I had no weapon against their multiplication. The noise lowered. Everything quivered. I moved slowly, as if under water, towards the edge of a bench. I sat down. The people who surrounded me kept glancing in my direction every now and again, as if discreetly trying to make sure I was still at the bar. I became aware of being watched by everyone, even when they were not looking at me. I became convinced that all had hidden and invisible eyes at the sides and backs of their heads. And it was only when I looked up at one of the men who was so tall his head seemed to almost touch the cobweb infested rafters that I knew the purity of fear.

The Famished Road, Ben Okri

Assignment

a What impression, if any, do you get of the narrator of each passage? How important are the feelings of the narrators in each case?

b What differences have you found in the styles used by the writers? Look at the words used: are they, in general simple and familiar, or are they strange and complex? Look also at the length of the sentences used. Once you have noted several differences between the passages, consider what effect these have on the impact the material makes on the reader.

c Picture a modern hiring fair. What emblems might be carried by the following workers: a plumber, an actor, a TV salesperson, a scientist, an astronaut?

d Write about a crowded scene where fear is the dominant emotion.

ACTIVITY

5e

Coursework – Speaking and Listening – Knowledge of Language

In the extract from *Precious Bane* given as Extract A in Activity D a number of Shropshire dialect words are used. Find them in the passage and decide by looking at the context what you think they might mean. Of course, if any of the words is used in your own locality you may be familiar with it already.

Attempt the following three activities to improve your knowledge of spoken language.

1   By listening carefully to the way people speak, collect other examples of dialect words either from your own or other areas of the United Kingdom. Having done that, draw up a questionnaire to find out whether people are familiar with the words you have found – or, indeed, whether they can add any of their own. You should think of no more than seven questions. Phrase them in simple, easily understood language.

2   Conduct a survey about regional accents and people's attitudes to them. Do your friends or fellow students have recognisable accents and do they have strong feelings about how they or other people speak? Have attitudes changed about the importance of 'BBC English', as 'Standard English' or 'Received Pronunciation' is sometimes called? What do you feel about current trends in attitudes towards accents?

3   Does a person's ethnic origin affect their accent and their use of dialect words? See how much you can find out about this by listening to the speech of people who are around you or on television. Australian soap operas may provide you with a source of both! Consider what is added to the diversity of the language through such variations.

ACTIVITY

5f

Reading – Research and Information Retrieval – Knowledge about Language

Do some research in your local library to find out about the following:

1   interesting or odd local place names. Find out what they mean and what language they originate from;

2   the etymology (origination) of unusual or interesting words. Consult the *Shorter Oxford Dictionary* or an etymological dictionary. Here are some suggestions of words you might like to look up: bungalow, chortle, plumber, asbestos, Aryan, moccasin, chocolate. Look up anything else that occurs to you, it can be fascinating.

ACTIVITY

5g

Optional Coursework – Writing Science Fiction

In the last two activities, although you've covered some important aspects of the National Curriculum, you have moved away from writing about crowds. For a final piece of work in this area you might want to think about writing something less realistic and more imaginative than in Activity B.

In the *Pern* books by Anne McCaffery there are descriptions of 'gathers' or fairs. In *Mort* by Terry Pratchett there is a hiring fair not unlike that in *Precious Bane* except it's on Discworld instead of Earth. If you saw the first *Star Wars* film you will remember that there was a splendid collection of aliens in the bar visited by Han Solo and Luke Skywalker. Similarly memorable is the scene in the first *Gremlins* film where the creatures behave like naughty kids when they take over the cinema.

Choose your location and people it with the creatures of your choice. Remember the suggestions about having a varied selection, behaving distinctively, in a setting brought to life by its own sounds and smells. Try to create a mood or atmosphere.

Drafting and Revising

As always, when you have written a draft, check and revise it both for content and accuracy. When you're happy, write it out neatly, head it appropriately and submit it to your tutor for assessment.

Review of Unit 5

- Activity A was preparation for writing.
- Activity B was reading and analysis (En 2.1, 4).
- Activity C was written coursework (En 2.4, En 3).
- Activity D was examination practice – reading and response (En 2.1, 4, En 3).
- Activity E was speaking and listening coursework (En 1.1, 4).
- Activity F was optional written coursework (En 3).

Making a Record

On your Coursework Index Form, write down the necessary information about the coursework in this unit. This was the written work in Activity C and the individual oral work in Activity E. If you chose to do Activity F, record the relevant details. Tick the relevant aspects of En 1, En 3 and En 3 on your Coursework Checklist.

What Should You Do Now?

Choose another unit in this chapter or turn to Unit 1 in another chapter.

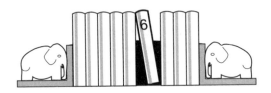

UNIT (**6**) *Far Away Places*

Describing interesting and exotic places can be both a pleasure and a challenge. The writers of the glowing accounts in holiday brochures are trying to persuade you to part with your hard-earned cash. Their accounts may not be unbiased, therefore.

ACTIVITY

(*6a*)

Reading – Knowledge about Language

Read the following description carefully and then answer the questions that follow.

> One of the most popular of international resorts on the Costa Dorada, Calella, welcomes you with a sparkling array of holiday attractions. The golden sands of the wide beach stretch out in front of the town and northwards up to Pineda. In the background, the rolling pine-covered hills contrast with the deep blue sea. And to the south, rocky headlands and small sandy coves await the keen swimmer and snorkelling enthusiast.
>
> Only a few years ago Calella was a small Catalan fishing village, centred around the tiny old church. The church is still there, and so is much of the town's original character, living happily side by side with the bustling personality of a modern resort.
>
> Tree-shaded avenues, interspersed with open-air bars, line the beach. Shops of all shapes and sizes are around every corner, offering a tempting assortment of bargains. And in the evening, the town bursts even more into life with its bars, restaurants, discotheques and nightclubs. And not to be missed is the super night out at the 'El Mas' barbecue.
>
> Calella is also a good centre for excursions – to Barcelona – to Montserrat – to Andorra or to cruise between the coastal resorts and see the unspoilt beauty of the Costa Brava. Or to simply get around by using the scenic railway that runs all along the coast.
>
> Only a mile away and yet in contrast to Calella is the picturesque little town of Pineda, with its beautiful main square and colourful gardens. Life is on a quieter note here, although there are enough bars and restaurants (and a disco or two) for when the mood takes you.
>
> Club Cantabrica Brochure, Holiday House (1992)

Questions

Now answer these questions.

a   What facts do we learn about Calella and the area around it?
b   Your tutor will discourage you from writing sentences that start with 'and'. Why do you think this writer does it so often?
c   What is wrong with the last sentence of the fourth paragraph? Consult Chapter 6, Unit 1.
d   Make two columns. List all the descriptive words (adjectives) used in the first five lines, up to 'sea', in the left-hand column. In the right-hand column put a word with the opposite meaning. For example:

popular   unpopular, shunned
sparkling   dull

Think also of words with the opposite meanings to replace 'welcomes', 'array' and 'attractions'. Write out the first part of the passage using your substitute words.
Read your new description of Calella. The travel firm wouldn't sell many holidays now, I suspect!
e   Look at the rest of the passage. Could there be another way of looking at the other features mentioned? For example, when we're told that the town 'bursts into life' it could mean that it's noisy and overcrowded. Try to find three or four similar instances of the description putting everything in the best possible light.
f   If it is feasible, in a small group discuss what you have found out from answering the previous questions.

ACTIVITY

6b

Writing a Parody or Pastiche

Look up the words 'parody' and 'pastiche' in a dictionary. What is the difference? Choose which of the two you will be writing in this activity.

Make a list of possible attractions in the area where you live. Be inventive. If you don't live in a recognised 'tourist spot', think of features that could be marketed in this way.

Write the entry on your district for a holiday brochure. Try to give that persuasive and enthusiastic tone to your work even if what you are describing is what one might call unusual!

Drafting and Revising

When you feel you've finished, read through your description carefully. Does it sound irresistible? Have you used plenty of exciting adjectives? If not, add more or revise until you're happy with it. Don't worry if it sounds a bit 'over the top'. It should do! Check for accurate spelling and punctuation (see Chapter 6).

ACTIVITY
6c

Informal Writing

Imagine that, lured by the glowing description in Activity B, someone spent a fortnight's holiday in your area. Writing as that person, compose a letter to a friend, saying how dreadful it was. Make it seem as bad as possible but keep it plausible and based on some semblance of reality. For example, if you live in an isolated country spot, someone else might loathe this – your 'relaxing solitude' might be their lonely nightmare! Remember how we twisted round the attractions of Calella? Colloquial expressions are acceptable here but spelling and punctuation must still be accurate. For the correct layout for the letter, see Chapter 6, Unit 6.

ACTIVITY
6d

Reading and Understanding

Read the following pieces of travel writing which were published in the *Observer* newspaper. Extract A is written by Robin McKie, and Extract B is by John Collee.

When you have read both passages thoroughly complete the assignment below.

Extract A

In the heart of the Highlands, there is a wilderness without peer in Western Europe. Stretching between Glen Nevis and Blair Atholl, and lined by Glens Spean and Coe to the north and south, it covers more than 250 square miles of bog, moor and mountain, a desolate plateau permanently inhabited by less than a dozen human beings.

This bleak land of peat hags and lochans has a distinguished pedigree. Scotland's ancient Royal hunting grounds were sited here; Bonny Prince Charlie hid with loyal Cluny on corrie-pocked Ben Alder after Culloden; while David Balfour and Alan Breck, the fictional heroes of Robert Louis Stevenson's *Kidnapped*, escaped the redcoats across Rannoch Moor, 'a wearier looking desert which man never saw'.

These words are typical, I have since discovered – as are John Macculloch's, an eighteenth-century traveller who described the lands of Courrour, Rannoch and Alder as 'a place of inconceivable solitude, a dreary and joyless land of bogs, a land of desolation and grey darkness'.

You get the picture, then. This is not a twee, comfortable landscape of rolling hills and elegant pastures. Its horizons are empty and austere. Equally they have a haughty beauty and grandeur. Even better, this magnificent vision has not changed a jot for two centuries, creating a wild unspoiled oasis in the middle of the suburban garden that is modern Britain.

The *Observer* 26 July 1992, Robin McKie

Extract B

'Vajra Hotel,' I said to the taxi driver as soon as I arrived in Katmandu.

We drove straight through the tourist quarter of Thamel, in so far as a taxi ever drives straight in Katmandu, nudging between rickshaws and flute sellers, world travellers, street hawkers and recumbent cows. We continued through Chhetrapati district, past a knot of students shouting political slogans, past a sunken pool festooned with startling clean laundry.

'Vajra,' I repeated. Chhetrapati had vanished behind us. We were free-wheeling downhill towards the river.

The road ended abruptly where the previous monsoon had swept away the bridge. We crossed the river on a makeshift pontoon of wood and sandbags. Black pigs rootled in the stinking shallows. I was about to tell the driver to turn back when we chuntered up the far bank and there, sure enough, was an oval sign with 'Hotel Vajra' in red letters. Behind its high brick walls, the Vajra was surprisingly beautiful, built in the Newar style with elaborate, carved windows and the tiled overhanging eaves of a Florentine palazzo.

There was a flowering tree outside my window with yellow flowers the size of party hats. From the roof terrace you could look west to where the sun was now dropping behind the distant golden stupa of the Monkey Temple. To the east lay Katmandu – a row of crazy brick tenements on the far side of the river. At sunset their zinc water tanks gleamed like pale beacons in the blue and pink haze. In the sky above them hung the thick white rope of the Himalayas. I knew I would be happy here.

The *Observer* 12 July 1992, John Collee

Assignment

a Make a list of the distinctive features of each of the places. Set these out down the page as you did with the adjectives in Activity A. Beside each item, note whether, in your opinion, the writer felt it was a good or bad aspect. Now compare the two. Do you feel that the writers' tastes are similar? Which place do you think you would prefer to visit? If it's practical, discuss your answer with other group members.

b The description of Calella in the holiday brochure seen in Activity A was written for a very specific purpose. What do you think the writers' purposes were when writing these articles?

c Both passages contain words whose meaning and/or usage may not be familiar to you. Looking up these words or phrases in a dictionary if necessary, explain their meaning in this context. From A look up: 'without peer'; 'lochans'; 'corrie'; 'austere'; 'unspoiled oasis'; 'suburban garden that is modern Britain'. And from B: 'recumbent'; 'festooned'; 'rootled'; 'pontoon'; 'stupa'; 'tenements'; 'beacons'. How effective is the use of these words, in your opinion? Can you think of alternative ways of saying the same thing?

ACTIVITY

6e

Reading – Research and Information Retrieval

1   Find out the exact location of Calella, Rannoch Moor and Katmandu by looking them up in an atlas. If you don't have one yourself, a college or public library will. Now see what else you can find out about them in books, magazines and holiday brochures. Look for photographs. Ask yourself whether these sources are designed for publicity or to give factual information.

2   Choose a far away place which is attractive to you but which you have never visited. Find out enough to allow you to write an informative factual article. You can use this research for Activity F.

ACTIVITY

6f

Coursework – Writing

Now it's your turn to be a travel writer.

A women's magazine has asked you to produce a short article (about 500 words) about somewhere you have visited.

The Editor's Requirements

This is what the editor would like you to do:

- Create an exact picture of what the place looks, sounds and smells like.
- Describe what it feels like to be there in terms of weather, climate and so forth.
- Convey a vivid impression of the atmosphere or ambience (check this word in a dictionary if you're not sure of its precise meaning).
- Give a strong impression of your attitude towards the place – whether you liked or disliked it.

Preparation

As this writing is for a women's magazine, you may wish to look at a few of these to investigate their approach. If you wish to specify a particular magazine for your article, that's fine.

Think about whether, in your opinion, certain aspects should be included or excluded because of the readers' likely interests and concerns. Be careful not to make assumptions – for example, that female readers only wish to know about shopping facilities!

Starting Effectively

Look back at the opening of Extract B. The writer starts with the moment of his arrival in Katmandu. He does not spend several paragraphs telling us why he decided to go there, where he bought the tickets and what he packed in his suitcase. In a short piece of writing there's no room for this. Decide on a good way to begin which takes us straight to the heart of your chosen place. An effective opening gets the readers' attention straight-away.

Drafting and Revising

Write a first draft. When you feel you have finished, check it through. You may wish to consult your tutor at this stage.

Content

Check with the editor's requirements given earlier. Have you remembered to include smells and sounds as well as sights? Have you conveyed your feelings about the place?

Structure

Is your writing in an order that is easy to follow – does it flow smoothly from one aspect to another? Is it in the most effective order? Would it be more interesting and lively if it was rearranged?

Accuracy

Check spelling, punctuation and expression (see Chapter 6). Does it make perfect sense?

Once you are happy with all the above points, prepare the final draft. Here are some suggestions:

Think of a catchy headline (see Chapter 5, Unit 3) and follow it by your name, for example DEVON IN THE DOWNPOUR by Sandy Clarke.

Look out any photographs that you may have taken. If none is available, perhaps you can find some in a brochure or a book about the area. A photocopy of one or more of these, strategically placed in your work, will make it look very professional.

If you have access to a word processor or typewriter you may wish to use it for this piece of work. Again this will give it a professional look.

Make sure you put the date of writing somewhere on your work for future reference.

Finally, read it all through again, looking for any remaining errors.

ACTIVITY

6g

Coursework – Speaking and Listening

Give a short talk on the place which you used for your written coursework. Aim to speak for between five and ten minutes.

Preparation

Provided you have sufficient material, preparation should be quite easy.

Here is some general advice.

Try, if possible, to include a bit of humour: this lightens the tone and creates interest. Think about what your audience will enjoy and use words and expressions that are suitable for them. Two basic rules are that your audience should be able to hear what you are saying and understand what you mean. You'll know by their response whether you've been successful or not.

Never write down a prepared speech and read it out. This is not at all the same as speaking aloud. The effect is stilted and boring as you have to look at your paper, not out towards your audience.

List headings for the various aspects which you will be describing. Put each one, with just a few words to remind you, on a small index card. Arrange these into the right order.

If you wish to refer to pictures and posters or wish to use maps or diagrams, work out where they must be so that they can be displayed or passed round. It is often interesting to have some illustrations. Ordinary photographs can be projected onto a screen using an episcope. If you can obtain one, you may wish to use it. Familiarise yourself with its working ahead of time, though. Similarly, it may be possible to use an overhead projector rather than a board to give information. Make sure you know how to operate this if you plan to use it.

Mark on your cards where references to visual material are to be made. You don't want to compile lots of maps and pictures only to find that you've forgotten to mention them!

When you're speaking, bear in mind the following:

- Try to look at the audience generally rather than just at your tutor. If you feel too shy, pick a spot on the wall somewhere behind them. Don't look at the floor or your notes all the time.
- Don't speak too fast. Gabbling to get it over and done with is not advisable.
- Speak loudly enough to be heard. Don't hide behind your hands, your hair or your notes as your voice will be muffled.
- Try not to use irritating and distracting mannerisms like twiddling your hair or jingling coins in your pocket.
- If you're enthusiastic about your subject matter, this will be communicated to your audience and your talk will be interesting.

You may wish to practise your talk beforehand using a tape-recorder (or someone in your family). Remember, everyone's voice sounds weird on tape – not just yours!

ACTIVITY

6h

Optional Further Reading

If you enjoyed the pieces of writing in this unit look out for similar ones in the Sunday newspapers. In addition, find the travel section in your local library. You'll find guide books and first-hand descriptions that make good reading even if you're unlikely to travel any further than your favourite armchair!

Review of Unit 6

- Activity A was reading and knowledge about language (En 2.2, 4).
- Activity B was writing (En 3).
- Activity C was writing (En 3).
- Activity D was reading and understanding (En 2.2, 4).
- Activity E was reading, research and information retrieval (En 2.3).
- Activity F was written coursework using research (En 2.3, En 3).
- Activity G was speaking and listening coursework (En 1).
- Activity H was optional further reading (En 2.1, 2).

Making a Record

On your Coursework Index Form, write down the necessary information about the coursework in this unit. This was the written work and research in Activity E and the individual oral work in Activity F. Tick all the relevant aspects of En 1, En 2 and En 3 on your Coursework Checklist.

What Should You Do Now?

Turn to Unit 1 of Chapter 2.

② Narrating

*I*N this chapter we look at narration. You will be telling stories, of various sorts and in various ways. Like describing, narrating can be seen as a form of personal writing. Most GCSE syllabuses expect candidates to have at least one example of this in their coursework folders.

This is what we will be working on:

- writing and speaking effectively about experiences and feelings;
- structuring effectively what is said or written;
- showing a sense of audience;
- adapting style of communication to achieve particular effects;
- revising and redrafting work so it is both interesting and correct;
- communicating a sensitive response to what is read.

Where Should You Begin?

Complete all the activities in Unit 1. When you have done this it is probably a good idea to select at least one more unit from this chapter but if you prefer, you may move on to another chapter in order to tackle a different kind of writing.

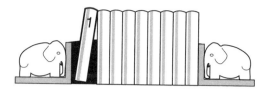

UNIT (**1**) Consequences

UNIT (**1**) Consequences

What is the main difference between narrating and describing? Doing Activity A should help you to understand the difference.

ACTIVITY

1a

Planning a Story

Think of the story of Little Red Riding Hood. You can sum it up by saying that it's about a little girl who goes to see her grandmother and is attacked by the wolf who has dressed up in Granny's clothes. Here we have two main ingredients – **characters** and **action**.

The story could be set out like this:

CHARACTERS
Little Red Riding Hood, Granny, Wolf

ACTION
Attack on Little Red Riding Hood by Wolf

Think of a story that you know well – it could be a story you remember from childhood or the plot of a film you saw recently. Set it out the same way using the headings, 'characters' and 'action'.

In a written version of Little Red Riding Hood, of course, a certain amount of description would be used – of the wood she walks through, of the wolf's hairy face and so on – but the plot and the characters are the most important aspects when it comes to story telling. Most stories will be about something that happens to someone.

Writing a good story requires careful preparation. In order to tell the story you have to know exactly what is going to happen, not just at the beginning, but also at the end. Many students start writing stories without having decided the final outcome, hoping that inspiration will come to them along the way. All too often it does not! The worst consequence of this is the 'dream' ending, hated violently by all teachers of English. You know how it goes: 'Then I found that it was morning and my mother was shaking me. It was all a dream!' In other words, having embroiled the central character in a ridiculous or impossible mess or having lost interest after two sides of writing, this is the only solution possible in a couple of sentences.

For the moment, then, instead of actually writing a story, let's just consider plots. We need one or more characters and for something to happen. We want to keep it simple because the story is going to be a short one. The length you are aiming at is about 500 words, not 500 pages!

Reading and Analysis

Consequences

You may have come across a game called 'Consequences' when you were younger. Each person involved has a piece of paper. They write a line on the piece of paper and then fold it over and pass it on to the next person. At each stage you're putting down one of a sequence of facts or events. At the end, because each person is writing 'blind', you have an improbable (and often rude) story on each piece of paper. The ingredients are something like this:

1 boy's name (a male character has now been identified);
2 girl's name (a female character has been added);
3 where they met (the setting is now established);
4 what he said to her;
5 what she said to him;
6 what he did;
7 what she did (stages 4 to 7 give us the action of the story);
8 the consequence of that was (this gives us the result of the action).

Look at the story below about a chocolate eclair and identify the eight steps above (they don't necessarily appear in the same order).

The Chocolate Eclair

It had been a terrible morning. Staggering under the weight of the shopping bags, I fought my way into the cafe. I would collapse for half an hour with a cup of coffee and then get the bus home.

The town that morning had been amazingly crowded. Everyone seemed to have decided, despite the rain, that winter was over and it was time to come out of hibernation. The queue in the bank had been miles long, the one in the Post Office ridiculous. Now, finally, with half of the produce of Gateway's bulging out of my carrier bags, I was going to treat myself.

'A cup of coffee, please,' I said to the girl behind the counter. Suddenly I weakened. 'And a chocolate eclair.'

Juggling my bags with difficulty, I looked round, only to realise that there were no empty tables. I approached one by the window which was occupied by a man engrossed in a newspaper. 'Sorry. Do you mind?' I asked, putting down my cup.

'Not at all,' he said, continuing to read.

I dropped my various bags, unbuttoned my coat and sank onto the chair. I stirred my coffee and drew a deep breath. That was better.

Suddenly, scarcely taking his eyes off his paper, the man reached forward, picked up the chocolate eclair from its plate and took a bite of it.

I couldn't believe my eyes. I stared at him open-mouthed. He appeared not to notice. He looked quite respectable too – he was dressed in a dark suit and a smart raincoat. Even his paper was an expensive one. What should I do? I wasn't going to be done out of my treat.

I looked round at the other tables to see if anyone had witnessed his disgusting behaviour. Everyone was absorbed in their own business – gossiping, wiping down children, laughing and talking.

With an outraged 'Huh!' I drew the plate closer towards me, picked up the eclair and took a large cream-filled bite. That would teach him.

This time it was his turn to look surprised. The paper froze in mid-rustle and he paused in the act of rearranging the pages. He glared at me, his dark brows meeting over his nose. He seemed to hesitate for a moment, then, to my fury, he pulled the plate over to his side of the table, lifted what was left of the eclair and took another bite.

That did it. I scrambled to my feet, gathered up my shopping, picked up the last of the eclair, stuffed it into my mouth and marched towards the door. I was half way through it when the most embarrassing words I have ever heard came towards me. I glanced back; there she was, smiling and waving a plate in my direction.

'Excuse me, love,' called the girl from behind the counter, 'you've forgotten your chocolate eclair!'

Realising with horror what had happened, I blushed scarlet and fled from the cafe in dismay.

Here, the consequence (the conclusion), is directly linked to the early part of the story.

Look back at the narrator. Although it isn't actually stated, there are strong suggestions that this character is female. What evidence can you find for this?

What happens in the story is directly linked to how she is feeling and to the story's setting. We are told that she is tired and that the town is extremely busy – consequently the cafe is crowded. Because she has lots of shopping she fails to notice that she hasn't picked up her eclair. The man does not object to her sharing his table, but takes no particular notice of her – consequently she does not realise that he already has an eclair of his own. The final result is that she rushes out in embarrassment having in fact done what she thought he was doing!

This story is based around two characters and a single incident. The setting is used as background and is not fully developed. The story is about 500 words in length. This relative simplicity is what you should be aiming at. But what was the writer's intention?

As the story is written in the first person (I), there is the possibility that the reader can identify with this person. It is likely that anybody could land him or herself in a similar situation. As readers we are meant to sympathise with the character's feelings, having imagined ourselves in her predicament.

ACTIVITY

1c

Coursework – Speaking and Listening

It is quite likely that you have experienced an occasion which has caused you embarrassment. This can provide an opportunity for a piece of oral coursework. Tell your story to a small group of fellow students, to your tutor or record it on audio tape.

Try to plan and structure what you say. There is no problem, here, about remembering to plan the end of the story – you **know** what happened, after all. You will still need to decide where to start, though. You might need to give some background information in order to set the scene. You then need to say precisely what happened. You also need to say how you felt and whether there has been any long-lasting effect. For example, I doubt whether the narrator of 'The Chocolate Eclair' would return to that cafe for some weeks after the incident. If it's helpful, you can write down key words to remind you what you intended to say. Don't write your story down and read it out. The idea here is to **tell** people and any words you write down should just serve to prompt you.

If you are working in a small group, you can follow up your stories with a discussion of each others' experiences.

ACTIVITY

1d

Planning a Plot

Often, in an English course, you'll be given a title and be expected to come up with an interesting and original story based on it. Three main problems tend to occur.

1. The Two-page Introduction

If you are aiming to write about 500 words (about two sides of A4 paper in average handwriting) you have to plunge pretty well straight into the important part of the story. If, for example, you are writing about 'The Big Match', you can't afford to spend two sides, or even one, describing where you first heard about it, how you luckily obtained the tickets, what you had for breakfast on the day, how you got stuck in a traffic jam: not if your intention is to write about the match itself. If the point of the story was that after looking forward to it so much, you finally missed it, some of this type of detail might be justified. Similarly, if you were writing about an incident at a party, spending a side or more describing how the central character went shopping to find an outfit, lay soaking in a bath for three hours, skilfully applied her make-up and then put on her new clothes, would be wasting time when you should have been telling the story.

2. The Standard Plot

It's an extraordinary fact that faced with a title, hundreds of people come up with the same idea. This tends to become a bit boring for anyone reading such work on a regular basis. You might quite reasonably ask, 'How will I know?' Your best bet is to discard the first idea that occurs to you – that's the one everybody else had – and try to develop something a little more unusual. A story called 'The Prisoner' immediately conjures up the picture of someone in a cell usually having been arrested for a crime committed by someone else. A more interesting alternative could be that the story appears to be about a prison cell but is actually about a budgie in a cage – complete with instruments of torture like the bell, the mirror, exclusion of light (the cover) and the plastic 'friend'. Or it could be about someone imprisoned in an unhappy relationship, or in a wheelchair as a result of an accident. In the story something could happen to show the character that there is some way to freedom, that life can be happy after all.

3. Lack of Realism Because of Limited Knowledge

Most people write best about what they actually know. Writers of thrillers have almost certainly researched such things as the effects of poisons, the characteristics of certain makes of gun and the speech patterns of New York cops. It is quite likely that you have not. If that's so, don't write about it! You may feel that you've read sufficient books of a particular type to be able to copy the style convincingly. I would still be dubious. One particular example I came across was a story about a plane crashing in the South American jungle. This immediately set various alarm bells ringing in my head. In this story (entitled 'The Crash') the aircraft had come down in dense forest; the pilot was flung out and trapped (somehow) beneath the fuselage. In order to attract the attention of other planes passing overhead, he decided to start a fire. Pinned down as he was this should have been tricky if not impossible, but no, he gathered fallen wood and soon had it alight. Should any plane happen to have been passing, it would probably have noticed the blaze as, presumably, the whole plane would have gone up in smoke, the pilot with it! Even had he, improbably, survived, of course there would have been few if any possibilities of a passing plane landing nearby and even fewer of a search party finding the wreck through impenetrable jungle! Be warned! A story about a pile up on the M1 in dense fog would not have been so exotic but I suspect it would have been a lot more plausible and realistic.

Bearing these three problems in mind, work out interesting and realistic plots to fit two of the titles which follow:

- The Dump;
- The Odd One Out;
- The Trap;
- A Perfect Partner;
- Lost;
- The Winner.

Don't forget the steps we looked at earlier. A sensible procedure would be to think of the following, although not necessarily in this order:

- main character;
- other characters (not too many);
- what the setting is;
- what happens, (stick to one major incident);
- what the consequences are.

Discuss your plots with other class members, your tutor or sympathetic friends and relations. Between you decide which is the most effective and whether it could be improved in any way. If you were working with other students were the ideas you came up with similar?

ACTIVITY

1e

Coursework – Writing

Having reached this stage, you have a few more decisions to make and then you can start writing your chosen plot into a full story.

Characters

If you haven't already done so, think of names and the background details of your main characters. You may not actually bring these into the story but you should know about them. You should decide on such aspects as their age, appearance, personality and job.

Setting

Decide where your story is set geographically (preferably somewhere you know); decide what time of year it is (you don't want to mention autumn leaves in one paragraph and daffodils in the next). If it's important to the story you are telling, decide what the weather is like.

Style of Narration

Are you going to assume the identity of a character in the story and write as 'I', i.e. in the first person? Alternatively are you going to write in the third person, i.e. about 'he' and 'she'?

Time and Tense

Most stories are told in the past tense – 'he said', 'she went', 'I felt'. If you want to do something different from this, be careful. You need to be consistent all the way through. If something happened before the beginning of the story you need to use a more distant past tense: for example, 'she thought **she had seen** him before'; 'he said **he had hated** them for years'. If you look at the first paragraph of 'The Chocolate Eclair' (**Activity B**) you will see this illustrated when she talks about what she had done in the town before going to the cafe.

Do you want to tell the story in a straightforward way, as it happens? This is probably best at this point in your course. Devices like flashbacks can be effective but it's probably wise to leave them for later.

Speech Punctuation

Almost inevitably, you will include speech in this story. Turn **now** to Chapter 6, Unit 4 and study the rules until you are confident that you can punctuate speech accurately. This is an area where many people make mistakes so try to ensure that you are not one of them.

Now you are ready to start writing.

Drafting and Revising

Write a first draft and see how it goes. When you've finished, read it through. Have you included the right amount of description to give the reader a picture of people and places? Does the end of the story appear to be a consequence of what went before? Is it realistic? Is it interesting? If you feel dissatisfied with any of these aspects, write an improved version.

Now check for accuracy. Have you punctuated speech correctly? Are all the end commas in place? Check again. Is your spelling correct? Have you written in sentences?

Once you are pleased with both content and accuracy, write it out neatly, put the title, your name and the date of writing at the top and hand it to your tutor for assessment.

ACTIVITY

1f

Optional Coursework – Writing

You may feel that you would be happier writing a story if you knew how it was to begin. Often getting started is the trickiest part. Use the title 'A Fresh Start' and use the paragraphs given below as the start of your story. You must still go through the plotting procedure outlined in Activity D but some of the information, though not the consequence or outcome, has been given to you.

A Fresh Start

Again there was nothing.

With a disgusted sigh, Barry flung one local newspaper on the floor and reached for the other one, mechanically turning the pages. What was he meant to do? It was six months now since he'd lost his job and most weeks there was nothing worth applying for either in the papers or at the Job Centre. This week seemed to be just the same. What he needed was a chance to show what he could do, to have a fresh start.

The advert caught his eye almost as if it had been conjured up by his thoughts.

'Boost your morale and gain useful qualifications,' he read. 'Middleton

College offers a fresh start for mature students.' Go to college? Could he? Barry remembered his school days all too clearly. There seemed to be so many better ways of spending a sunny afternoon than cooped up in a dusty classroom. Like most of his mates he'd left finally without any paper qualifications . . .

Clearly there is going to be some important development in Barry's life because of seeing the advert. Try to make it interesting but at the same time probable. He could do brilliantly and go on to university. He could be employed as a caretaker or he could fall in love with his beautiful Maths teacher. It's up to you. Don't write, though, about how many trout he catches when he goes fishing on a Sunday unless this can be directly traced back in some way to the opening of the story.

Drafting and Revising

As before, check content and accuracy when you think you have finished the story. Revise to improve both as necessary. When you're happy with the result, put the appropriate headings and submit your story for assessment.

ACTIVITY

1g

Optional Further Reading

To see sound plotting in operation, look at any good detective novel. Writers like P.D. James, Ruth Rendell and Dorothy Sayers will provide you with good illustrations. You also might want to look at *The Day of the Jackal* by Frederick Forsyth and any novel by Dick Francis. These light and approachable novels will demonstrate how a plot can gradually unfold, leading to carefully planned consequences.

Review of Unit 1

- Activity A was preparatory work.
- Activity B was reading and analysis (En 2.1, 4).
- Activity C was speaking and listening coursework (En 1.1, 2, 3).
- Activity D was preparatory work.
- Activity E was written coursework (En 3).
- Activity F was optional written coursework (En 3).
- Activity G was optional further reading (En 2.1).

Making a Record

Now find your Coursework Index Form and write down all the relevant information. Write down the number of the piece according to how many you have now done and put the chapter, unit and task number for reference. Note the date and put a title or brief description, then list the ATs covered in the final column. The relevant tasks here are the individual and group oral work in Activity C and the written work in Activities E and F.

When you have done that, tick the relevant aspects of En 1 and En 3 on your Coursework Checklist.

What Should You Do Now?

Either choose another unit from this chapter or turn to the first unit of a different chapter.

The other units in Chapter 2 are as follows:

Unit 2 – Letter Line

This unit is about writing stories in the form of or inspired by letters.

Unit 3 – It's a Mystery

In this unit you look at the techniques used in stories involving suspense, then put these into practice in your coursework.

Unit 4 – Play for Today

Instead of using letters, in this unit you will be writing stories in play form.

Unit 5 – Once upon a Time

In this unit you look at examples of and techniques used in traditional stories and write one yourself using what you have learned.

(**2**) *Letter Line*

If you decide to work on this unit, this is what you should do: complete Activities A and B which prepare you for later work. Do Activity C which is speaking and listening coursework, then move on to Activity D which is written coursework. When you have completed Activity D you may, if you wish, turn to another unit in this chapter or to the first unit of another chapter. It is a good idea, however, to complete the two further tasks in this unit. Activity E is an opportunity for further written coursework, this time using a letter as the starting point for a story. Activity F gives you the chance of reading and responding to an extract from Shakespeare's *Romeo and Juliet*. Studying pre-twentieth century literature is necessary if you hope to achieve a higher level than 7 (level 8 is GCSE grade B).

Stories in letters

You may not know this, but many of the earliest novels written in English consisted of letters being written from one character to another thus telling a story from more than one point of view.

In this unit we're going to use letters as the basis or starting point for various different stories.

ACTIVITY

(**2a**)

Preparation and Planning

Virtually everyone will have read the problem page of a magazine or newspaper at some time. Often it's the first page people turn to.

Imagine the scene: You're sitting in the dentist's waiting room. You pick up a magazine and find the problem page. To your annoyance, someone has cut out an advert on the previous page which means that the first 'Dear Jo' letter is missing. All that's left is this reply:

> Dear Christine,
> Many people feel the same. It's not an easy situation. Perhaps there is a local organisation which provides a point of contact for others like you in your area. It's sometimes a question of getting out of the house for part of the day so that you are able to think of other matters and get things into perspective. If there is no support group around, you might think of starting one. This, in itself, would allow you to meet other people and provide you with other activities. For further help and advice, telephone freefone 0800 45678.

What do you think the missing letter to Jo is about?

Let's consider the clues. This person, Christine, is obviously confined to her home for long periods of time. This could be because she has a particular illness or disability. Jo suggests that she should get out each day or start a support group – does that suggest that it is less likely that Christine herself is incapacitated? What are the other possibilities? Perhaps she is unemployed and feels that she has no goal in life. Would lack of money prevent her, then, from actually starting something up? Alternatively, she could be caring for someone else: a young or handicapped child, an elderly person or someone who has been disabled by illness or accident. Are there any other possibilities?

Decide what Christine's problem is and write her letter to 'Dear Jo'.

ACTIVITY

2b

Writing a Series of Letters

You pick up another copy of the magazine and find that the advert cutter has been busy again. This time the reply to one of the letters is missing. This is the 'Dear Jo' letter.

> Dear Jo,
>
> My parents are driving me mad. I'm seventeen years old and nearing the end of a course at college. I have quite a lot of friends who are older than me. They work at the local hospital and most evenings I join them at the staff social club. I often don't get in until after midnight but I sleep in the next day. I rarely bother with family meals these days because my Mum just uses this time to nag at me and anyway I'm overweight. I smoke quite heavily and like to have some drinks (alcoholic) with my friends. I'd like to move out and get a place of my own but I haven't any money. What should I do?
> Sarah
> North London

What is Sarah complaining about, exactly? What does she want to be allowed to do? How should the agony aunt approach her in the reply? If she is too critical of Sarah's various activities she may sound as if she's nagging, just like Mum. Try to find the right tone – not sharp, but not patronising either.

Letter 1. *Write Jo's Reply*

If you're carrying out this activity with other students it might be interesting to compare your answers. Through this you will have a better idea of the suitability of your version. You may wish to revise yours in the light of what you've seen.

It could be that Sarah's mother might also feel inclined to write to a problem page. Let's think about the situation from her point of view. Her daughter is missing college and so is likely to fail her exams, being 'led astray' by older friends, smoking, drinking under age, not eating properly (potentially anorexic), and considering 'running away'. Sarah is also probably being rather rude and unpleasant to her mother on the odd occasions she sees her.

Letter 2. The Mother's Letter to Jo

Having thought this through from the other point of view, write the mother's letter to 'Dear Jo'. Make it sound as realistic as possible.

When you have done that, think about Jo's reply. She might talk about Sarah's case as a typical example of teenage rebellion. She might suggest having a word with her college tutors to see how bad the problem is, asking them to speak to Sarah about a future career if she does fail her exams. She might tell you not to over-react and not to worry unnecessarily.

Letter 3. Jo's Reply

When you think you've decided what would be said, write Jo's reply.

This is only part of the story. You have Sarah's situation as she sees it and also her mother's point of view. You have advice to both of them from a third party. The question is, what happened? Did Sarah moderate her behaviour in the light of Jo's reply? Did she fail her college course? Did she make herself ill? Or was she actually doing all the work she need-ed to, getting herself a good job at the hospital a few months later and a shared house with friends because of her contacts there? Did the mother stop fretting and allow Sarah to go her own way, or did she try to insist on her staying in on weekday evenings and eating a decent meal once a day, at least until her course was over and she was eighteen?

Letter 4. Letter to a Friend

Three years have passed. As EITHER Sarah OR her mother, write a letter to a friend who is currently in the situation you were in then. Talk about what happened in your case. Say how you feel now about that time and discuss how each of you behaved, assessing whether it was right or wrong. Give your friend the appropriate advice in the light of your experience.

ACTIVITY

2c

Coursework – Speaking and Listening

Armed with the letters which you have written for Activity A, discuss, in a small group, the behaviour and attitudes of everyone involved: the daughter, the parent, the 'agony aunt'.

Appoint someone as 'group leader', whose job it is to keep the discussion moving without anyone either 'hogging' it or staying too silent. The following questions may be a useful basis for this activity.

● What different views did group members have about what would happen in the future (as used in letter 4)?

- How do views differ on the right way to handle someone like Sarah?
- Do these differences reflect the comparative ages of group members?
- What have individuals' experiences been of this sort of conflict, whether as offspring or as parents?
- Were there differences in opinion between those who had experienced such a problem as parents, and those who had experienced the problem as children?

ACTIVITY
2d

Coursework – Writing

Here are two other situations along the same lines. Choose the one of these which most appeals to you and write the suggested sequence of letters.

Situation A

The letter below appeared on the problem page.

> Dear Jo,
>   I have just come home early from a visit to my son Mike and his wife who live in America. I was really looking forward to the trip, but when I got there it was so different from what I expected. They were friendly enough to start off with but then I felt that I was in the way, only useful when they needed a baby-sitter. They all seem to lead such busy lives nowadays. Once we were a close and loving family. They've only been in America for nine months.
>   J.D.
>   Northampton

Sequence of Letters for You to Write

1   Write a letter from the son, Mike, to his parent (decide whether J.D. is his mother or father) saying that he is going to take a job in America.
2   Write a letter from Mike to a friend describing his mother or father's reaction to his decision to live and work abroad.
3   Write a letter from Mike persuading his parent to come and visit.
4   Write a letter from Mike's wife (invent a name) to a friend or relation, describing the visit of her parent-in-law.
5   Write a letter to the parent from either Mike or his wife trying to smooth things over and restore a friendly relationship.
6   Write the parent's reply to (5). This letter should really finish things off – either patching up the quarrel or breaking off communication for ever.

Situation B

The letter below from Angie appeared on the same page: use it if you prefer it to that given for Situation A.

> Dear Jo,
>   My life isn't worth living. For the last six months I have been in love with someone I believed to be the most wonderful man in the world. Now I've found out that he's married and his feelings for me were all lies. I don't know what to do. I just sit at home and mope. I'll never love or trust anyone else.
>   Angie
>   Macclesfield

The Sequence of Letters for You to Write

Write the following sequence of letters:

1   Write a letter from Angie to a friend describing how she first met the man (give him a name).
2   Write the man's letter to a friend also describing the early part of their relationship. Make his feelings clear. He could genuinely care about Angie or he could just be using her. Show his intentions with regard to telling her about his wife.
3   Write an anonymous letter to Angie informing her that he is married. Decide who this informant is and why this letter is being written (i.e. the motive behind it – it could be for Angie's good or through self-interest). Don't include this information in the letter. You need to know this so you can word the letter appropriately.
4   Write a letter from the anonymous author of (3) to a friend, explaining why this action has been taken.
5   Write Angie's reply to the man after receiving the anonymous letter. She should finish the relationship in this letter.
6   Write his reply to her. This letter should resolve the situation finally, one way or another.

Drafting and Revising

Once you have finished a first draft of either sequence of letters, check your work carefully. Have you used an identifiably different 'voice' for each author of a letter? Have you made the content consistent with the character you have created? Is each letter believable and interesting? Make any necessary improvements in the light of a critical read through.

   Now check the accuracy of your work. Check that your spelling is correct and that you have punctuated your work appropriately. Consult Chapter 6, Unit 6 for the correct layout for the letters. These are all in formal letters but you should put in the sender's address and a date on each one. You can show the timescale by careful choice of dates.

Producing the Final Version

Once you are totally satisfied that you have done this as well as you can, write the letters out neatly, each one on a separate sheet of paper. If you want to make this seem real you could use a different style of paper and handwriting for each character involved. You may not feel this is worth-while, however.

What You Might Do Now

You may, at this point, turn to another unit or chapter but two further tasks are now offered. It is a good idea to work through them even if you decide not to submit the written work for assessment. If you have decided to move on to another unit, turn first to the final page of this unit to see what you have covered in order to make an accurate record.

ACTIVITY

2e

Coursework – Writing

Here is another opportunity for a piece of imaginative personal writing.

This is the situation. Pat has recently died, leaving her daughter Mary to inherit the family home. Pat's husband Robert had died some years ear-lier, his heart having been weakened by fighting in the war. Mary is clear-ing the drawers of her mother's bureau when she comes across a packet of letters, tied with blue ribbon. This is the final letter in the sequence.

> 6 Fairfield Cottages
> Bassingbourn
> Cambs
>
> 8th May 1945
>
> Dear Stan,
> What you ask is impossible; it just wouldn't be fair. If I left Mary I'd never forgive myself. She means more to me than anyone else in the world, even you, my love. And Robert adores her too. If I took her with me, I'd be stealing her from him. He's done nothing to deserve that. In his letters he's always asking about her and wanting photographs. He can hardly wait to see her again. America is too far for a weekend.
> So you see, my dear, I've no choice. I can't leave her and I can't take her away from her Dad.
> Please send back my letters so that I can keep them with yours. It's not going to be easy, in the future, but perhaps I can look at them and remem-ber these months, the happiest time of my life. I'll never forget you.
> Pat

Use this as the basis for a story. Work out what happened, both before and after this letter – how she met Stan, who he was, what he looked like, what their feelings for each other were and what he was proposing.

You may either write the story 'straight' (perhaps in the first person, speaking as Pat) or write it in the form of letters between Pat, Stan and any other characters you wish to include (for example, a friend of each one).

Try to find out the significance of the date used and also the location. If you make any references to the War or the setting, be sure to check their accuracy.

Drafting and Revising

As always, when you've written a draft, check both the content and the accuracy. When you are happy, write it out neatly and hand it to your tutor for assessment.

ACTIVITY

2f

Written Response to Pre-Twentieth–Century Literature Coursework

If possible, see a live production or watch a video of Shakespeare's *Romeo and Juliet*. This will allow you to respond to the play as a whole. Even if this is impractical, look carefully at the following extract from Act IV, Scene I.

At this point in the play, Romeo has killed Juliet's cousin and has been banished. He has secretly married Juliet but her parents are insisting that she now marry Count Paris. She is confiding her troubles to Friar Lawrence who performed the marriage ceremony.

> *Juliet:* If, in thy wisdom, thou canst give no help,
> Do thou but call my resolution wise,
> And with this knife I'll help it presently.
> God join'd my heart and Romeo's, thou our hands;
> And ere this hand, by thee to Romeo's seal'd,
> Shall be the label to another deed,
> Or my true heart with treacherous revolt
> Turn to another, this shall slay them both.
> Therefore, out of thy long-experienc'd time,
> Give me some present counsel; or, behold,
> 'Twixt my extremes and me this bloody knife
> Shall play the umpire, arbitrating that
> Which the commission of thy years and art
> Could to no issue of true honour bring.
> Be not so long to speak; I long to die,
> If what thou speak'st speak not of remedy.

> *Friar Lawrence:* Hold, daughter; I do spy a kind of hope,
> Which craves as desperate an execution
> As that is desperate which we would prevent.
> If, rather than to marry County Paris,
> Thou hast the strength of will to slay thyself,
> Then is it likely thou wilt undertake

A thing like death to chide away this shame,
That cop'st with death himself to scape from it;
And, if thou dar'st, I'll give thee remedy.

Juliet: O, bid me leap, rather than marry Paris,
From off the battlements of any tower,
Or walk in thievish ways, or bid me lurk
Where serpents are; chain me with roaring bears,
Or hide me nightly in a charnel house,
O'er-cover'd quite with dead men's rattling bones,
With reeky shanks and yellow chapless skulls;
Or bid me go into a new-made grave,
And hide me with a dead man in his shroud –
Things that, to hear them told, have made me tremble –
And I will do it without fear or doubt,
To live an unstain'd wife to my sweet love.

Friar Lawrence: Hold, then; go home, be merry, give consent
To marry Paris. Wednesday is tomorrow;
Tomorrow night look that thou lie alone,
Let not the nurse lie with thee in thy chamber.
Take thou this vial, being then in bed,
And this distilled liquor drink thou off;
When presently through all thy veins shall run
A cold and drowsy humour; for no pulse
Shall keep his native progress, but surcease;
No warmth, no breath, shall testify thou livest;
The roses in thy lips and cheeks shall fade
To paly ashes, thy eyes' windows fall,
Like death when he shuts up the day of life;
Each part, depriv'd of supple government,
Shall, stiff and stark and cold, appear like death;
And in this borrow'd likeness of shrunk death
Thou shalt continue two and forty hours,
And then awake as from a pleasant sleep.
Now, when the bridegroom in the morning comes
To rouse thee from thy bed, there art thou dead.
Then, as the manner of our country is,
In thy best robes, uncovered on the bier,
Thou shalt be borne to that same ancient vault
Where all the kindred of the Capulets lie.
In the meantime, against thou shalt awake,
Shall Romeo by my letters know our drift,
And hither shall he come; and he and I
Will watch thy waking, and that very night
Shall Romeo bear thee hence to Mantua.
And this shall free thee from this present shame,
If no inconstant toy nor womanish fear
Abate thy valour in the acting it.

Romeo and Juliet, William Shakespeare (Alexander Text)

If there are unfamiliar words in this passage, look them up in a dictionary. Notice the difference in the way Juliet and Friar Lawrence speak. She is very young (only about fourteen). Look how emotional she is and how she threatens lots of extreme actions. He is much older and wiser as well as being a monk. He also knows of a solution to her problem.

Letters for You to Write

1   Using the style of letters to a problem page, write a letter from Juliet to Friar Lawrence asking for his advice. Take material from both of Juliet's speeches. Try to convey her desperation by including some of her wilder statements about what she will do to avoid having to marry Paris. You could use modern English or you might want to retain the flavour of the original.
2   When you have written this letter, write Friar Lawrence's reply. You can assume that the vial of liquid has been sent to her with the letter. In this case, of course, you are not writing for publication in a magazine. You are giving detailed advice about what she must do. Keep the style and tone appropriate to the character.
3   Write the letter, referred to in the extract, from Friar Lawrence to Romeo, explaining the situation. Romeo is also young and hot-headed, highly likely to want to rush back to Verona and kill Paris, thereby being arrested and ruining everything. Make sure, therefore, that you prevent him from taking this or any other rash course of action. Tell him precisely what he is to expect and what he must do. You probably know that it all goes wrong and the play ends in tragedy. This is not because Friar Lawrence wrote an ineffective letter, merely that Romeo didn't receive it.

If you have been able to look at the play as a whole, rather than just this extract, this piece of work may be submitted in your folder as a response to literature. If not, here you are studying pre-twentieth century literature (a requirement) and also practising responding to material in a way which may be similar to the examination (although you are unlikely to meet a Shakespeare extract there).

Drafting and Revising

As always, check your work thoroughly, writing more than one draft to improve content and style. Set the letters out appropriately. When you have written the final version, put a title, your name and the date. If you are writing coursework in response to literature, include this in the heading and put *Romeo and Juliet* by William Shakespeare.

ACTIVITY

2g

Optional Further Reading

Obtain a copy of Helene Hanff's novel *84 Charing Cross Road*. This tells the story, through letters, of her relationship with Frank, an antiquarian bookseller. It has been made into both a play and a film.

Review of Unit 2

- Activity A was preparatory work.
- Activity B was writing.
- Activity C was speaking and listening coursework (En 1.1, 2, 3).
- Activity D was written coursework (En 3).
- Activity E was written coursework (En 3).
- Activity F was reading and response to a pre-twentieth-century text and possible written coursework (En 2.1, En 3).
- Activity G was optional further reading (En 2.1).

Making a Record

Write down the necessary information about the coursework in this unit. This was the group oral work in Activity C and the written work in Activities D, E and F. Tick the relevant aspects of En 1, En 2 and En 3 on your Coursework Checklist.

What Should You Do Now?

Choose another unit in this chapter or turn to Unit 1 in another chapter.

UNIT (**3**) *It's a Mystery*

If you choose this unit you should complete all the tasks set.

Mystery Stories

The mystery story is one type which you're likely to want to try writing. This is a chance to pit your wits against the reader. Can you build up suspense, create a fascinating puzzle and finally provide a satisfying conclusion?

When writing this type of story you have to be careful. There's often a temptation to use a plot and setting which you know too little about. Careful planning is a must. You can't leave the outcome to chance. You will also have to think about how to tell the story as effectively as possible, dropping hints along the way and building up atmosphere and suspense.

ACTIVITY

(3a)

Preparation – The Plot

You may have come across the brain-teaser type of mystery where you're given a set of improbable facts and are invited to make sense of them by asking questions, the answers being restricted simply to 'yes' or 'no'. These can take hours to solve unless you hit on the right line of questioning or have the right sort of mind. Do you know this example?

The Mystery of Anthony and Cleopatra

Antony and Cleopatra are lying on the floor dead. Around them is a puddle of water and pieces of broken glass. What happened?

You might ask whether the window is broken. The answer is no. Is there anyone else in the room? No. Are there any wounds visible on the bodies? No. Did they take poison? No. Is the water important? Yes. Has a pipe burst? No. Is the window open? Yes. Is the water rain? No. Eventually you might happen to ask whether Antony and Cleopatra are human. The answer 'no' to that starts you on the right line of thinking. You finally discover that they are goldfish whose bowl has fallen off the windowsill because of a sudden gust of wind coming in. The bowl has broken, hence the glass and the spilt water. They have died because of being out of the water.

Roald Dahl wrote an interesting short story about a woman who kills her husband by hitting him on the head with a frozen leg of lamb. She then cooks the murder weapon and the police are totally mystified as they can find no clue about what weapon was used. They tuck into delicious lamb sandwiches while discussing the case with the 'distraught' widow!

Here are two short extracts (A and B) from mystery stories. Read the material then decide on an explanation for what happened or what is going on. If you can think of more than one possibility, so much the better. Jot down the ideas in note form. At this stage don't worry about how a story should be told.

Extract A

I was on the dark side of the road, in the thick shadow of some garden trees, when I stopped to look round. On the opposite and lighter side of the way, a short distance below me, a policeman was strolling along in the direction of the Regent's Park. A carriage passed me – an open chaise driven by two men. 'Stop!' cried one. 'There's a policeman. Let's ask him.' The horse was instantly pulled up, a few yards beyond the dark place where I stood.

'Policeman!' cried the first speaker. 'Have you seen a woman pass this way?'

'What sort of woman, sir?'

'A woman in a lavender coloured gown . . .'

'No, no,' interposed the second man. 'The clothes we gave her were found on her bed. She must have gone away in the clothes she wore when she came to us. In white, policeman. A woman in white.'

'I haven't seen her, sir.'

'If you or any of your men meet with the woman, stop her, and send her in careful keeping to that address. I'll pay all the expenses and a fair reward into the bargain.'

The policeman looked down at the card that was handed to him. 'Why are we to stop her, sir? What has she done?'

'Done! She has escaped from my Asylum. Don't forget; a woman in white. Drive on.'

The Woman in White, Wilkie Collins

Here you have to decide who the hidden observer is – it could be the woman in white. Why has she escaped? What motives does the man have for keeping her locked up there? Was she in need of treatment? She seemed, initially, to have come to the asylum of her own free will. Is she dangerous or is it the man who is? Make up as many plausible explanations as you can.

Extract B

Extract B is taken from a play called *The Exorcism* by Don Taylor. First, here's a description of the cottage which is the setting.

Edmund: Anyway it was a beautiful evening, so we decided to go for a walk. We followed a footpath across the fields – about three-quarters of a mile back over there – and then we saw the cottage, half hidden in the trees. It looked so completely isolated – no other house was in sight for miles – that we decided to go across and investigate. We'd always said that if ever we did manage to get a weekend cottage in the country we'd make damn sure it really was in the country, surrounded by trees and fields and emptiness, not twenty yards from a main road. So we climbed a style, crossed a ditch, scratched our legs to bits and had a look.

Dan: It's getting harder and harder. All the decent ones get snapped up in no time.

Edmund: It wasn't much more than a ruin really. Doors and windows boarded up, and nettles three feet high, right up to the door. But we liked the area, it's reasonably convenient for London, and anyway, Rachel fell in love with it.

[The following newsflash appears at the end of the play.]

The Newsflash

Newsreader: Finally, news has come in of a bizarre Christmas tragedy. In a remote country cottage, four apparently healthy people in their late thirties have been found dead. An air of mystery surrounds the story at the moment, said a spokesman from Scotland Yard, but foul play is not suspected. The four bodies, when found, were in an extremely emaciated condition, and although the house was full of food and drink, and a sumptuous Christmas dinner was laid on the table, almost untouched, all four people appeared to have died of starvation.

The Exorcism, Don Taylor

What happened? In this case, you may feel, a supernatural element is involved. As before, try to think of plausible explanations for this mystery.

Put these ideas on one side. You'll be returning to them later.

ACTIVITY

(3b)

Looking at Techniques for Creating Suspense

When writing a mystery story you are trying to provoke a strong reaction from the reader. You want them to have that shiver of fear creeping up the back of their neck. How are you going to achieve this?

Setting

Firstly the setting is important, in terms of place, time and weather. It's not accidental that in the extracts we have looked at so far, one was set on a dark road at night and the other in an old and isolated cottage. These are ingredients you frequently find in such stories. It is far more difficult to create a sinister atmosphere in a suburban housing estate at three o'clock on a sunny afternoon, although I dare say it is possible.

Think of classic horror stories such as *Dracula* and *Frankenstein's Monster*. You find mysterious happenings at night in crumbling isolated castles with timely thunderstorms. You may not want to go quite this far as these features have been overused and have become clichés.

Choice of Language

Next your choice of language will be important. In this sort of story you're likely to use quite a lot of description, both of people and places. You might like to look back at Chapter 1, especially Units 1, 3 and 6 to remind yourself about how to write this effectively. You need to choose fresh and interesting words which say precisely what you mean and which also sound right. You can help to build up atmosphere by choosing words starting with the same letter (this is called alliteration), for example 'the snake slid slowly over the polished floor, slithering silently'.

Length of Sentences and Pace

Finally, you'll need to think about length of sentences. You will probably want to use a variety of lengths, longer when you're building up an atmosphere, short and sharp when something happens.

ACTIVITY

3c

Reading and Response – Knowledge about Language

Look at Extract A which is taken from *Jane Eyre* and at Extract B from *Devices and Desires* and analyse the authors' techniques by answering the questions which follow each passage. There are more questions here than you would find in the written examination but this activity is a good preparation for that. Don't give yourself a limited time – spend as long as necessary in order to answer the questions thoroughly.

Extract A

I had forgotten to draw my curtain, which I usually did, and also to let down my window-blind. The consequence was, that when the moon, which was full and bright (for the night was fine), came in her course to that space in the sky opposite my casement, and looked in at me through the unveiled panes, her glorious gaze roused me. Awakening in the dead of night, I opened my eyes on her disc – silver white and crystal clear. It was beautiful but too solemn: I half rose and stretched my arm to draw the curtain. Good God! What a cry!

The night – its silence – its rest, was rent in twain by a savage, a sharp, a shrilly sound that ran from end to end of Thornfield Hall.

My pulse stopped: my heart stood still; my stretched arm was paralysed. The cry died, and was not renewed. Indeed, whatever being uttered that fearful shriek could not soon repeat it: not the wildest winged condor on the Andes could, twice in succession, send out such a yell from the cloud shrouding its eyrie. The thing delivering such utterance must rest ere it could repeat the effort.

It came out of the third storey; for it passed overhead. And overhead – yes, in the room just above my chamber ceiling – I now heard a struggle: a deadly one it seemed from the noise; and a half-smothered voice shouted – 'Help! Help! Help!' three times rapidly.

'Will no one come?' it cried; and then while the staggering and stamping went on wildly, I distinguished through plank and plaster:

'Rochester! Rochester! For God's sake come!'

A chamber door opened; some one ran, or rushed, along the gallery. Another step stamped on the flooring above and something fell: and then was silent.

Jane Eyre, Charlotte Bronte

Questions on Extract A

a   Write down the time of day and the weather. Do these have mysterious overtones?

b   Write down any words associated with death.

c   Write down the words used to refer to the attacker who has also made the first cry. What associations do these words have?

d   Find all the words beginning with 's'. Are they placed together to create an effect? What effect do you think they create? Do the same for words starting with 'r'. What is the effect this time?

e   With a pencil, draw a line vertically through each full stop. Are the sentences long or short? Does Charlotte Bronte vary their length?

f   What is the effect of sentence length on the pace (how fast the story moves)? Does this change later in the passage? Notice how in the sentence which begins 'My pulse . . . ' there are three short abrupt statements. These are nearly the same length but there is one more word in each than in the previous one.

Notice how the narrator here is just as mystified as we are and that she is describing the events to us as she experienced them so we are invited to share her feelings.

Extract B

Extract B is take from *Devices and Desires* by P.D. James. A killer known as 'the Whistler' has killed three women in the area. Valerie is trying to catch the last bus home.

She wanted to break into a run but managed to resist. The creature, man or beast, crouching in the undergrowth was already sniffing her fear, waiting until her panic broke. Then she would hear the crash of the breaking bushes, his pounding feet, feel his panting breath hot on her neck. She must keep walking, swiftly but silently, holding her bag tightly against her side, hardly breathing, eyes fixed ahead. And as she walked she prayed: 'Please God, let me get safely home and I'll never lie again. I'll always leave in time. Help me to get to the crossroads safely. Make the bus come quickly. Oh God, please help me.' And then, miraculously, her prayer was answered. Suddenly, about thirty yards ahead of her there was a woman. She didn't question how, so mysteriously, this slim, slow-walking figure had materialised. It was sufficient that she was there. As she drew nearer with quickening step she could see the swathe of long, blonde hair under a tight-fitting beret, and what looked like a belted trenchcoat. And at the girl's side, trotting obediently, most reassuring of all, was a small black and white dog, bandy-legged. They could walk together to the crossroads. Perhaps the girl might herself be catching the same bus. She almost cried aloud, 'I'm coming. I'm coming,' and, breaking into a run, rushed towards safety and protection as a child might to her mother's arms.

And now the woman bent down and released the dog. As if in obedience to some command, he slipped into the bushes. The woman took one swift backward glance and then stood quietly waiting, her back half turned to Valerie, the dog's lead held drooping in her right hand. Valerie almost flung herself at the waiting back. And then, slowly, the woman turned. It was a second of total, paralysing horror. She saw the pale, taut face which had never been a woman's face, the simple, inviting, almost apologetic smile, the blazing and merciless eyes. She opened her mouth to scream, but there was no chance and terror had made her dumb. With one movement the noose of the lead was swung over her head and jerked tight and she was pulled from the road into the shadow of the bushes.

Devices and Desires, P.D. James

Questions on Extract B

a Note down the way in which P.D. James describes the setting.

b Look at Valerie's thoughts about the attacker in the first paragraph. How is he made to sound frightening?

c Look at the sentence in the first paragraph which starts 'Then she would hear . . .' How do the words sound? Notice the use of repeated first letters and the effect created.

d Look at the frequency of words beginning with 's'. Where are they used and what is the effect? Compare this to those used in Extract A. Also find words starting in 'r'. Notice that James uses some of the same words as Bronte.

e Mark the full stops as you did in Extract A. Notice the length of sentences, usually fairly short, often broken up by commas, mirroring the girl's feelings. Look particularly at the last paragraph. What effect is created?

f Now look at the sentence 'And then, slowly, the woman turned.' If this was rearranged it wouldn't have the same effect. Try placing the word 'slowly' at different points. The way James makes us pause by placing it in the middle, divided off by commas, allows the horrific truth to start to dawn on us too.

Although this piece is written in the third person, it is still told entirely through Valerie, the main character. Her feelings are what we are experiencing. The tactic here is to make us, like the character, feel falsely reassured by the sight of the woman and dog. These are not associated with danger. It is therefore all the more chilling when the true identity of the figure is revealed. Don't forget this technique. You may want to use it later.

Coursework – Writing

Now you are ready to write a mystery story. Choose one of the options below.

1   You could choose to write up, as a piece of coursework, one of the plots which you thought of in Activity A about *The Woman in White* or *The Exorcism*.

2   You might like to use this idea. A young couple get married and go with friends to their large country house for their honeymoon. They play a game of hide-and-seek. The bride finds the perfect hiding place – an old trunk in the attic. She pulls down the lid and it shuts fast (possibly she could be 'helped' by someone else in the party). The trunk is airtight. She suffocates and her husband and his friends never find her. You could write this from the bride's point of view, from the husband's or part of the story from each. You might want to start off with someone today buying the house and coming across the body when clearing out the attic.

3   You might wish to write a story which includes these words: 'She thought she was safe . . . but she was wrong'.

4   Choose a mystery story which has recently appeared in the news: about a disappearance, a murder or anything else which captures your imagination. Write the story explaining what really happened from the point of view of someone involved. A programme such as *Crimewatch* might give you some ideas.

5   If none of these appeals, think up a story yourself but include in it both mystery and fear.

Which ever you choose, don't make it too long and complicated. This is only a short story, not a full length novel. You might want to look back at Unit 1 of this chapter, especially Activities D and E to remind yourself of potential pitfalls.

Drafting and Revising

When you have worked out your plot fully, write the story. Think carefully about the techniques which you looked at earlier in this unit. Try to build up fear and tension by using language effectively. Make a shiver run down the spine of someone reading it.

When you think you have finished, read it through. Does it make sense? Does the explanation fit with other details which you've given? Have you written a satisfactory ending? Have you created the effects you intended? If necessary, make improvements or rewrite your story.

Check for Accuracy

When you are happy with the content, think about accuracy. Have you written in proper sentences even where you are trying to express fear and suspense? If you have used speech, have you punctuated it correctly? Check the appropriate units in Chapter 6 to make sure. Is your spelling accurate? Look in a dictionary.

Write the Final Version

When you are satisfied that this story is as good as you can make it, write it out neatly and hand it to your tutor for assessment. Don't forget to put your name, the title and the date of writing at the top.

ACTIVITY

3e

Coursework – Speaking and Listening

Find a mysterious and frightening short story. You might want to try one by Edgar Allan Poe whose stories are published in paperback. There are also various collections of ghost and horror stories from which you could find something suitable.

Alternatively, if you have read novels of the type written by authors such as Stephen King or Thomas Harris choose a suitably chilling chapter.

Read your chosen piece aloud, trying, by the way you say the words, to make it as effective as possible. Practise doing this on your own until you feel you can read it really well. Use a tape recorder to assess how effective your reading is. You may be able to borrow tapes of actors reading stories from your local library. Listen to examples and try to pick up some tips.

When you're happy, give a final reading of it. Your audience could be a small group of friends or fellow students or just your tutor. You might want to tape record your performance to make assessment easier.

Review of Unit 3

- Activity A was preparatory work.
- Activity B was preparatory work.
- Activity C was reading and knowledge of language (En 2.1, 4).
- Activity D was written coursework (En 3).
- Activity E was speaking and listening coursework (En 1.2, 3).

Making a Record

Write down the necessary information about the coursework in this unit. This was the written work in Activity D and the individual oral work in Activity E. Tick the relevant aspects of En 1 and En 3 on your Coursework Index Form.

What Should You Do Now?

Now choose another unit from Chapter 2 or turn to the first unit of a different chapter.

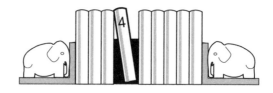

UNIT **4** *Play for Today*

If writing in play form sounds interesting to you, this is what you should work on in this unit:

- Activity A involves reading extracts from plays.
- Activity B is written coursework – do both A and B.
- Activity C is an addition or an alternative to Activity B.
- Activity D is speaking and listening coursework.

When you have completed Activity D you may, if you wish, turn to another unit in this chapter or to the first unit of another chapter. It is a good idea, though, to complete the final task in this unit which is further written coursework.

Narrating through Plays

Putting an incident into a scene of a play is very different from telling a story in the normal way. In a play you only have the characters' spoken words and their actions. You don't have description of people or places or any narrative saying what happened before and what will happen next. You may also have to restrict the action to certain key settings. This will be discussed more specifically at a later point.

ACTIVITY

4a

Reading and Analysis – Knowledge about Language

Let's look at an extract from a play and see how it's written, particularly noticing how it differs from a story told in the usual way. Read the passage and answer the questions which follow. This task is useful preparation for the written exam. Don't worry about setting yourself a time limit, though – take as long as you need.

This piece is taken from *Stepping Out* by Richard Harris. It is about a varied group of women (and one man) who attend a tap-dancing class in North London. Here they are chatting while waiting for their class to begin. Read the extract and answer the questions which follow. If possible, this could be read aloud by four people, each one taking a part.

<blockquote>

[*Sylvia comes out of the changing room*]

Sylvia: She's only at it again.

Maxine: Who is?

Sylvia: Wassername – Vera.

[*She sits on the floor, taking out a pair of new tap shoes*]

</blockquote>

Maxine:	What is it this time?
Sylvia:	She's only sticking up a list of instructions about the toilet facilities.
Maxine:	Like your shoes, Sylv.
	[*Rose, now in her dancing gear, comes out of the changing room, giggling to herself*]
Sylvia:	What are you so cheerful about?
Rose:	Nothing, nothing.
Maxine:	Vera's just given her nine out of ten for toilet training.
Rose:	[*Rose sits and, still smiling to herself*]
	Do you ever make love first thing in the morning?
Sylvia:	Are you kidding? He can't do a thing until he's had a cooked breakfast.
Maxine:	Your boy got himself a job yet, Rose?
Rose:	Everywhere he try, it's the same story.
Sylvia:	I think it's bleeding lousy for kids nowadays.
	All the time he was at school we kept telling him – no qualifications, no work.
Sylvia:	If you ask me all this qualifications lark is just an excuse,
	[*tapping her head*]
	It's what you've got up here – right, Geoffrey?
Rose:	[*insisting*]
	He should have paid more attention at school.
Maxine:	Do any of 'em?
Rose:	For some, it's more important than others.
Sylvia:	He'll sort himself out, don't worry.
Geoffrey:	What about the Youth Training Scheme?
Rose:	He say it's slave labour.
Sylvia:	He's right an' all.
Geoffrey:	Well I would have thought it at least . . .
Rose:	And the way he talk to his father. We never bring up our children to talk like that.
Maxine:	They're all the same. Look at Wonderboy: one minute he's in a pop group and the next minute he's in a coma. D'you know what the latest is? He's decided he wants to go to art school. Art school? He can't even draw a deep breath without fainting.

Stepping Out, Richard Harris

Consider the following questions on the extract from *Stepping Out*.

a   Because this is from a play, it is through the dialogue that we learn about the characters. Write down what you have discovered about each of these characters, their likely personality, family circumstances, social class, and so on, from the way they speak. For example Rose is Afro-Caribbean. Is there anything which suggests this?

b   These people are just chatting; nevertheless some more serious issues are touched on. What are they? You will see by looking at your answer that you can write about different attitudes to an issue by having various characters, with differing points of view, talking about it in this way.

c   Here is part of the extract, no longer in play form. Write down the main differences between the dramatised version and the version in story form.

> Sylvia came out of the changing room with a disgusted expression on her face.
> 'She's only at it again,' she said.
> Maxine, sitting at her ease on the far side of the room, looked up.
> 'Who is?' she enquired.
> 'Wassername – Vera.' Sylvia squatted down on the floor at the front of the room, gave herself a critical glance in the mirror then pulled a new pair of tap shoes from her brightly coloured plastic bag.
> 'What is it this time?' Maxine said, an amused note in her rather deep voice. Sylvia explained that she'd just seen her in the changing rooms pinning up a list of instructions headed 'Toilet Facilities'. They both laughed, remembering how Vera seemed to spend all her time cleaning up after everyone in the class. She emptied ashtrays, removed empty juice cartons and gave everyone unwanted advice.
> 'Like your shoes, Sylv,' Maxine commented just as Rose came out of the changing room door, smiling to herself.
> Sylvia didn't answer. It was nice of Maxine to say that, especially when she had masses of flashy gear – she was a brilliant dancer, too, unlike Sylvia who might make a big joke of having two left feet but she still felt envious of the other's skill.

In the play version, facial expressions, tones of voice and actions have to be indicated in the stage directions and then carried out by the actors. It's not necessary to describe every little thing a person does. A good actor will study the character and build up a range of suitable gestures and expressions as well as using an appropriate voice, with regard to tone and accent.

In the play version, actions are written in the present tense. They are happening now.

In the story version, it is possible to describe what a character is thinking and feeling. This is only shown by actions and expressions in the play. It is impossible to show that Sylvia and Maxine are remembering other similar actions by Vera unless they say something about it. It is impossible for Sylvia's exact feelings about Maxine and her dancing ability to be conveyed. She might make some fleeting facial expression which suggests these thoughts, but that's all.

Sometimes a playwright will describe exactly what a character should look like or be wearing but it may be left fairly vague. Editions of Shakespeare, for example, have no such detailed instructions. A character's physical appearance is seen when the actor playing the part comes on stage. In a story, all this has to be conveyed to the audience in writing.

The set, too, is seen rather than described in a play. The mirror in *Stepping Out* is at the front of the stage, on the supposed 'fourth wall'. It is not really there but its existence is suggested by the way it is looked into by characters. In the story it has to be described.

Coursework – Writing

In this section we will turn a story into a play and a play into a story.

Turning a Story into a Play

Read the following extract from *The Joy Luck Club* by Amy Tan. Change it from its present form into a scene from a play. You may add extra spoken words if you like. Waverly Jong, accompanied by her young daughter, Shoshana, has brought her new American boyfriend, Rich, to dinner at her mother's home.

Extract A

When I offered Rich a fork, he insisted on using the slippery ivory chopsticks. He held them splayed like the knock-kneed legs of an ostrich while picking up a large chunk of sauce-coated eggplant. Halfway between his plate and his open mouth, the chunk fell on his crisp white shirt and then slid into his crotch. It took several minutes to get Shoshana to stop shrieking with laughter.

And then he helped himself to big portions of the shrimp and snow peas, not realising that he should have taken only a polite spoonful until everybody else had had a morsel.

He had declined the sautéed new greens, the tender and expensive leaves of bean plants plucked before the sprouts turn into beans. And Shoshana refused to eat them also, pointing to Rich: 'He didn't eat them! He didn't eat them!'

He thought he was being polite by refusing seconds, when he should have followed my father's example, who made a big show of taking small portions of seconds, thirds and even fourths, always saying he could not resist another bite of something or other, and then groaning that he was so full he thought he would burst.

But the worst was when Rich criticised my mother's cooking, and he didn't even know what he had done. As is the Chinese cook's custom, my mother always made disparaging remarks about her own cooking. That night she chose to direct it toward her famous steamed pork and preserved vegetable dish, which she always served with special pride.

'Ai! This dish not salty enough, no flavour,' she complained, after tasting a small bite. 'It is too bad to eat.'

This was our family's cue to eat some and proclaim it the best she had ever made. But before we could do so, Rich said, 'You know, all it needs is a little soy sauce.' And he proceeded to pour a riverful of the salty black stuff on the platter, right before my mother's horrified eyes.

The Joy Luck Club, Amy Tan

Before you start to write, look at Chapter 6, Unit 6, which gives advice about presentation and layout in a play.

When you are looking at the extract, you may find it helps to underline all the words which are spoken in one colour, all the actions in another and to cross out all the thoughts and feelings which cannot be conveyed except through facial expressions. Do this only if the book belongs to you! You may feel you wish to start your piece by saying who is present and where they are. You will probably wish to add more lines of dialogue and also specific directions about actions and behaviour.

Drafting and Revising

Write your new piece out first of all in rough. Have you left anything out? Can you add any more to give interest or more information? When you are pleased with the content, check your spelling and punctuation. Convention demands that you put a colon(:) after the character's name before a speech. Have you done this? Does each spoken line end with the appropriate punctuation mark? It's all too easy to leave this out. When you have checked carefully write it out neatly according to the guidelines given in Chapter 6, Unit 6.

Turning a Play into a Story

The next extract is also about a meal which goes wrong. It is taken from Alan Ayckbourn's play *How The Other Half Loves*. Mary and William, quiet and retiring people, are having dinner at Teresa and Bob's house. Unfortunately Bob is still at the pub and Benjie, their two-year-old, has had a hand in the cooking. Teresa brings in the soup but then rushes out, asking them to help themselves, as she smells burning.

This time, you are going to change the format from play to story.

Extract B

Mary:	[*after a pause, starting to serve the soup*]
	Soup, William?
William:	[*taking a bowl*]
	Thank you.
	[*he sniffs the soup*]
Mary:	What are you doing?
William:	It smells of air freshener.
Mary:	No.
William:	Definitely air freshener.
Mary:	Well, try and eat it. She's gone to a lot of trouble.
William:	You know what happens to my stomach with badly cooked food.
Mary:	Yes, dear. I know. . .
	[*Teresa enters from the kitchen*]
Teresa:	That stove. That damned stove. I have asked Bob a hundred times – well I'm not waiting for him. He can damn well starve.
Mary:	Is there anything the matter, Terry?
Teresa:	Matter? Matter? Good heavens no. Come on, then. Let's enjoy ourselves. Eat up.

Mary:	Right. This looks delicious. [*She picks up her spoon*] [*William continues to gaze at his plate, dubiously*]
Teresa:	William?
William:	Er – yes, thank you . . .
Teresa:	I hope you enjoy this soup. I stood over it for hours. [*William and Mary dip their spoons in the soup*] I've put practically everything in it I could lay my hands on. [*William and Mary each take a mouthful*] Benjie helped me with it a little bit. [*William and Mary choke*]
Mary:	[*recovering*] Aren't you having any?
Teresa:	I couldn't face it just at the moment. Don't mind me. I'll just get drunk. . . . [*there is a pause*]
Teresa:	How is it?
Mary:	Wonderful.
William:	Very unusual.
Teresa:	[*picking up the ladle*] I can't resist it. I'll have to try it. [*She sips the soup, replaces the ladle and stares at it*] It tastes like anti-perspirant.
Mary:	Oh.
William:	Well . . .
Teresa:	Doesn't it taste like that to you? It must do.
Mary:	No . . .
William:	Yes, it does.
Teresa:	Then what the hell are you eating it for, for God's sake? Here, let me pour it back. [*She snatches their plates*]
Mary:	[*resisting*] No, it's . . .
Teresa:	Give it to me. [*A tug of war*] Come on. [*She gets their plates and pours the soup back into the tureen*] Well, that's that. End of the meal.
William:	Oh? Why is that?
Teresa:	The chops are completely burnt and I don't know how you feel about raw potatoes.
William:	Ah.
Mary:	Oh dear.
Teresa:	[*cheerfully*] Never mind. There's always the wine, isn't there? The least we can do is to behave like civilised human beings. I don't know about you two but I'm going to enjoy myself. [*She starts to sing loudly and discordantly*]

How the Other Half Loves, Alan Ayckbourn

This time instead of adding dialogue, you may wish to generalise in places about what is said, rather than giving every word. You will be adding description – of the characters involved and of their thoughts and feelings. What do you think William and Mary look like? How do they feel as Teresa pulls their plates away and tells them that dinner is over? Why is she behaving like this? What is her mood? How do you think she is dressed?

Drafting and Revising

Write a first draft of your story version. Look in Chapter 6, Unit 4 to make sure you remember how to punctuate direct speech. As always, once you have come to the end of your draft, check that the content is as good as you can make it and that you have written as accurately as possible.

Produce the Final Version

Put your adaptations of A and B together. Think of a relevant title to link both – something about the subject matter. Write this title, your name and the date at the top and hand it to your tutor for assessment.

ACTIVITY

4c

Alternative Coursework – Writing

Make up a scene about a meal which goes disastrously wrong. You could use a misunderstanding based on different cultures, as in the extract from *The Joy Luck Club* or a situation where some of the people present are behaving extraordinarily as in the extract from *How the Other Half Loves*.

Perhaps you have had personal experience of something which you could use. A friend of mine was once so bored when visiting his dreary next-door neighbours for a meal that he fell asleep – at the table!

Drafting and Revising

As always, write a first draft and then read it through carefully. Could the content be improved? Have you made errors in spelling and grammar? Write further drafts until you are satisfied then write out a final version adding the necessary headings.

ACTIVITY

4d

Coursework – Speaking and Listening

You may select either 1 or 2 but you may wish to do both the tasks suggested here.

Task 1

Choose one or more scenes from a play to read or perform in a group.

You will find that your college or local library stocks a few well-known plays. There should be a larger collection, including sets of plays, some-where in your county or borough. Your local library will be able to tell you where it is.

Reading a play aloud can be very enjoyable. Performing it can be more so. If you are doing this you will need to work out moves and collect fur-niture and smaller articles to use (these are known as 'props', short for properties, as you probably know). If you are prepared to learn the words, so much the better. Holding a book severely restricts your free-dom of movement. Your performance could be shown to the rest of your class, including your tutor. Alternatively, if this is impractical it could be video taped (or even audio taped) for assessment.

Task 2

Improvise a scene. This time, with your group of friends or fellow stu-dents, instead of using a script, work out the basic outline of the scene and then make it up as you go along. Some planning is necessary or your scene may move in the wrong direction. Try to decide in advance what the outcome or conclusion is supposed to be. You can run the scene through several times, improving on it and discussing it in between. Show your final version to your tutor as above.

What You Might Do Now

When you have completed Activity D you may, if you wish, turn to another unit in this chapter or to the first unit of another chapter. It is advisable, however, to complete the final activity in this unit even if you decide you do not wish to use this piece in your coursework folder.

If you have decided to move on to another unit, turn to the last page of this unit in order to make an accurate record of your achievements so far.

ACTIVITY

(4e)

Coursework – Writing About a Serious Issue

As you will have seen in Activity A, it is possible to write a scene which debates a controversial or topical subject. Here are two extracts which do this. Look at them carefully to see how the issue is handled.

Extract A is taken from David Hare's play *Racing Demon*. The play explores the value and role of religion in modern British society, espe-cially that practised by the Church of England. Here Stella, an Afro-Caribbean woman, is discussing her traumatic abortion with the local vicar, Lionel Espy.

Extract A

Lionel:	. . . Now please tell me what happened next.
	[*She waits a moment, recovering, then starts*]
Stella:	Well after I got out, I was feelin' terrible. So I started takin' these pills.
Lionel:	Who gave them to you?
Stella:	A doctor. I dunno. I never seen 'im again.
Lionel:	The same doctor?
Stella:	Oh no. I din' never meet that doctor.
	[*Lionel nods*]
Lionel:	I see.
Stella:	They just let you in, there's a nurse, and then they knock you out. Then you wake up and it's over. 'Cept for me it wa'n't.
Lionel:	What do you mean?
Stella:	I 'ad to 'ave another one. They 'en't done a proper scrape.
Lionel:	Uh-huh.
	[*pauses again, waiting*]
	Where was this?
Stella:	Lewisham. I din' understand it. They said they couldn' find it. So they 'ad to take another look.
Lionel:	Yes. How long between the two?
Stella:	Oh, it was a Monday. Monday's the slow day, it's the only day they'll let me off.
	[*Beginning to cry again*]
	So it was Monday, then Monday.
Lionel:	I see. Two Mondays.
Stella:	We 'ad to pay twice.
Lionel:	Who paid?
Stella:	My 'usband. 'E got money. 'E jus' din' wanna 'ave kids.
	[*Crying now*]
	The second Monday they found it, then they threw it away.
	[*Lionel watches*]
	I might 'ave coped, you know. 'Cept 'e gets so angry. Now I cry all the time. That's what drives 'im mad. 'E jus' gets angrier, an' 'e says, will you never stop cryin'? An' I say, I'd like to, I can't.
Lionel:	Can you go somewhere else? Do you want to leave him?
Stella:	I a'n't got no money. I've nowhere to go.
	[*Looks at him now*]
	What does the Church say?
Lionel:	What does it say? About abortion?
	[*Pauses a moment, very quiet*]
	Abortion is wrong.
	[*he looks at her unapologetic*]
Stella:	I couldn' 'elp it.
Lionel:	I know. I'm not saying **you** were wrong. You had no choice.
Stella:	I don' wanna leave him.
Lionel:	I know. And also it's a marriage. We want your marriage to last. Is there a chance your husband might come in and see me?

[*She looks at him mistrustfully*]
It's a stupid question, I'm sorry.

Racing Demon, David Hare

The issues discussed here are whether Stella was right to have an abortion and whether she should leave her husband. She states her reasons for acting as she did and Lionel gives the Church's position on the subject. By having two very different people talking about this, more than one view point can be expressed. This makes it a good way of looking in an un-biased way at a subject which often arouses strong feelings.

Extract B is taken from *Whose Life is it Anyway?* by Brian Clark. Ken has been paralysed from the neck downwards in a car accident. He wants to be given the right to decide for himself whether to go on living. He would need constant medical care to survive. He can do nothing for himself at all. He is discussing his situation with the judge brought in to make a final ruling.

Extract B

Judge:	But, surely, wishing to die must be strong evidence that the depression has moved beyond a mere unhappiness into a medical realm?
Ken:	I don't wish to die.
Judge:	Then what is this case all about?
Ken:	Nor do I wish to live at any price. Of course I want to live, but as far as I am concerned, I'm dead already. I merely require the doctors to recognise the fact. I cannot accept this condition constitutes life in any real sense at all.
Judge:	Certainly, you're alive legally.
Ken:	I think I could challenge even that.
Judge:	How?
Ken:	Any reasonable definition of life must include the idea of its being self-supporting. I seem to remember something in the papers – when all the heart transplant controversy was on – about it being all right to take someone's heart if they require constant attention from respirators and so on to keep them alive.
Judge:	There also has to be absolutely no brain activity at all. Yours is certainly working.
Ken:	It is, and sanely.
Judge:	That is the question to be decided.
Ken:	My Lord, I am not asking anyone to kill me. I am only asking to be discharged from this hospital.
Judge:	It comes to the same thing.
Ken:	Then that proves my point; not just the fact that I will spend the rest of my life in hospital, but that whilst I am here, everything is geared just to keeping my brain active, with no real possibility of it ever being able to direct anything. As far as I can see, that is an act of deliberate cruelty.
Judge:	Surely it would be more cruel if society just let people die, when it could, with some effort, keep them alive.

Ken:	No, not **more** cruel, **just** as cruel.
Judge:	Then why should the hospital let you die – if it is just as cruel?
Ken:	The cruelty doesn't reside in saving someone or allowing them to die. It resides in the fact that the choice is removed from the man concerned.
Judge:	But a man who is very desperately depressed is not capable of making a reasonable choice.
Ken:	As you said, my Lord, that is the question to be decided.

Whose Life is it Anyway?, Brian Clark

Here Ken is invited to put forward his point of view. The Judge questions this and comments on it but his final opinion is not at present being revealed. The issue is whether Ken is sane enough to decide for himself. What do you think about a dilemma like this? Often the patient is unable to speak on his or her own behalf and others have to make this difficult decision for him or her.

Writing a Scene to Debate an Issue

Write a scene containing debate about a serious issue. You may use one of those touched on here if you like. Other subjects are aired in Chapter 5. You might like to look through that chapter to find further appropriate material. If you already feel strongly about a particular issue, use that. Try to bring the scene to some sort of conclusion if that's possible. Examples could be someone reaching a decision, whether right or wrong, about a course of action; someone could be leaving in disgust; a fight might be developing. Any setting is possible but state what it is and give a brief statement about the characters. Make your writing as effective as possible.

Drafting and Revising

As always, write a draft first then check for good content and accuracy.

Review of Unit 4

- Activity A was reading and analysis – knowledge about language (En 2.1, 4).
- Activity B was written coursework (En 3).
- Activity C was written coursework (En 3).
- Activity D was speaking and listening coursework (En 1.2, 3).
- Activity E was written coursework (En 3).

Making a Record

Write down the necessary information about the coursework in this unit. This was the written work in Activities B, C and E and the group oral work in Activity D. Tick the relevant aspects of En 1 and En 3 on your Coursework Checklist.

What Should You Do Now?

Choose another unit from Chapter 2 or turn to the first unit of a different chapter.

Once Upon a Time

In this unit you will be looking at folk or fairy tales and telling one of your own. If this sounds interesting, this is what you should do:

Complete all activities up to and including Activity C. If you wish you may then turn to another unit in this chapter or the first unit of a different one. It is a good idea, though, to complete the further activities in this unit.

ACTIVITY

(5a)

Reading and Analysis

You may think that folk or fairy tales are solely for children but there's no reason why that should be so. We probably only come across them in attractive collections with lots of illustrations or as the basis for a Christmas pantomime – *Aladdin, Puss in Boots* or whatever. This wasn't the case in days gone by and isn't now in some other parts of the world. Often these are stories which are told rather than written. Surprisingly there seem to be 'common' ingredients which appear worldwide, perhaps because they are variations of the same story spread by travellers or because there are only so many basic plot ideas, making similarity inevitable.

The first thing to do is to look at such a story and see what elements it contains.

The Frog Prince

Once upon a time, there was a little princess with golden hair who lived in a castle with her father, the King, and her mother, the Queen. She had no sisters or brothers, but when she had finished her lessons she would play quite happily by herself in the gardens of the castle. Her favourite toy was a shiny golden ball. When she threw it into a hedge or lost it in a bed of flowers, one of the gardeners would find it for her.

One hot day, the Princess ran out of the castle garden into the cool green forest carrying her golden ball. She came to a mossy glade where a broad oak tree threw its shade, and near this lay a great pool with the broad leaves and waxen cups of water lilies floating on its water. The Princess sat down under the tree and started tossing her ball in the air. She tossed and caught it six times over but the seventh time she did not catch it. The golden ball fell, splash, into the pool.

The Princess ran to the edge of the pool and began to cry. 'My golden ball!' she wept. 'It has sunk to the bottom and I shall never see it again!'

'Don't cry, Princess,' croaked a sad voice. 'What will you give me if I fetch your ball from the bottom of the pool?' The Princess looked round in all directions, but she saw nobody except a big green frog sitting on a broad water lily leaf and staring at her with small bright eyes.

'Will you fetch my ball?' she cried.

'Yes, I will dive to the bottom of the pool and bring you your golden ball if you promise to give me what I ask for,' answered the frog.

'Oh, I will give you anything you ask!' cried the Princess. 'I will drop a silver penny into the pool for you, or even my pearl ring!'

'I have no use for silver pennies or jewels,' croaked the frog. 'But let me be your companion. Promise me that I can sit at your table, eat from your silver plate, drink from your crystal goblet, and sleep on your silken pillow. Then I will dive down into the water and find your golden ball.'

'I promise!' said the Princess and at once she heard a splash and saw bubbles in the water as the frog dived off the lily leaf into the pool.

'What a silly old frog to ask for such foolish things,' she said to herself. But she smiled for joy when she heard another splash and saw the frog hop back onto the leaf with the golden ball in his mouth. He threw the ball onto the grass at her feet and without even pausing to thank him, the Princess picked it up and ran away home.

'Wait for me!' croaked a sad voice behind her. 'I cannot run like you. I can only hop.'

But the Princess took no notice and ran back to the castle as fast as she could.

That night the Princess sat at supper with the King and Queen and all the ladies and gentlemen of the court. The candles were lit in the tall silver candlesticks and the candlelight shone on the silver dishes and the ladies' jewels. In a gallery, the musicians made soft music. But when the music stopped for a few minutes, the Princess raised her head and looked towards the door as if she were listening to something. Everybody else stopped talking and listened too.

It was only a soft little sound they heard through the door, a sound like 'Hop, hop, hop,' coming nearer and nearer up the marble staircase. The Princess turned pale.

Hop, hop, hop, they heard, and a minute later there came a soft little tap on the door.

'Lovely Princess, open to me.' croaked a voice outside.

'Who can it be?' asked the King in surprise. 'Go and see, my dear.'

The Princess went slowly to the door, opened it about half an inch, looked through and shut the door again very quickly. 'Who was it?' asked the King.

'Only an ugly frog,' answered the Princess, trying to smile.

'A frog!' exclaimed the King, more surprised than ever. 'Whatever can he want?'

But even as he spoke they heard another tap at the door and the frog croaked, 'Don't you remember the promise you made?'

'What is he talking about?' asked the King.

'Well, you see,' said the Princess, 'I lost my golden ball in the pool and the frog brought it back to me. I promised him that he could be my companion, so he followed me home. I shall tell somebody to throw him downstairs, the ugly creature.'

The King looked severely at the Princess.

'Whatever promise you made, you must keep,' he said. 'Even a promise to an ugly frog.'

Then the Princess, looking quite sulky, went to open the door. The frog came in, hop, hop, hop, over the carpet; hop, hop, hop, right up to the Princess's chair.

'I can't reach the table,' he croaked. 'Lift me, Princess.' Pouting, the Princess set the ugly frog on the linen tablecloth where he sat blinking his small, sad eyes at the candlelight.

'Give me my supper,' he croaked.

'There isn't a plate,' said the Princess.

'But, Princess,' said the frog, 'have you forgotten? You promised I should eat off your own silver plate.'

The King looked sternly at the Princess, so she pushed her beautiful silver plate nearer the ugly frog, who ate some of her supper. The Princess ate nothing, but she picked up her goblet of crystal to sip some wine.

'Give me a drink,' croaked the frog.

'You can drink water from a saucer,' said the Princess. 'Princess, have you forgotten? You promised I should drink from your own crystal goblet.'

So the poor Princess, looking more sulky than ever, passed her goblet to the frog who took several sips of wine. Then he sighed, looked round with his sad, beady eyes, and croaked, 'Where is your bed? I am tired.'

'Take him upstairs to rest,' said the King severely. 'He helped you when you were in trouble, so you must keep the promise you made to him.'

The Princess shivered at the very thought of the ugly frog hopping into her bedroom, but she dared not disobey the King. 'You can hop upstairs. I will find you a bedroom,' she said to the frog.

The frog closed his eyes sleepily.

'You must carry me; I am too tired to hop any further. Don't forget you promised I should sleep on your own silk pillow.' So the Princess had to pick up the frog in her fingers and carry him up another flight of stairs to her bedroom where she put him in a dark corner hoping he would go to sleep. Tired and hungry, she herself got into her little white bed and laid her head down on the silk pillow. In a few minutes she was fast asleep.

Hop, hop, hop. Hop, hop, hop. A soft little noise woke the Princess. There sat the ugly frog in the middle of the floor. She could see him quite plainly in the rays of moonlight that fell through her window.

'Princess,' he croaked, 'remember your promise. Let me sleep on your pillow.'

Then the Princess flew into a rage and cried, 'You've eaten from my silver plate and you've drunk from my crystal goblet. But I will not let an ugly – cold – green – frog sleep on my silk pillow! Go and sleep in the fountain in the garden! Better still, go back to your pool!'

The frog sat on the cold stone floor and tears fell from his sad beady eyes.

'You promised, Princess,' he croaked.

As she looked at him, sitting there, she suddenly stopped feeling cross and sulky. He **had** rescued her treasure – and she **had** promised.

'I'm sorry, frog,' she said. 'I shouldn't have said those horrid things.'

She climbed down from the bed, lifted him carefully and placed him on her silken pillow. 'It can't be much fun being a frog,' she said. Bending down she placed a gentle kiss on the top of his little green head.

To her amazement, at that moment, the frog vanished. In his place was a young handsome Prince.

'Thank you, kind Princess,' he said. 'You have freed me from the spell of a wicked wizard who transformed me into a frog many years ago.'

The Princess was delighted by what had happened. When she was older, she married the Prince and they lived happily ever after.

Having read the story carefully, answer these questions.

a   How does the story start and finish? Write down the phrases used. Are these the traditional phrases used in English stories of this type?

b   Identify the characters involved. Are these typical? Think of one or two examples of other stories, from England or elsewhere which have similar characters involved; write down the title and list the characters. Do the characters have certain recurring physical characteristics, like colour of hair? What is the family group in this story? Is this typical? Think of other family structures which are often found in traditional stories – for example, a king with three daughters.

c   In addition to the main events of this story there is some description. Find where this occurs. Write down some of the adjectives used. What do you think their effect is? What picture is created in your mind?

d   Do you think this version of the story was written for an adult or a child reader? Find examples to back up the conclusions you have drawn.

e   In a story like this there is often a particular style of storytelling. Often certain words and phrases are repeated. Find examples of this. Often the same colours and substances are mentioned: golden, silver, green – do they appear here?

Similarly a year and a day is often a standard length of time; the numbers three and seven seem to be preferred to others. Is this the case in this story? What is the effect and what is the purpose of these features?

f   Does the story have a message or 'moral'? If so, what is it? Think of other stories which teach you a lesson. Note down some examples.

ACTIVITY

5b

Coursework – Writing

Think of a traditional story which you know and write it down. You may check the plot by re-reading it if you like, but put the book away when it comes to writing. Don't write in simple language aimed at a child, just try to write effectively. Use the techniques which you have identified in *The Frog Prince* – repeating phrases, using traditional colours and so on, even if the version of the story with which you are familiar does not. Make sure the moral is clear. When you have finished a first draft, read your story through carefully. Have you told it in an interesting way?

At this point, if you like, you could rewrite the story, bringing it up to date. What would the modern equivalent of a handsome prince be? A city banker? A film star? Could the castle turn into a Beverly Hills mansion and the forest into urban Manchester? What would the poor woodcutter be? This up-dating process can be quite fun. Try to retain the original moral, even if it is now in a modern context.

Choosing your Coursework

Now decide what you are going to put into your final draft. It could be:

- the original story, written down as effectively as possible, by you;
- a modernised version of that story;
- a completely new story, displaying the same narrative techniques as the traditional ones, but invented by you as 'A Fairy Story for our Times'. Here you are using a modern setting and characters and making the moral appropriate for today.

Drafting and Revising

Checking for accuracy

Don't forget to check your writing thoroughly for inaccuracies before you hand it in. The spelling should be correct as should the punctuation. Check the rules of speech punctuation in Chapter 6, Unit 4, if you are at all unsure. Now check your own work again to see whether you have made any mistakes.

Producing the Final Version

Once the work is as interesting and accurate as possible, put your name, the title and the date of writing at the top and submit it to your tutor for assessment.

ACTIVITY

5c

Coursework – Speaking and Listening

This time, instead of writing a story down, you are going to tell it aloud. Again it is up to you whether you choose to tell a traditional tale which you know or whether you wish to modernise or invent one. To a certain extent your choice may depend on who your audience is likely to be. It would be ideal to tell your story to a group of young children if that were a practical possibility. They would probably be a very responsive audience and you would be less likely to feel embarrassed.

For telling a story orally you need to think about how to arouse feelings by the way you perform. If you are describing a hoard of jewels, you will wish to make your audience visualise the beauty and splendour of it.

You can do this by having a glowing description with outsize comparisons (for example, rubies as big as hens' eggs) but also by the expression in your voice. If you wish to create fear or suspense, lowering your voice, speaking in a hushed whisper and looking round furtively will help to create such feelings in your audience.

You may feel you need to have the 'bones' of your story written down, so you don't get lost. Restrict yourself to a few words on a piece of card – about twenty at the most. Never write the whole thing out and try to memorise it; this is very restrictive. Professional storytellers (and there has been a revival of this skill in recent years) vary their story according to the audience response. Storytelling is thus a two way process. As your audience react to what you say, you use words and techniques to make them react even more. The friendly visiting aunt who tells your young child a ghost story just before bedtime is likely to pile on the horror more and more as the child becomes round-eyed with terror. A sleepless night for the unfortunate parent is often the result! This is, however, effective storytelling.

Work out your story. Decide on your audience. Rehearse it and then tell it. If you produce an audio-tape you can use it as coursework.

What Should You Do Now?

If you wish, you may now turn to another unit in this chapter or to a different chapter. It is a good idea, however, to complete Activity D in this unit even if you decide finally that you do not wish to include this piece in your coursework folder. Look also at the suggestions for further reading in Activity E. If you decide to move on to another unit, turn now to the last page of this unit to see what you have achieved so far.

ACTIVITY

5d

Coursework – Reading and Writing in Response to Literature

So far, the stories we have looked at have been written in prose. A lot of traditional stories take the form of ballads which are meant to be sung. A ballad is normally written in verses containing four lines; usually every other line rhymes.

A version of the story in the anonymous ballad below occurs in Denmark, Sweden and Greece as well as in England and Scotland. The Greek version, from Crete, goes back more than two thousand years. Read the ballad through then look at the commentary printed alongside it. When you have done that, answer the questions.

TAM LIN

1   O I forbid you maidens all,
    That wear gold in your hair,
    To travel to Carterhaugh,
    For young Tam Lin is there.

► Here we have gold mentioned again as in *The Frog Prince.*

2   There's none that goes by Carterhaugh.
     But they leave him a pledge,
     Either their mantles of green
     Or else their maidenheads.

► 'Carterhaugh' is associated with magic. The colour green is too.

3   Janet has tied her kirtle green
     A bit above her knee,
     And she's gone to Carterhaugh
     As fast as go can she.

► This is the first time this verse (also called a 'stanza') occurs.

4   She hadn't pulled a double rose
     A rose but only two
     When up then started young Tam Lin,
     Says, 'Lady, pull no more!

► Janet seems to be trying to get his attention. The rose is associated with love or romance.

5   'Why come you to Carterhaugh
     Without command from me?'
     I'll come and go by Carterhaugh
     And ask no leave of thee.'

6   Janet has tied her kirtle green
     A bit above her knee.
     And she's gone to her father's hall
     As fast as go can she.

► Something happens between the end of stanza 5 and this one! Note the repeated opening lines.

7   Out then spoke her father dear
     And he spoke meek and mild;
     'O and alas, Janet, he says,
     'I think you go with child.'

8   'If that be so,' Janet said,
     'Myself shall bear the blame;
     There's not a knight in all your hall
     Shall get the baby's name.

9   'If my love were an earthly knight
     As he's an elfin grey,
     I'd not change my own true love
     For any knight you have.

► Tam Lin is a supernatural or magical being.

10   'The steed that my true-love rides on
     Is lighter than the wind;
     With silver shod before
     With burning gold behind.'

► Silver and gold are used in the description of his steed.

11   Janet has tied her kirtle green
     A bit above her knee.
     And she's gone to Carterhaugh
     As fast as go can she.

► This is the same as stanza 3 – this is repetition.

12 'O tell me, Tam Lin,' she says,
     'How came you here to dwell?'
     'The Queen of fairies caught me
     When from my horse I fell.

► Tam Lin is the victim of enchantment.

13 'Ay at the end of seven years
     They pay a tithe to Hell;
     I am so fair and full of flesh
     I'm feared it be myself.

► Notice the use of number seven.

14 'But tonight is Hallowe'en
     And the fairy folk ride.
     They that would their true love win
     At Miles Cross they must bide.

► Halloween is associated with witchcraft and enchantment.

15 'O first let pass the horses black
     And then let by the brown;
     But quickly run to the milk-white steed
     And pull the rider down.

► Tam Lin's horse sounds special compared to the others. White is associated with purity.

16 'For I'll ride on the milk-white steed
     Nearest to the town;
     Because I was an earthly knight
     They give me that renown.

► Notice the repetition of 'milk-white'. Why is this done?

17 'They'll turn me in your arms
     Into a newt and a snake;
     But hold me fast and fear not;
     I am your baby's father.

► These sorts of transformations quite often occur in traditional tales.

18 'They'll turn me in your arms
     Into a lion bold;
     But hold me fast and fear not
     As you shall love your child.

► In longer versions of this ballad, all the transformations (st. 17, 18, 19) are repeated here.

19 'At last they'll turn me in your arms
     Into a naked knight;
     Then cloak me with your mantle
     And keep me out of sight.'

20 Gloomy, gloomy was the night
     The clouds were riding low,
     As fair Janet in her green mantle
     To Miles Cross she did go.

21 About the middle of the night
     She heard the bridles ring.
     She heeded what he did say
     And young Tam Lin did win.

22 Out then spoke the Fairy Queen
    And an angry queen was she,
    'Woe betide her ill fared face
    And an ill death may she die!

▶ A cruel and vindictive female character, sometimes a Queen, is a recurring character in such tales.

23 'Had I known, Tam Lin,' she said,
    'What this night I see,
    I'd have plucked out thy two grey eyes
    And put in two of tree.'

▶ 'two of tree', i.e. she would blind him, replacing his eyes with wooden ones.

Anonymous

1. Analysis

a   Identify in this ballad any of the elements, either to do with the story itself or how it is written, which are similar to *The Frog Prince*.
b   Identify any other elements which you think may be traditional which did not appear in the other story. Say why you think this is so.

2. Writing

You may wish to try both of these suggestions or, alternatively, choose the one which you find most appealing.

a   At present the story revolves around Janet's actions and feelings. Rewrite this story, in prose, from **Tam Lin's point of view**, adding any extra description which you feel would make the new version effective. For example, you could write about Tam Lin's first sight of Janet at Carterhaugh, about his fears at Halloween that she will be unable to rescue him from enchantment.
b   Take a well-known story or invent one along traditional lines and write it in ballad format. You may shorten and simplify the story if you like.

When writing the verse, this may be a useful guide. If you count up, there are usually eight syllables in the first and third lines and six in the second and fourth. Here is an example:

She – had – n't – pulled – a -doub – le – rose [8 syllables]
A – rose – but – on – ly – two [6 syllables]
When – up – then – start – ed – young – Tam – Lin, [8 again]
Says, – 'La – dy,- pull – no – more! [6 again]

Sometimes, the verse goes slightly wrong and there's only seven – check for yourself.

Don't worry about trying to be too exact, but bear this syllable number in mind when you're writing. Also, usually the second and fourth lines in a verse rhyme, (knight and sight, stanza 19, low and go, stanza 20). Often the best way to judge whether a verse is right or not is to read it aloud and hear what it sounds like.

Drafting and Revising

As always when you have finished the first draft of a piece of written work, check it through carefully. Is the content as good as you can possibly make it? Is the story interesting? Is it along traditional lines? Have you used the techniques which you have identified and become familiar with? When you are happy with your story, check the accuracy. Spelling and punctuation must be correct. The normal rules apply, even in ballad form. Re-read your work closely, correcting any errors which you find.

Producing the Final Version

When you are satisfied with your work, write it out neatly, put the title, your name and the date of writing at the top and submit it for assessment.

ACTIVITY

5e

Reading – Research and Information Retrieval

1   In the children's section of your local library, find collections of fairy tales or folk tales from countries or cultures **other than your own**. When you read them, see whether you can find similarities with stories which you have grown up with.

2   In a library, find and read other examples of traditional ballads. The biggest collection is *The English and Scottish Popular Ballads* edited by Child. This gives information about origins and several different versions of most ballads. A simpler book is *Border Ballads* edited by James Beattie. If your library does not stock these, ask the librarian to advise you.

3   In a library, find a volume of narrative poetry (i.e. poems which tell stories). Several selections exist. Ask for help from the library staff if you're not sure where to look. Notice how often the ballad format is used, even by relatively modern poets – why do you think that is? Try to spot some of the techniques which we have identified.

Review of Unit 5

- Activity A was reading and analysis – knowledge about language (En 2.1, 4).
- Activity B was written coursework (En 3).
- Activity C was speaking and listening coursework (En 1).
- Activity D was written coursework in response to pre-twentieth-century literature (En 2.1, 4, En 3).
- Activity E was reading, research and information retrieval and knowledge about language (En 2.3, 4).

Making a Record

Write down the necessary information about the coursework in this unit. This was the written work in Activities B and D and the individual oral work in Activity C. Tick the relevant aspects of En 1, En 2 and En 3 on your Coursework Checklist.

What Should You Do Now?

Turn now to the first unit of another chapter.

3 Responding to Literature

Y̶OU must have work in response to literature in your coursework folder. It is also necessary to study a whole work by Shakespeare (this can be a short poem rather than a play) and, if you are hoping to achieve level 7 (GCSE grade C or above) or higher, you must read other pre-twentieth century literature. The units in this chapter give you the opportunity to fulfil these requirements.

This is what you will be working on:

- reading a range of literature;
- developing and demonstrating a personal response to what is read;
- showing understanding of devices and techniques used in literature;
- comparing techniques used by different writers;
- developing an understanding of the changes in language over time, seeing how words and their use differs from one period to another and the effect of this on a reader.

In Unit 3 of this chapter there will also be an opportunity to respond to films and television programmes, developing an awareness of the techniques and devices used in this medium.

What Should You Work on Now?

You must complete Unit 1 and work on the first part of Unit 2. I would strongly recommend that you then select at least one more unit from this chapter. There is coursework in response to literature elsewhere in the book. You will find a list showing where it occurs in the Appendix.

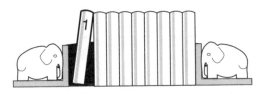

UNIT *Five Minute Fiction*

Unlike the other chapters in this book, here you are not concentrating on writing yourself in a particular way. You will be looking at some of the techniques professional writers use and then showing your understanding of them by either writing about these techniques or by using them yourself.

ACTIVITY

1a

Reading

Read Asimov's introduction to his short story 'Insert Knob A into Hole B', then read the story itself.

Introduction

In some ways this story has the strangest background of any I ever wrote. It is also the shortest story I ever wrote – only 350 words. The two go together.

It came about this way. On August 21, 1957, I took part in a panel discussion on means of communicating science on WGBH, Boston's educational TV station. With me were John Hansen, a technical writer of directions for using machinery, and David O. Woodbury, the well-known science writer.

We all bemoaned the inadequacy of most science writing and technical writing and there was some comment on my prolificity [large output]. With my usual modesty, I attributed my success entirely to an incredible fluency of ideas and a delightful facility in writing. I stated incautiously that I could write a story anywhere, any time, under any conditions within reason. I was instantly challenged to write one right then and there with the television cameras on me.

I accepted the challenge and began to write, taking for my theme the subject of discussion. The other two did not try to make life easier for me, either. They deliberately kept interrupting in order to drag me into their discussion and interrupt my line of thought, and I was just vain enough to try to answer sensibly while I continued scribbling.

Before that half hour programme was over I had finished and read the story (which is why it is so short, by the way) and it was the one you see here as 'Insert Knob A into Hole B'. In his own introduction to the story when it appeared in *The Magazine of Fantasy & Science-Fiction*, Mr Boucher, the editor, said he was printing it just as it was (I had sent him the hand-written script after typing a copy for myself) 'even to the retention of its one grammatical error'. I have kept that error here, too. It's yours for the finding.

I cheated, though. (Would I lie to you?) The three of us were talking before the programme started and I somehow got the idea that they might ask me to write a story on the programme. So, just in case they did, I spent a few minutes before its start blocking out something.

Consequently, when they asked me, I had it roughly in mind. All I had to do was work out the details, write it down and then read it. After all, I had twenty minutes.

Insert Knob A into Hole B

David Woodbury and John Hansen, grotesque in their space suits, supervised anxiously as the large crate swung slowly out and away from the freight-ship and into the airlock. With nearly a year of their hitch on Space Station A5 behind them, they were understandably weary of filtration units that clanked, hydroponic tubs that leaked, air generators that hummed constantly and stopped occasionally.

'Nothing works,' Woodbury would say mournfully, 'because everything is hand assembled by ourselves.'

'Following directions,' Hansen would add, 'composed by an idiot.'

There were undoubtedly grounds for complaint there. The most expensive thing about a spaceship was the room allowed for freight so all equipment had to be sent across space disassembled and nested. All equipment had to be assembled at the Station itself with clumsy hands, inadequate tools and with blurred and ambiguous direction sheets for guidance.

Painstakingly Woodbury had written complaints to which Hansen had added appropriate adjectives, and formal requests for relief of the situation had made its way back to Earth.

And Earth had responded. A special robot had been designed, with a positronic brain crammed with the knowledge of how to assemble properly any disassembled machine in existence.

That robot was in the crate being unloaded now and Woodbury was trembling as the airlock closed behind it.

'First,' he said, 'it overhauls the Food-Assembler and adjusts the steak-attachment knob so we can get it rare instead of burnt.'

They entered the station and attacked the crate with dainty touches of the demoleculizer rods in order to make sure that not a precious metal atom of their special assembly-robot was damaged.

The crate fell open!

And there within it were five hundred separate pieces – and one blurred and ambiguous direction sheet for assemblage.

'Insert Knob A into Hole B'
from *Nightfall and Other Stories*, Isaac Asimov

Understanding and Analysis

There are two questions you can ask about any piece of literature:

1 What is it about?
2 How is it written?

What is 'Insert Knob A . . . ' About?

Probably, if you were asked to sum this up in a single sentence you would say that it was about two men in a space station with an unsolved problem.

In this particular story, the problem is more important than the two men. Their being on a space station is a major contributory factor, however. What is the problem?

Asimov says in the introduction that this story is about communication difficulties, the subject being discussed on the TV programme. How does he explore this idea?

First, there is the situation that the two men are in. Their equipment breaks down and they have to mend it with insufficient guidance. This is one example of bad communication. They don't have good instruction sheets which give clear unambiguous directions.

Second, what they do about this is to write to their base on Earth. Either the comprehension of those in charge on Earth or the letters written by the men must have been at fault as the supposed solution is not one at all. Those on the base do not understand what **can** be sent (because of space problems that are explained in the story) and those dispatching the robot don't appreciate the problem. This is bad communication.

Third, the instructions sent with the robot are 'blurred and ambiguous' just like the other ones they have had to deal with. This again is an illustration of bad communication.

How is 'Insert Knob A . . . ' Written?

Any story will probably use **characters**, a **setting** and a **plot**. It will also use **language** in a deliberate way to give information and create interest for the person reading the story.

Characters

Two characters are used in the story. What is the origin of their names? What do we know about the characters? Picking up evidence from the story we can make some deductions.

Woodbury seems to be a little less forceful as he speaks 'mournfully' about their problems and writes 'painstakingly' to Earth. He also seems to care about food because he has cooking equipment at the top of his repair list. He also seems quite emotional as he 'trembles' as he waits for the crate.

Hansen seems to be more impatient and critical. He says the instructions are 'composed by an idiot' and he adds 'appropriate adjectives' to Woodbury's letter – strong or abusive ones, probably.

Setting

The setting here is a space station. This is important because the distance and expense involved in shipping goods to the station is the source of the men's problems. It also explains why the robot is finally transported to them in the way it is. Another setting, even a remote region on Earth, wouldn't cause the same difficulties.

How does Asimov establish the setting?

In the first sentence of the story he uses particular phrases which make this clear to the reader. The men are 'grotesque in their spacesuits'; there is a reference to a 'freight-ship' and an 'air-lock'. He then refers to the place as 'Space Station A5' which tells us that this is one of many. There are also, presumably, A1, A2, etc. and quite likely B5, K3 and so on. This tells us that this is a future time when space travel is routine. The men evidently are in a regular term of duty. They are stationed there for several years at a time apparently, 'nearly a year of their hitch . . . behind them'.

Earth is clearly some distance away but it is the planet they originate from and their requests are sent there. Asimov uses advanced scientific sounding words which contribute to this impression of a technologically developed future world: 'hydroponic tubs', 'positronic brain', 'Food-Assembler', 'demoleculizer rods', etc.

All this quickly and efficiently, using a minimum number of words, gives us a precise impression of where and when this is set.

Plot

The story is constructed in such a way that we can understand how the men feel. Asimov uses suspense. He also provides clues as to what may be going to happen so that, by the end of the story, we are either surprised by the outcome or we are not, depending on whether we guessed what was going to be in the crate.

Structure

First, he tells us that the men are waiting for the delivery. Then he explains what their problems are on the Space Station and, by telling us how long they've been there, allows us to feel sympathy for their difficulties. He describes the lengths to which they have gone to complain and the 'perfect' solution that has been devised.

We are then told about their eager anticipation that everything will be put right. This makes the reader, in turn, eager to find out if it will be put right and, probably gives the reader suspicions that it may not be that simple.

The long sentence describing their cautious handling of the crate keeps us waiting just as the men themselves are. Then the awful truth is communicated to us abruptly. The short sentence 'The crate fell open!' contrasts with the sentence of thirty-three words which comes before it. This marks a change and prepares us for the final sentence revealing the crate's contents. This is a seventeen word sentence broken in the middle by a dash. This makes it sound like two factual statements. The first, telling us that the robot is in five hundred pieces is bad enough; the second, saying that there is only a blurred and ambiguous instruction sheet makes it that much worse.

The story has thus travelled in a circle: the men are no better off at the end than they were at the beginning and in some ways they are worse off because their hopes have been raised and then shattered.

Language

When you look back at what we have said so far about character, setting and plot, you will see that Asimov chooses words that convey the right information to the reader in the shortest space possible. The introduction makes it clear that when writing this story he could not afford to use a single 'extra' or unnecessary word.

He has also arranged those words in order for us to obtain the information in the right order. It would spoil the story completely if we were told about the robot being disassembled right at the beginning. He is therefore using language to affect the reader in a precise way: to arouse interest and create suspense.

The length of sentences varies in order to make the pace vary. When you are reading, you slow down or speed up depending on whether there are short sharp statements or longer more flowing ones. Notice how the narration is broken up by the characters' comments and speeches. This adds variety which again creates interest.

Did you spot the grammatical error? It should be that the written complaints and formal requests for help made **their** way, not **its** way, back to Earth.

Now that you have looked at these different aspects, you should have a good understanding of how the story is written as well as what it is about.

When you are analysing a piece of literature, this is what to look at:

What is it About?

- Describe the story or situation
- Identify any deeper issue involved
- Decide whether there is a 'message' and what it is.

How is it Written?

- Who are the characters and what are they like?
- What is the setting and how is it established?
- What is the plot – what happens – and what does this show?
- How is it structured? In what order is information given?
- What techniques are used to create interest?

- What can you observe about the use of language – words and their arrangement into sentences for particular effect?

Your understanding of these aspects is called **knowledge about language** and can be demonstrated in discussion or in your written work.

Whenever you are studying literature, remind yourself of this list. It may be a good idea to copy it down, keeping it with your English work. You can then refer to it more easily when working on another page of the book.

ACTIVITY

1c

Coursework – Speaking and Listening

Working in a small group with your tutor, discuss what you consider Asimov's intentions were in writing this story. Do you think he wrote it simply because of the challenge to do it or is he making a serious point?

How did you react to the story's ending? Did you expect it to end in this way?

How effectively do you think the story is written? Pick out specific examples of parts you like or dislike.

Are there disadvantages to the story being so short? Are there any areas that you would have liked Asimov to have expanded upon?

In conclusion, do you think it is a successful short story?

ACTIVITY

1d

Coursework – Writing in Response to Literature

To demonstrate your understanding of this story, choose one of the options below for a piece of coursework.

Whichever you choose, you must:

- make the characters have the same personalities as those in the original story;
- use the characters' feelings as originally shown;
- keep the setting the same;
- bear in mind the original plot if appropriate;
- remember what Asimov was demonstrating about communication.

You will need to **re-read the story** before you start work.

Options

1 Write one or more earlier episodes in the men's time at Space Station A5. This should be where items of equipment start going wrong. If you like, you could use an incident with the Food-Assembler with its steak-attachment knob, which is mentioned in the story. You can probably think up various other devices which might have broken down. You may like to include the characters' failed attempts at mending these and their growing feelings of frustration.

There could be a touch of humour in your work – it doesn't seem as if the breakdowns are actually life threatening – but also try to show understanding and appreciation of the men's difficulties.

2   Write the episode where Woodbury is writing to Earth and Hansen is strengthening his letters by adding further pithy adjectives. They seem to send begging letters as well as formal requests (which could be written as memos – see Chapter 6, Unit 6). You could include extracts from these or quote them in full. Try to contrast the style and tone in which the different ones are written: the begging letters might be quite emotional and more informal than the requests where you would use much colder 'official' language. (See Chapter 6, Unit 5.) You might like to write your response solely in the form of these communications and the replies from Earth (see Chapter 2, Unit 2, Activities A and B about writing stories in the form of letters).

3   What happens next? Carry on from the end of the story. What do the characters say? What do they do? Can they work out the instructions and assemble the robot or is there any other solution? Write another 400 to 500 words bringing matters to some sort of conclusion.

4   Write an alternative ending. Bearing in mind that the story is about poor communication and misunderstandings, write a different ending, starting with the sentence 'The crate fell open!' Work out the possibilities before you start to write. Don't try to work it out as you go along. (Remind yourself about this by looking back at Activity D in Unit 1 of Chapter 2.)

Drafting and Revising

When you have finished your chosen piece, read Asimov's story again. Have you included anything which doesn't seem to fit, which contradicts it or is inconsistent? Are the characters and setting the same as in the original? Are your additions probable and believable? Re-read your work to double check.

Content

Is this as good as you can possibly make it? Have you written enough (at least 400 words) but not so much that your work is rambling and repetitive? Is it interesting?

Style

Have you expressed yourself clearly? Have you thought about the words you have chosen and tried to use particular arrangements of words and lengths of sentences to achieve specific effects?

Accuracy

Have you used correct punctuation and spelling throughout? If you used letters and memos, did you set them out correctly? If you included direct speech is the punctuation accurate? Check in your work and, if necessary, in the appropriate section of Chapter 6.

Revise and redraft your work until you are satisfied that you have achieved the best possible result.

When you have written out your final draft, put your name, an appropriate title according to which option you chose, and the date of writing at the top. You should also put these words as an additional heading: 'Work in response to "Insert Knob A into Hole B", a short story by Isaac

---

Review of Unit 1

Asimov.'

- Activities A and B were reading, understanding and analysis (En 2.1, 4).
- Activity C was speaking and listening coursework (En 1 and En 2.1, 4).
- Activity D was written coursework in response to literature (En 2.1, 4, En 3).

Making a Record

Now find your Coursework Index Form and write down all the relevant information. Write down the number of the piece according to how many you have now done and put the chapter, unit and activity number for reference. Note the date and put a title or brief description, then list the ATs covered in the final column. The relevant activities here are the group oral work in Activity C and the written work in Activity D.

When you have done that tick the relevant aspects of En 1, En 2 and En 3 on your Coursework Checklist.

What Should You Do Now?

The other units in this chapter are as follows:

Unit 2 – Aspects of Love

This unit looks at various writers' approaches to relationships between the sexes. You must complete the first part of this because studying a work by Shakespeare is compulsory.

Unit 3 – Review

Unit 3 gives you the chance to write about your own choice of reading. You also have the opportunity here of writing about films and television programmes.

Unit 4 – Images of War

This unit presents differing views of the First World War and invites you to respond to these in a variety of ways.

Unit 5 – Baby Beware

In this unit there are various poems addressed to or about very young children. The poems expose the hopes and fears writers have about the societies into which children are born.

Turn first, then, to the beginning of Unit 2. Once you have completed the compulsory section you will probably want to finish that unit. When you have finished your work in Unit 2 it is advisable to select another unit from this chapter. When you have done sufficient work in response to literature you should turn to Unit 1 of another chapter. You may, of course, wish to work on a different type of writing for a while, returning to literature later in the course.

UNIT (**2**)   *Aspects of Love*

Part 1: Shakespeare

You must complete all the activities set in this part of the unit because studying Shakespeare is a requirement for GCSE/Keystage 4.

When you have finished Part 1 you will probably wish to carry on to the end of this unit. If you prefer, after Part 1 you may choose another unit from this chapter or you may move on to a different chapter.

ACTIVITY

(2a)

Reading, Understanding and Analysis – Pre-Twentieth Century Literature

The following four short poems are sonnets by William Shakespeare about different aspects of love (he wrote 154 in total). Read each one carefully then look at the questions and comments about it. When you feel you understand the poem as fully as possible, move on to the next one.

Poem A

Sonnet 130

My Mistress' eyes are nothing like the sun;
Coral is far more red than her lips' red;
If snow be white, why then her breasts are dun;
If hairs be wires, black wires grow on her head.
I have seen roses damask'd, red and white,
But no such roses see I in her cheeks;
And in some perfumes is there more delight
Than in the breath that from my Mistress reeks.
I love to hear her speak, yet well I know
That music hath a far more pleasing sound;
I grant I never saw a goddess go –
My Mistress when she walks treads on the ground.
And yet, by heaven, I think my love as rare
As any she belied with false compare.

Comments

Here the poet is remembering all those overused and exaggerated phrases that tend to appear in poems addressed to an admired lady: eyes like the sun, lips like coral, snowy breasts, roses in her cheeks, breath like perfume, a voice like music and a walk like that of a goddess. He is refusing to use these terms to describe his mistress. Is he insulting her? Or is he still praising her? Look at the last two lines. What does he mean by 'rare'? What is he getting at when he says that the other women were 'belied (i.e. lied about) with false compare'?

When you are thinking about how Shakespeare tries to create interest here, consider also how someone who was used to reading the conventional sort of poem would react to this one. Look at the statement in the first line – he's intending to shock, isn't he? Are there words here which are surprising or even insulting? Why does he use them?

Poem B

Sonnet 91

Some glory in their birth, some in their skill,
Some in their wealth, some in their body's force;
Some in their garments, though new-fangled ill;
Some in their hawks and hounds, some in their horse;
And every humour hath his adjunct pleasure,
Wherein it finds a joy above the rest;
But these particulars are not my measure:
All these I better in one general best.
Thy love is better than high birth to me,
Richer than wealth, prouder than garments' cost,
Of more delight than hawks and horses be;
And, having thee, of all men's pride I boast –
Wretched in this alone, that thou mayst take
All this away, and me most wretched make.

Comments

This poem is set out in a very carefully structured way. In the first four lines he describes what some people value. In the second block of four he is basically saying 'each to his own but it's not for me'. In the third block of four lines he compares her love to each of the items valued by others in the first four lines (and he deals with them in the same order). What is his conclusion when he does this? The 'crunch' then comes in the last two lines: if she is the source of all his happiness, she can take it all away and leave him the worst off instead of the best. The most significant point is thus saved for last. The effect of this is to make the reader's final reaction stronger: saying that she is everything to him is quite normal in a love poem – this changes it a bit.

Notice here how Shakespeare uses lots of repetition to stress certain statements in the poem: for example 'some' in the first four lines. Notice how the rhyme of 'take' and 'make' in the final two lines links the words together and makes it sound very final – and not very pleasant.

Poem C
Sonnet 116

Let me not to the marriage of true minds
Admit impediments. Love is not love
Which alters when it alteration finds,
Or bends with the remover to remove.
O, no! it is an ever-fixed mark,
That looks on tempests and is never shaken;
It is the star to every wand'ring bark,
Whose worth's unknown, although his height be taken.
Love's not Time's fool, though rosy lips and cheeks
Within his bending sickle's compass come;
Love alters not with his brief hours and weeks,
But bears it out even to the edge of doom.
If this be error, and upon me prov'd,
I never writ, nor no man ever lov'd.

Comments

The thought behind this poem is quite subtle. Let's follow it through carefully. The first two lines say that no 'impediment' – hindrance or obstruction – can be allowed in (admitted) to the union of totally compatible and right thinking minds. He then goes on to say that love doesn't change even when one of the lovers changes, if it does, it isn't love. In the second group of four lines he goes on to list various extreme forces which cannot change it. It is described as a fixed star by which you can navigate ('bark' here means ship). You may be able to calculate its height but its worth is still unknown, in other words it can't be measured. In the next block of four lines Shakespeare says that Time can't change it even though the lovers' youthful looks ('rosy lips and cheeks') may be altered when they are cut down by Time's 'sickle' or scythe – in other words as they grow older. What do you think he's saying in the last two lines? It's something like, 'If I'm wrong, I'll eat my hat'!

What sort of attitude towards love is Shakespeare expressing here? Do you agree with what he is saying?

Poem D
Sonnet 138

When my love swears that she is made of truth,
I do believe her, though I know she lies,
That she might think me some untutor'd youth,
Unlearned in the world's false subtleties.
Thus vainly thinking that she thinks me young,
Although she knows my days are past the best,
Simply I credit her false-speaking tongue;
On both sides thus is simple truth suppress'd:
But wherefore says she not she is unjust?
And wherefore say not I that I am old?

O, love's best habit is in seeming trust,
And age in love loves not to have years told.
Therefore I lie with her, and she with me,
And in our faults by lies we flattered be.

Comments

This is subtle in a different way. Let's follow the argument through carefully.

In the first two lines he says he deliberately believes the lady when she swears she's telling the truth (and that she is faithful to him), although he knows she's lying.

He then gives the reason: it's so that she'll think he's young and naive (although he isn't!).

He thus vainly, i.e. because of his vanity and in vain (for no useful reason) – allows himself to think she's deceived, and she thinks he is. They are both thus suppressing 'simple truth' (line 8).

But why should they want this, he asks in lines 9 and 10? He answers that it is wiser to only appear to trust someone and that admitting your age is the last thing you want to do if you're older, and in love.

In the second last line there is a double meaning. In Shakespearean English, to lie with someone means to go to bed with them, to be their lover. It also, of course, means to tell lies to them. The final line suggests that their lies keep them both happy.

What is the attitude in this poem? How does it differ from the attitude in poem C? Which do you think is more realistic?

General Observations

Having looked at all four poems, you can probably see some similarities in the way they're constructed. A sonnet always has fourteen lines. Usually Shakespeare's sonnets are organised into three groups of four lines, with a main area of the argument or idea explored in each group. Within the group, every other line rhymes. There is then a concluding statement in the final two lines which often contains a twist, a surprise or a new angle on the subject. These lines rhyme with each other. This is, as it were, the punch line.

Because a sonnet is so short, it is necessary to use language in a very precise and concise way. This is why they give the impression of being crammed full of thought. Usually sonnets are written about romantic love.

ACTIVITY

2b

Coursework – Speaking and Listening

If it is possible, work in a group of four. Each person in the group should choose one of the sonnets to read aloud.

Agree who will do which and then practise on your own until you feel you can convey the meaning and the mood of the poem effectively. Don't be distracted by its being a poem: the punctuation marks should guide you as usual. You don't stop at the end of a line if there is no mark indicating a pause.

For example:

Let me not to the marriage of true minds
Admit impediments,

You just carry straight on as if 'Admit' was on the same line as 'minds'.

Read your poem aloud to your group. When you have read the poems, discuss which poems you preferred. Was one, in your opinion, more effective than others? Discuss why. Discuss any advantages or disadvantages which you have found in the length of the poems and the language in which they are written.

ACTIVITY

2c

Coursework – Writing in Response to Literature

Choose **one** of the four sonnets for a written response. What you will do depends on which poem you choose. Re-read the poem before you start to write.

Poem A

Write a letter to someone you love (this can be an invented person if necessary!). In the letter make use of typically over-sentimental phrases which are used nowadays to express love. Then try to think of more original and real ways to say what you feel.

Poem B

Write a letter to your love (real or imagined). Write about what, these days, is valued by many people: foreign holidays, fast cars, and so on, and write about how your love is more valuable to you. Try to put in a 'twist' at the end of the letter.

Poem C

Write a definition of true love, modern style. (See also the poem 'Love is . . . ' by Adrian Henri on the next page.

Poem D

Write a conversation between two people who are trying to deceive both each other and themselves about aspects of their relationship. Either use correctly punctuated direct speech (see Chapter 6, Unit 4) or set it out like a play (see Chapter 6, Unit 6).

Optional Extra

Try your hand at writing a sonnet on the subject of love. Use the same structure and rhyme pattern. You should have about ten syllables per line.

Drafting and Revising

When you have written a first draft, check it through. Have you followed the instructions carefully? Does it express similar ideas to those in the Shakespeare poem? Change what you have written if necessary.

Is your work correct? Check your spelling and punctuation carefully. Write further drafts, improving the content and accuracy until you are satisfied.

When you have written the final draft, put your name, the date of writing, and a suitable title at the top. Also include the words 'Written in response to a sonnet by Shakespeare' as part of your heading.

Now you have completed the first three activities in this unit, you may, if you choose, turn to another unit in this chapter or to a different chapter. You will find further work in this unit on the theme 'Aspects of Love'. If you find this interesting, please continue.

If you decide to move on to another unit, turn now to the last page of this unit to see what you have achieved. You can then make an accurate record.

Part 2: Other Writers

You may choose **one** activity from D, E or F or tackle each in turn until you feel you would like to move to another unit.

ACTIVITY

2d

Coursework – Reading and Response

Read the following poem by Adrian Henri

Love is . . .

Love is feeling cold in the back of vans
Love is a fanclub with only two fans
Love is walking holding paintstained hands
Love is

Love is fish and chips on winter nights
Love is blankets full of strange delights
Love is when you don't put out the light
Love is

Love is the presents in Christmas shops
Love is when you're feeling Top of the Pops
Love is what happens when the music stops
Love is

Love is white panties lying all forlorn
Love is a pink nightdress still slightly warm
Love is when you have to leave at dawn
Love is

Love is you and love is me
Love is a prison and love is free
Love's what's there when you're away from me
Love is . . .

What aspects of love does this poem explore?

Perhaps it could be said that the first stanza (verse) is about the willing sacrifices you make when you love someone: getting cold, getting paint on your hands. Stanza two is about the strange and special delights you might find. The third stanza is about how you feel and the fourth about the memories and associations involved. What do you think he means in the final stanza when he says 'love is a prison and love is free'?

The poem is written without including any punctuation (only permissible when you are a professional writer – not when you're hoping to acquire GCSE!). Why do you think this is? What is the effect? Notice that the phrase 'Love is' is repeated many times and ends each stanza. Why do you think that is done? The first three lines in each stanza rhyme with each other. What effect does this have on the sound of the poem? Apart from the final line of each stanza and the first two lines of the last stanza, the lines in the poem are roughly the same length.

Having seen what the poem is saying and how it's written, you are now going to produce your own version.

1   Get ideas from friends and relatives about their definition of what 'love is'. What is the greatest sacrifice, the biggest thrill, the most unusual association or memory? (I once had a boyfriend who was a gardener: I associate him with the smell of rotting lawn mowings and engine oil!)

2   Collect further ideas from songs (for example, 'These Foolish Things Remind Me Of You', both the straight and 'spoof' versions), films, TV programmes, books of stories, sayings and poems; sentimental or comic birthday cards, valentines and so on.

3   From your own experience, think of definitions which are true to life and original. Someone once said that true love was sharing a toothbrush. What do you think?

4   If you are doing this activity with other students, compare your findings. Discuss and share your ideas, thus acquiring even more information.

5   Select from what should now be an extensive list and put it into a similar form to that used by Henri. You may wish to retain the repetition of 'Love is' when introducing the items and also when finishing each stanza. You can use a four line stanza like he does or vary it to suit yourself. You can use rhyme in the same way as the original, adapt or abandon it. Your intention is to make your poem sound right. Try to have a progression of ideas through your poem like in Henri's.

Drafting and Revising

Write and rewrite your poem until you are happy with both what it says and the way that it is written. Use conventional punctuation, please. Check your spelling. Put the appropriate headings at the top: name, date, 'written in response to "Love is . . . " by Adrian Henri', your own title.

Reading Aloud

When you are happy with the final version of your poem, practise reading it aloud. When you feel you can read it well, either read it aloud to your tutor and/or classmates or record it onto audio tape. This can be assessed as Speaking and Listening Coursework. If you are working in a group with other students, discuss the rival merits of the poems you have listened to. Whose poem worked best and why?

This activity covers **all** Attainment Targets!

What Should You Do Now?

When you have completed this activity, you may turn to another unit in this chapter or to a different chapter. You may wish to go on to do Activity E.

If you decide to move on to another unit, turn now to the last page of this unit to see what you have achieved. You can then make an accurate record.

ACTIVITY

2e

Coursework – Reading and Response

Read the following short story by James Joyce.

Eveline

She sat at the window watching the evening invade the avenue. Her head was leaned against the window curtains and in her nostrils was the odour of dusty cretonne. She was tired. Few people passed. The man out of the last house passed on his way home; she heard his footsteps clacking along the concrete pavement and afterwards crunching on the cinder path before the new red houses. One time there used to be a field in which they used to play every evening with other people's children. Then a man from Belfast bought the field and built houses in it – not like their little brown houses, but bright brick houses with shining roofs. The children of the avenue used to play together in that field – the Devines, the Waters, the Dunns, little Keogh the cripple, she and her brothers and sisters. Ernest, however, never played: he was too grown up. Her father used often to hunt them in out of the field with his blackthorn stick; but usually little Keogh used to keep 'nix' and call out when he saw her father coming. Still they seemed to have been rather happy then. Her father was not so bad then; and besides, her mother was alive. That was a long time ago; she and her brothers and sisters were all grown up; her mother was dead.

Tizzie Dunn was dead, too, and the Waters had gone back to England. Everything changes. Now she was going to go away like the others, to leave her home.

Home! She looked round the room, reviewing all its familiar objects which she had dusted once a week for so many years, wondering where on earth all the dust came from. Perhaps she would never see again those familiar objects from which she had never dreamed of being divided. And yet during all those years she had never found out the name of the priest whose yellowing photograph hung on the wall above the broken harmonium beside the coloured print of the promises made to Blessed Margaret Mary Alacoque. He had been a school friend of her father. Whenever he showed the photograph to a visitor her father used to pass it with a casual word:

– He is in Melbourne now.

She had consented to go away, to leave her home. Was that wise? She tried to weigh each side of the question. In her home anyway she had shelter and food; she had those whom she had known all her life about her. Of course she had to work hard, both in the house and at business. What would they say of her in the Stores when they found out that she had run away with a fellow? Say she was a fool, perhaps; and her place would be filled up by advertisement. Miss Gavan would be glad. She had always had an edge on her, especially whenever there were people listening.

– Miss Hill, don't you see these ladies are waiting?

– Look lively, Miss Hill, please.

She would not cry many tears at leaving the Stores.

But in her new home in a distant unknown country, it would not be like that. Then she would be married – she, Eveline. People would treat her with respect then. She would not be treated as her mother had been. Even now, though she was over nineteen, she sometimes felt herself in danger of her father's violence. She knew it was that that had given her the palpitations. When they were growing up he had never gone for her, like he used to go for Harry and Ernest, because she was a girl; but latterly he had begun to threaten her and say what he would do to her only for her dead mother's sake. And now she had nobody to protect her. Ernest was dead and Harry, who was in the church decorating business, was nearly always down somewhere in the country. Besides, the invariable squabble for money on Saturday nights had begun to weary her unspeakably. She always gave her entire wages – seven shillings – and Harry always sent up what he could but the trouble was to get any money from her father. He said she used to squander the money, that she had no head, that he wasn't going to give her his hard-earned money to throw about the streets, and much more, for he was usually fairly bad of a Saturday night. In the end he would give her the money and ask her had she any intention of buying Sunday's dinner. Then she had to rush out as quickly as she could and do her marketing, holding her black leather purse tightly in her hand as she elbowed her way through the crowds and returning home late under her load of provisions. She had hard work to keep the house together and to see that the two young children who had been left to her charge went to school regularly and got their meals regularly. It was hard work – a hard life – but now that she was about to leave it she did not find it a wholly undesirable life.

She was about to explore another life with Frank. Frank was very kind, manly, open-hearted. She was to go away with him by the night-boat to be his wife and to live with him in Buenos Ayres where he had a home waiting for her. How well she remembered the first time she had seen him; he was lodging in a house on the main road where she used to visit. It seemed a few weeks ago. He was standing at the gate, his peaked cap pushed back on his head and his hair tumbled forward over a face of bronze. Then they had come to know each other. He used to meet her outside the Stores every evening and see her home. He took her to see 'The Bohemian Girl' and she felt elated as she sat in an unaccustomed part of the theatre with him. He was awfully fond of music and sang a little. People knew that they were courting and, when he sang about the lass that loves a sailor, she always felt pleasantly confused. He used to call her Poppens out of fun. First of all it had been an excitement for her to have a fellow and then she had begun to like him. He had tales of distant countries. He had started as a deck boy at a pound a month on a ship of the Allan line going out to Canada. He told her the names of the ships he had been on and the names of the different services. He had sailed through the Straits of Magellan and he told her stories of the terrible Patagonians. He had fallen on his feet in Buenos Ayres, he said, and had come over to the old country just for a holiday. Of course, her father had found out the affair and had forbidden her to have anything to say to him.

– I know these sailor chaps, he said.

One day he had quarrelled with Frank and after that she had to meet her lover secretly.

The evening deepened in the avenue. The white of two letters in her lap grew indistinct. One was to Harry; the other was to her father. Ernest had been her favourite but she liked Harry too. Her father was becoming old lately, she noticed; he would miss her. Sometimes he could be very nice. Not long before, when she had been laid up for a day, he had read her out a ghost story and made toast for her at the fire. Another day, when their mother was alive, they had all gone for a picnic to the Hill of Howth. She remembered her father putting on her mother's bonnet to make the children laugh.

Her time was running out but she continued to sit by the window, leaning her head against the window curtain, inhaling the odour of dusty cretonne. Down far in the avenue she could hear a street organ playing. She knew the air. Strange that it should come that very night to remind her of the promise to her mother, her promise to keep the home together as long as she could. She remembered the last night of her mother's illness; she was again in the close dark room at the other side of the hall and outside she heard a melancholy air of Italy. The organ-player had been ordered to go away and given sixpence. She remembered her father strutting back into the sickroom saying: – Damned Italians! coming over here!

As she mused the pitiful vision of her mother's life laid its spell on the very quick of her being – that life of commonplace sacrifices closing in final craziness. She trembled as she heard again her mother's voice saying constantly with foolish insistence:

– Derevaun Seraun! Derevaun Seraun!

She stood up in a sudden impulse of terror. Escape! She must escape! Frank would save her. He would give her life, perhaps love, too. But she wanted to live. Why should she be unhappy? She had a right to happiness. Frank would take her in his arms, fold her in his arms. He would save her.

She stood among the swaying crowd in the station at the North Wall. He held her hand and she knew that he was speaking to her, saying something about the passage over and over again. The station was full of soldiers with brown baggages. Through the wide doors of the sheds she caught a glimpse of the black mass of the boat, lying in beside the quay wall, with illumined portholes. She answered nothing. She felt her cheek pale and cold and, out of a maze of distress, she prayed to God to direct her, to show her what was her duty. The boat blew a long mournful whistle into the mist. If she went, tomorrow she would be on the sea with Frank, steaming towards Buenos Ayres. Their passage had been booked. Could she still draw back after all he had done for her? Her distress awoke a nausea in her body and she kept moving her lips in silent fervent prayer.

A bell clanged upon her heart. She felt him seize her hand: – Come!

All the seas of the world tumbled about her heart. He was drawing her into them: he would drown her. She gripped with both hands at the iron railing.

– Come.

No! No! No! It was impossible. Her hands clutched the iron in frenzy. Amid the seas she sent a cry of anguish!

– Eveline! Evvy!

He rushed beyond the barrier and called to her to follow. He was shouted at to go on but he still called to her. She set her white face to him, passive, like a helpless animal. Her eyes gave him no sign of love or farewell or recognition.

'Eveline', from *The Dubliners*, James Joyce

Now that you have read the story of Eveline, it is necessary to look at what it is about and how it's written. Make notes in answer to the following questions:

1   The main characters in the story are Eveline, her father and Frank. Write each name in turn as a heading. List under the heading, as much about the character as you can, using evidence from the story.

2   What are the conflicting pressures on Eveline? Divide your page into two columns. Put at the top of one column 'Reasons for staying at home' and at the top of the other 'Reasons for going to Buenos Ayres'. List all the arguments you can find in the appropriate place.

3   Why do you think she chooses to stay behind? Look at your list. Is there anything else in the story which you haven't considered so far?

4   The setting of this story is Dublin. Eveline is a Roman Catholic. Does this make a difference to her decision, in your opinion? What would the Church's attitude be towards her going off with Frank?

5 Did you think, early in the story, that Eveline would leave? Try to explain why you thought as you did. Does she make the right or wrong decision?

6 What is the mood of the story? How is it created?

7 How did you feel at the end of the story? Try to explain why. What message do you think Joyce is trying to convey? What aspects of love are looked at here? Consider love within the family as well as romantic love.

8 Joyce disapproved of speech marks, calling them 'perverted commas'. This is why they don't appear in the story. What interesting or unusual use of words have you noticed here? The story was published in 1914.

Speaking and Listening

If you are working with a group of students, discuss your answers to the questions.

Writing

Choose **one** of the following as a written response to the story. Re-read the story before you start to write.

1 Imagining that you are Eveline, write several diary entries (probably five is the minimum number), over a period of time. The earliest could be about the picnic when her mother was still alive; another could be the day her mother died. You could then write about the first time she saw Frank, and when they went to the theatre. The last entry could be the day he left or even some time afterwards showing her feelings then.
   Try to enter into Eveline's character and put yourself in her place. Write about the other characters using what the story says as a guide to what they are like. Put a suitable date at the top of each as a heading showing how much time has passed. Avoid putting 'Dear Diary' and a signature after each entry. Write at least 400 words.

2 Frank has returned to Buenos Ayres. Let's imagine that Eveline feels that she gave him an insufficient explanation of her behaviour. Imagining that you are Eveline, write a letter to Frank explaining the conflicting thoughts and feelings which led you to stay in Dublin. Say how you feel now. Perhaps suggest any possible future action on your part with regard to Frank. Use the information in the story to make your letter as believable and full as possible. Aim to write at least 400 words in total.

3 Joyce's story is told solely from Eveline's point of view. Rewrite the story using Frank as the central character. You could write this in the form of a simple narrative or you might like to write it as Frank's diary entries over the time of his acquaintance with Eveline (see the advice given in 1 above). You should write about the first time he met her, how his feelings for her grow and what he thinks about her father.

4   What happens next? Write about Eveline's return home. How does she feel? Her father will have read the letter she left for him; perhaps he has been drinking and 'goes for her'. Describe all this using what you have learned about the characters in the story. Write at least 400 words.

Drafting and Revising

When you have finished a first draft of the response you have chosen, check it through carefully. Improve both the content and accuracy by revising and redrafting. Look back at the original story and make sure you have not made the characters think and behave out of character. Check your spelling and punctuation.

When you have written a final draft, put your name, the date of writing, a suitable title and 'work written in response to "Eveline" by James Joyce' at the top.

Review of Unit 2

- Activity A was reading and analysis of a pre-twentieth-century text (En 2.1, 4).
- Activity B was speaking and listening coursework in response to literature (En 1; En 2.1, 4).
- Activity C was written coursework in response to literature (En 2.1, 4; En 3).
- Activity D was speaking and listening and written coursework in response to literature (En 1, En 2, En 3).
- Activity E was speaking and listening and written coursework in response to literature (En 1, En 2.1, 4; En 3).

Making a Record

Write down the necessary information about the coursework which you have done in this unit. The oral work was individual and group in Activity A and group oral work in Activities B and C. The written coursework work was in Activities C, D, and E.

When you have made a record on your Coursework Index Form, tick the relevant aspects of En 1, En 2 and En 3 on your Coursework Checklist. You have now studied a work by Shakespeare and some pre-twentieth century literature.

What Should You Do Now?

Turn to another unit in Chapter 3 or to the first unit of another chapter.

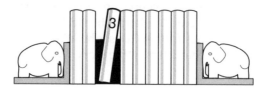

UNIT **3** *Review*

In this unit, instead of responding to pieces of literature which have been provided, you are going to decide what to write about. Essentially, you are going to write a review of a book you have read.

If you have chosen to work on this unit, you must complete all the activities up to and including Activity C.

After completing Activity C you may, if you wish, turn to another unit or to a different chapter. A further four activities are offered, however.

- Activity D is a written film review.
- Activity E is a spoken film review.
- Activity F is a written review of a television programme.
- Activity G offers various written coursework opportunities on soap operas.

ACTIVITY

3a

Reading and Understanding

First of all let's look at extracts from a couple of book reviews.

Extract A

This is from *Company Magazine* and is a short review of a book called *The Way Men Act* by Elinor Lipman.

> [This book is] Set in the small college town of Harrow, USA. We meet 30 year old Melinda, recently returned to her home town from the big wide world to lick her emotional wounds. After a broken romance and disillusioned dreams, she hopes to discover a new quality to her life. She starts work in her cousin's florist shop and meets up with an old school friend, Libby, who has a boutique next door. Both women are on the lookout for a permanent relationship, and both get what they're after – in a roundabout way. Lipman has the story telling power of Joanna Trollope and the readability and charm of Penelope Lively. Wonderful.

Extract B

This is from the *Independent on Sunday's* review section. It is from a much longer review by Mary Morrissy of *St Patrick's Daughter* by Margaret Mulvihill.

The first paragraph talks generally about Mulvihill's work. This is the second paragraph:

> Margaret Mulvihill's tale focuses on Jacinta Murphy, daughter of the feckless Eugene, who is sent by her mother to London to make a career for herself. But those expecting a rite-of-passage novel – innocent Catholic girl coming of age in godless Albion – are mercifully disappointed. Jacinta is not the product of your standard Irish girlhood. For a start, her parents are separated. Hapless Ma works in Dublin keeping the dead files in a hospital and takes lovers whose suitability is tested by whether they can get cash refunds on the ill-fitting shoes for which she has a weakness. Father boards at a lodging house in Camden, living off his one moment of fame – a role as St Patrick in a never completed film saga about Ireland's patron saint.

Morrissy continues to give an account of the main characters and to summarise the plot of the novel for a further three paragraphs. These are the last two paragraphs:

> All, of course, ends badly with Eugene's untimely death (a jogger's leap). His ribald wake is attended by all the women in his life, each desperate to claim their portion of him. Jacinta emerges, if not older and wiser, then clear of his rakish shadow, and by far the most mature character in the midst of a host of juveniles passing themselves off as adults.
>
> Mulvihill has a deft comic touch and a sure hand with verbal slapstick. The irreverent subtext, littered with the superstitious vocabulary of the catechism – purgatory, baptisms of desire, the children of Fatima – brings alive the world of Irish Catholicism, in all its richness and trumpery, far more effectively than a grim dose of realism. And the author's refusal to rein in her comic world, to make it conform, renders this novel as gloriously chaotic as life itself.

When you look carefully at these two very different reviews of two very different books, the basic structure of each is the same:

- there is an introductory statement about the author or the setting;
- the main character is introduced, information is given about what her situation is and what she is expected to achieve;
- further relevant characters or developments of the plot are discussed;
- there is a statement about the ending;
- there is a brief analysis of the way the book is written;
- the reviewer's opinion is given.

This, with the exception of the final personal opinion, is also very similar to the guidelines about how, in general, to look at literature. This was given in Activity B of Unit 1 of this chapter and you were advised to copy it down.

ACTIVITY

3b

Coursework – Writing a Review

Think of a book which you have read recently or, if you prefer, read something specifically for this activity. Choose a novel rather than a piece of non-fiction.

1   Write an introductory statement. If you have read other books by the same author or if you know some interesting facts about him or her, this might be a good place to start. Alternatively, write about the setting of this book. Keep this short and to the point: write no more than 100 words.

2   Write briefly about the main character. Tell the reader about what his or her situation seems to be and what he or she is expected to do about it.

3   Go on to talk about other relevant characters and give a **short** summary of the plot. You will need to miss out a lot of detail so just concentrate on the main events. Write no more than about 200 words for (2) and (3) together.

4   Write about the ending. You may feel that you don't want to give too much away. Talk about what sort of ending it is: expected and conventional, unusual, moving or whatever is appropriate. Keep this short and to the point: no more than 50 words.

5   Write about the way the book is written. How does the writer try to create interest? What is the tone and mood of the book? Has the writer used language in an interesting or original way? You could write about 100 words here.

6   Now you should give your opinion.

    a   Talk about the aspects of the book which you felt were good: perhaps you liked one or more character, perhaps you felt the story was gripping or moving or whatever. Write about 50 words on this.

    b   Talk about any disappointments – aspects which were not so well tackled and which you didn't like so much. You could write another 50 or so words on this. (Notice in the examples given earlier, no negative comments were made.)

    c   Finally write a short statement saying who you would recommend the book to – what sort of person would enjoy it?

Do not put the numbers given above in your work. They are just a guide to the structure. If you write the number of words suggested about each aspect, you will have written about 500 words in total.

Drafting and Revising

When you have completed a first draft, look at it critically. Is it too long? Have you included too much of the story? Does it ramble? Would someone who has not read the book understand what you are saying? Would this person find it interesting? You may find that your opinion, either enthusiastic or the reverse, shows clearly in the way you have written about the story. This may be acceptable but try, as far as possible, to be objective, i.e. unbiased and reasonable. Save your praises or scorn for the conclusion. Have you remembered to include something about the way the book is written (i.e. its style)? Adjust the content as necessary.

How is your written style? Have you used correct sentences and accurate spelling? Check it through very carefully and improve it if necessary.

When you are satisfied that both content and accuracy are of an acceptable standard, write out your final draft. Put your name, the date of writing and 'Review of . . . (put the title of the book and its author)'. Also put the heading 'Work in response to literature.'

Alternative Written Coursework

If you have a favourite author, several of whose books you know well, you could choose to write about the author's work in general rather than just about one book. The same basic structure can be kept but it needs to be adjusted a little as set out below.

1   It would be sensible to write a short introduction about the writer. This could include a few biographical details and a general comment about the sort of books written by him or her.
2   Here instead of giving a summary of one novel, you could write a short account of two or three books, stressing their similarities or differences.
3   As with one book, here you could write about the author's particular and distinctive written style with specific examples.
4   You could conclude by saying why you like this writer's work so much – what you particularly enjoy.
5   You can recommend the writer to other readers.

ACTIVITY

3c

Coursework – Speaking and Listening

Now you are going to give a spoken rather than a written review.

Ideally, you should carry out this activity in a small group – four or five people is about the right number. If possible you should each have read the same book but this doesn't necessarily have to be the case. This will be a little bit like the sort of situation you may have seen on television or heard on the radio leading up to some literary award like the Booker Prize.

Each person is going to make a statement, along the same lines as the written review, about the book he or she has read. If you have each read the same book, it is not necessary to give a summary of what it's about. (If you have read different books you will have to, though.) You should give your opinion supported by examples drawn from the book. When everyone has expressed an opinion, there can be a general discussion and a verdict about the book's merits can be given.

Preparation

You should **not** write out in full what you are going to say and then read it out. You may make yourself a few notes, preferably on small index cards so that they're easy to handle. If you wish to refer to pages and passages in the book, note the page numbers on your cards but also put a marker in the book itself and mark the relevant passage with a pencil line.

Either present your spoken review when a teacher can hear and assess you, or tape-record it.

What Should You Do Now?

When you have finished Activity C you may move on to another unit if you wish. You will probably choose to complete at least one more of the activities in this unit. Either work through them in order or select the one which looks most interesting to you.

If you decide to move on to another unit, turn now to the last page of this unit to see what you have achieved. You can then make an accurate record.

ACTIVITY

3d

Coursework – Writing a Film Review

If you are a movie fan, this may be a very suitable piece of work for you. The principle is exactly the same as that set out in Activity C except that you are writing about a film rather than a novel. Don't feel obliged to write or talk about new films, though, old ones would be just as acceptable.

You may feel it's useful to have a look in magazines or newspapers to see what reviewers are saying about the newest film releases. Use these as a guide for your written style. The structure of your work is likely to be very similar to that discussed earlier. Here are some suggestions.

1 First of all you want to give the person reading your review a 'flavour' of what you're going to tell them about. Give the title and a brief description of what sort of film it is. You may wish to say here what your reaction to it was.
2 Give a **simple** outline of the **basic** plot – don't go into too much detail as it could be very confusing. (Aim to write no more than 150 words here.)
3 This may be merged with (**2**) above. Write about the personalities of the main characters, who played the roles and how well they acted the parts. (Write about 100 words.)
4 Discuss, probably giving your personal opinion, the direction, the camera work, script, items of special interest, music, original features and so on. It is necessary to do this to show that you appreciate the techniques and conventions used in a film rather than in a piece of literature. (Write up to 150 words.)
5 Give your verdict about the film's quality: talk about its strengths and weaknesses and assess whether it's likely to be a hit at the box office (if it's a new film). Say what type of audience it would be suitable for (Write about 50 words).

As with the book review, don't actually use numbered sections but do write your review in proper paragraphs covering the points in this order. The total length should be about 500 words.

Drafting and Revising

As always, check both the content and accuracy of your work before completing a final draft. The words 'Work in response to a media text' should be at the top along with your name, the date and the title 'A review of . . . (name of film)'

ACTIVITY

3e

Coursework – Speaking and Listening

This activity is exactly the same as Activity C except you are going to talk about films rather than books. You have probably watched television programmes which give a critical analysis of each new film which is brought out. You are now going to do this. If you prefer, rather than several people each reviewing one film, one person could review several and you could cut out the discussion element.

If you rarely go to the cinema, this activity will either be unsuitable for you or, perhaps, prompt you to change your ways!

You will find the advice given for Activity C useful for completing this activity.

ACTIVITY

3f

Coursework – Writing about Television

In just the same way as you used a film rather than a book in Activities D and E, you can use television programmes as the basis for both written and oral coursework.

You could write about an individual programme or you could choose three varied programmes to assess: a documentary, a sitcom and a sports programme, for example. You could choose to compare and contrast two or three programmes of the same type but on different channels.

Choose one of these suggestions and write a review. Follow the same structure as was suggested for Activity D. If you are writing about more than one programme you will have to write one or two paragraphs on each one, covering 'story', intention and so on as well as the technical aspects. Redraft and revise as necessary, checking both content and accuracy. Include the words 'written in response to a media text' in your heading.

ACTIVITY

3g

Writing about a Soap Opera

One very popular type of television programme is the so called 'soap opera'. These originally acquired the name because the programmes were sponsored by the manufacturers of soap powders. They were screened in the afternoons to catch the 'housewife' audience. Their features seem to be that they are about the everyday lives of their characters and that episodes are shown frequently, sometimes daily, at the same time.

What soap operas are popular at present?

Some of the long-running soaps like *Coronation Street* are watched by millions. *Coronation Street* gained new popularity with teenage viewers in the 1980s by changing its image and introducing more young characters. The Australian soaps have also enjoyed enormous successes in Britain.

Find out the viewing figures for the four or five currently most popular soaps.

It is by no means inevitable that a soap opera is going to be a 'hit', however. The short career of BBC 1's *Eldorado* is a good example of this.

The first episode was screened on 6 July 1992. There was some outrage in the press that the BBC had spent a rumoured £10 million on building a replica of a Spanish village in the hills near Malaga. According to the *Guardian's* John Naughton, the set cost only £1.5 million. The larger sum was the investment necessary to make 150 episodes per year. The early reviews in the tabloids concentrated on the programme's apparent obsession with sex. John Naughton from the *Guardian* was initially prepared to be open-minded:

> One cannot judge a book by its cover, nor a soap by its opening episodes, which are bound to be dire as characters are introduced and a scenario established. *Eldorado* may come to be as popular as *Eastenders* or it may bomb like *Chateauvallon* and only time will tell, for ratings move in mysterious ways. I am not the best judge of these things, by the way, for I once predicted the demise of *Neighbours*. But for what it's worth, my impression of *Eldorado* is that it seems terribly contrived, somehow. It looks like the product of market research which recommends pandering to the interests and appetites of Basildon Man. This is a creature who owns a house with an en-suite bathroom, drives an XR2, wears shell-suits, reads a tabloid, votes Tory, owns a microwave – and aspires to own an apartment or a timeshare on the Costa del Sol. Accordingly, *Eldorado* – with its video shop, Texas Homecare, tacky bar, stuccoed apartments and heart-shaped pool – is essentially by Basildon out of Torremolinos. The characters are likewise stereotypical grotesques.

John Naughton, The *Guardian*, 7 July 1992

The timing of the launch was felt by some people to be unfortunate. Usually new series are screened after Easter or in the autumn. The intention, apparently, was to catch the audience who had tuned in for the Olympics. Viewing figures were never high. The *Daily Mirror* at the end of July 1992 said the programme was 'less popular than *Panorama*'.

There were problems with the script in the early days and many of the actors were young and inexperienced. The set caused problems when it came to recording dialogue as the houses had not been sound proofed. Because there were three episodes a week there was a huge workload with filming going on for as much as sixteen hours a day with little or no time for rehearsal. Juliet Smith, the show's original producer, announced her departure on 1 August 1992.

There is a scale on site for recording audience figures. Its high point is 15 million which was never achieved and its low point is 5.5 million. One episode only attracted 2.8 million, well off the scale. It was announced on 12 March 1993 that the series would end in July 1993. The audience numbers then were about 8.5 million.

There was some very strong opposition from the actors and production team about the cancellation of the series. It was felt that there had been significant improvements in the script and that many difficulties had been overcome.

Alan Yentob, responsible for the BBC's decision to scrap the programme said, 'I cancelled it because I did not see it growing into a show that I feel would work in five years' time. Not because it is a populist soap opera, but because those characters still seem to me to be living in a bubble. They still do not appear to grow out of the environment.'

Robert Chalmers, writing in the *Observer* of 4 April 1993, quotes Leslee Udwin who played Joy Slater, owner of the Eldorado wine bar, 'Let's not beat about the bush: we became a byword for crap. The low point came when somebody faxed out an advert for a haemorrhoid ointment which claimed that "this makes even sitting through an episode of *Eldorado* tolerable"'.

Where did it go wrong?

Coursework – Writing

Choose **one** of the following four suggestions for a piece of written work.

1   Perhaps you used to watch *Eldorado* and have some clear recollections about it. Using what you do remember about the programme and with reference to the information given above, write a report, drawing conclusions as to why it failed. For the way to set out a report, see Chapter 6, Unit 6.

2   Write about the appeal of the two or three most popular current soap operas. Use the information about why *Eldorado* was a failure as a source of suggestions for why other soap operas are successful. In each case say what they are about, where they are set and what sorts of characters and situations they present. Try to explain what you believe to be the secret of their success. It may be that you yourself are a fan and watch them on a regular basis. If you are not, you will have to watch some episodes. It may also be a good idea to speak to other people about what they think of the programmes. You could draw up a questionnaire to find out this information in a structured and organised way.

3   The new smash hit. Think of an original idea for a soap opera. *Eldorado* was supposed to be the first Euro-soap. *Riviera*, a similar idea made with a French co-production team, went down so badly in France that it was never shown on British television. Now it's your turn. Pick a theme which has European connections. Invent a cast of characters designed to appeal to a wide audience, think of a suitable setting and give the package a snappy title. You might even want to write part of the dialogue for the first episode.

4   Look out for a new or recently imported soap opera. Watch an episode or two and write a review of it. (Follow the guidelines in Activity D.) Predict its chances of long-term success, giving clear reasons to back up your expectations. Monitor its progress in the

future to see if you were right. If you were, you may have a rosy future in programme planning!

Drafting and Revising

When you have finished your chosen piece of written work, check through to see whether you can make any improvements. When you are happy with both content and accuracy, write it out neatly. At the top you must put your name, the date of writing, an appropriate title and 'Work in response to a media text'.

Review of Unit 3

- Activity A was reading and understanding (En 2.2, 4).
- Activity B was written coursework in response to literature (En 2.1, 4; En 3).
- Activity C was speaking and listening coursework in response to literature (En 1, En 2.1, 4).
- Activity D was written coursework in response to a media text (En 2.2, 4; En 3).
- Activity E was speaking and listening coursework in response to a media text (En 1, En 2.2, 4).
- Activity F was written coursework in response to a media text (En 2.2, 4; En 3).
- Activity G was written coursework in response to a media text (En 2.2, 4; En 3).

Making a Record

Write down the necessary information about the coursework in this unit. This was the written work in Activities B, D, F and G. The oral coursework was in Activity C (group) and Activity E (individual and/or group).

When you have recorded this, tick the relevant aspects of En 1, En 2 and En 3 on your Coursework Checklist.

What Should You Do Now?

When you have completed this unit, move on to another unit in this chapter or to the first unit of another chapter.

UNIT (**4**)   *Images of War*

In this unit you are going to read five poems which create differing images or pictures of the First World War, sometimes referred to as the 'Great War'.

Before you start reading the poems you might like to know a bit more about this war. It began on 1 August 1914 when Germany declared war on Russia. Britain and France joined forces against Germany on 4 August.

After the first month or two it settled into a pattern of trench warfare. This means that each side dug trenches several feet deep, facing each other across a space of a few hundred yards known as 'no-man's land'. Coils of barbed wire were put here to try to prevent one side from being able to rush across and capture the opposing trench. When the order to attack was given, the wire was shelled from behind the lines in order to break it up. This was supposed to allow easy access. All too often the bombardment fell short (killing their own soldiers), overshot the target or was just ineffective. The soldiers were then caught in the wire and were easily shot down. The trenches were constructed in parallel lines with lateral communication trenches running back to the support area behind. A one-way system operated so that the dead or wounded along with those whose duty at the front had finished used one communication trench. The fresh troops came up to the front line using another so that they would not be disheartened by seeing the condition of their comrades.

Some strategically important areas such as Vimy Ridge (which was next to a valuable coalfield) were continually being taken by one side then re-taken, with further loss of life by the other side who then, in turn, were ousted again.

There were enormous numbers of casualties. On the first day of the first Battle of the Somme in 1916 there were 57,000 casualties. In that battle in total there were 600,000 Allied soldiers killed and 650,000 Germans. In the Battle of Passchendaele in 1917 there were 245,000 British casualties. The Allied Generals had calculated that as they had more troops than the Germans the Allies would eventually be victorious even if one Allied soldier was killed for each German one. The total number of dead, from both sides, over the four years of the conflict was eight and a half million. The War ended on 11 November 1918.

ACTIVITY

(**4a**)

Reading, Understanding and Analysis

Read each poem carefully then move on to analyse what it is saying. Decide what aspect of the war is being looked at in each case. Also decide what you feel the poet's attitude is towards the conflict. Once you feel that you understand the poem thoroughly, move on to the next one.

Poem A, The Soldier

If I should die, think only this of me:
That there's some corner of a foreign field
That is forever England. There shall be
In that rich earth a richer dust concealed;
A dust whom England bore, shaped, made aware,
Gave, once, her flowers to love, her ways to roam,
A body of England's breathing English air,
Washed by the rivers, blest by suns of home.

And think, this heart, all evil shed away,
A pulse in the eternal mind, no less
Gives somewhere back the thoughts by England given;
Her sights and sounds; dreams happy as her day;
And laughter, learnt of friends; and gentleness,
In hearts at peace, under an English heaven.

Rupert Brooke, *The Collected Poems*

What is this poem about? Look at the first sentence: what does it mean?

The idea seems to be that the spot where the English soldier is buried will be a little fragment of England. Not only that, but according to the next one and a half lines, the earth of that grave will be enriched by containing within it the 'richer dust' of his English body.

The poet then gives us some pictures of the 'English' experiences which the soldier has had: flowers; ways to roam – presumably pretty country lanes; fresh English air; rivers; English sunshine – a sense of home.

What general picture is created of England through these images? It's quiet, peaceful and protective, isn't it?

In the second part of the poem Brooke goes further. It's almost as if the dead soldier is now part of God's mind – 'a pulse in the eternal mind' and is able to give back to God the thoughts which he has been given by England. There is another list of English experiences: happy dreams, friendly laughter, peaceful gentle hearts, all under a friendly blue sky which Brooke describes as 'an English heaven'. What pictures are created in your mind here? I can visualise tea shops, cricket on the village green, cosy panelled studies and young men in flannel trousers and straw boaters. He seems to be almost suggesting that God is English and England a sort of earthly paradise.

What do you feel the poet's attitude is towards the soldier dying in the war? Surely it is almost doing the 'foreign field' a favour to enrich it like this. England certainly sounds worth dying for, doesn't it?

What is the tone of the poem? Is it gloomy and depressed or is it optimistic and positive? Notice the first phrase: 'If I should die, think only this . . . ' It sounds as if the soldier is accepting the idea that he may have to die but can look on the bright side of it. This is reinforced by the last words of the poem: 'at peace, under an English heaven' – this appears to be what is in store for him once death has 'shed away' the evil in his heart.

It sounds as if dying for England is a really good thing, doesn't it?

Poem B, The Three Lads

Down the road rides a German lad,
Into the distance grey;
Straight toward the north as a bullet flies,
The dusky north, with its cold, sad skies;
But the song he sings is merry and glad,
For he's off to war and away.
'Then hey! for our righteous king!'(he cries)
'And the good old God in his good blue skies!
And ho! for love and a pair of blue eyes,–
For I'm off to war and away!'

Down the road rides a Russian lad,
Into the distance grey;
Out toward the glare of the steppes he spurs,
And hears the wolves in the southern firs;
But the song he sings is blithe and glad,
For he's off to war and away.
'Then hey! for our noble tzar!'(he cries)
'And liberty that never dies!
And ho! for love and a pair of blue eyes,–
For I'm off to war and away!'

Down the road rides an English lad,
Into the distance grey;
Through the murk and fog of the river's breath,
Through the dank, dark night he rides to his death;
But the song he sings is gay and glad,
For he's off to war and away.
'Then hey! for our honest king!'(he cries)
'And hey! for truth, and down with lies!
And ho! for love and a pair of blue eyes,–
For I'm off to war and away!'

Elizabeth Chandler Forman

What is Forman saying here? Each of the lads in this poem is pleased to
be 'off to war and away'. Each one seems to believe that the ruler of his
country is worth supporting whether he's a righteous, honest king or
noble tzar. Each soldier thinks that right is on his side: he's on the side of
God, fighting for liberty or for truth. But the soldiers in this poem are not
all fighting on the same side in the conflict so it can't be as simple as this.

   Why does each soldier feel pleased to be going and that he's on the
right side? He will have been told this by newspapers and posters at
home. Is each lad thinking about the reality of war or just some dream of
glory?

   Notice how Forman makes the point that young soldiers, whether from
Germany, Russia or England, are just the same. She does this by making
the wording of each poem very similar. The first two lines of each stanza
(verse) are identical apart from the nationality of the soldier. The third
and fourth lines mainly deal with the landscape each is marching

through. In the final stanza, she says specifically that the soldier is going to his death, perhaps so that the reader has no illusions about what is in store at the end of the march.

In the fifth line of each stanza, about the soldier's song, she varies one word but in each case the word chosen is a jolly, happy, carefree one. In lines six and seven the exact nature of the country's ruler and the good cause for which they are fighting, is varied just a little, according to the soldier's nationality. The final two lines of each stanza are identical. Each soldier has a dream of love and a taste for 'a pair of blue eyes' – perhaps this emphasises their youth and humanity, making it more of a waste when they are killed. Each is happy to be 'off to war and away', with no thought about what is awaiting him.

The tone of each soldier's song is just as optimistic and proud as the beliefs of Rupert Brooke's soldier. Is this the mood of the poem as a whole? This time, isn't the reader aware that the lads are wrong? Look at the fourth and fifth lines of the final stanza: 'Through the dank, dark night he rides to his death; But the song that he sings is gay and glad' Here his cheerful song is placed next to the statement that he is going to die. The word 'but' becomes stronger. The lad doesn't know, but we do.

What point do you think Forman is making about war? What is her attitude towards the conflict?

The next two poems are by Wilfred Owen. He was on active service in the front line for much of the war. He therefore had first hand knowledge of the reality of life in the trenches. He was killed one week before the war ended.

'Dulce et decorum est pro patria mori' is a saying which means 'it is a sweet and suitable thing to die for the sake of your country'.

Poem C, Dulce Et Decorum Est

Bent double, like old beggars under sacks,
Knock-kneed, coughing like hags, we cursed through
    sludge,
Till on the haunting flares we turned our backs,
And towards our distant rest began to trudge.
Men marched asleep. Many had lost their boots,
But limped on, blood-shod. All went lame, all blind;
Drunk with fatigue; deaf even to the hoots
Of gas-shells dropping softly behind.

Gas! GAS! Quick, boys! – An ecstasy of fumbling,
Fitting the clumsy helmets just in time,
But someone still was yelling out and stumbling
And floundering like a man in fire or lime. –
Dim through the misty panes and thick green light,
As under a green sea, I saw him drowning.

In all my dreams before my helpless sight
He plunges at me, guttering, choking, drowning.
If in some smothering dreams, you too could pace

Behind the wagon that we flung him in,
And watch the white eyes writhing in his face,
His hanging face, like a devil's sick of sin;
If you could hear, at every jolt, the blood
Come gargling from the froth-corrupted lungs,
Bitter as the cud
Of vile, incurable sores on innocent tongues, –
My friend, you would not tell with such high zest
To children ardent for some desperate glory,
The old Lie: Dulce et decorum est
Pro patria mori.

Wilfred Owen

Let's look at the image of war which is being presented here. Look at the impression we are given of the soldiers in the first stanza. Soldiers are usually seen as marching briskly with straight backs, gleaming buttons and highly polished boots. What picture is given here?

They are bent double, they are coughing, they are almost asleep on their feet and many have no boots. What picture do you get from the phrase 'blood shod'? The men are going back from the front line to rest. An impression of the muddy conditions is given in the phrase 'we cursed through sludge'. Far from moving quickly and efficiently they 'trudge' and 'limp' and are 'drunk with fatigue'. Already this is a very different image from those we have seen in the other two poems.

At the end of the first stanza, Owen says that the men are 'deaf even to the hoots of gas shells dropping softly behind'. He puts in this phrase quietly and without explaining its implications. It is almost as if we too are oblivious to these lethal shells. The pace of the poem has been quite slow, mirroring the weariness of the soldiers. Now it is as if everyone suddenly has to wake up with a jolt. At the beginning of the next stanza, the cry 'gas!' is intensified. The first time the word is printed in lower case letters; the second it is in capitals as if the cry is louder, more urgent. There is then the intense frantic attempt of the soldiers to fit their gas-masks, successful except for in one man's case. The picture we are given of this man is as if it is seen through the thick glass of the mask and green haze of the chlorine gas. When you think of the effect of breathing in a poisonous vapour, the word 'drowning' seems an appropriate choice. It is hardly surprising that the narrator tells us that he has nightmares about having had to watch this man die.

The final stanza is one very long sentence. It starts off by saying **if** we could see this terrible sight – and he describes the slow agonising death of the soldier – **then** we would not be quite so keen to fill children's minds with ideas about the glory of war. Notice that Owen uses the word 'lie'. He doesn't merely suggest that the old saying is a bit misleading; he says it is a **lie**, i.e. that it is **not** a sweet and suitable thing to die for your country.

So, what aspect of the war is being looked at here? What is this poet's attitude towards the conflict? What is the tone of this poem?

Poem D, Exposure

Our brains ache, in the merciless east winds that knive
    us.
Wearied we keep awake because the night is silent . . .
Low, drooping flares confuse our memory of the salient
    . . .
Worried by silence, sentries whisper, curious, nervous,
But nothing happens.

Watching, we hear the mad gusts tugging on the wire,
Like twitching agonies of men among its brambles.
Northward, incessantly, the flickering gunnery rumbles,
Far off, like a dull rumour of some other war.
What are we doing here?

The poignant misery of dawn begins to grow . . .
We only know war lasts, rain soaks, and clouds sag
    stormy.
Dawn massing in the east her melancholy army
Attacks once more in ranks on shivering ranks of grey,
But nothing happens.

Sudden successive flights of bullets streak the silence.
Less deadly than the air which shudders black with
    snow,
With sidelong flowing flakes that flock, pause and renew,
We watch them wandering up and down the wind's
    nonchalance,
But nothing happens.

Pale flakes with fingering stealth come feeling for our
    faces –
We cringe in holes, back on forgotten dreams, and stare,
    snow-dazed,
Deep into grassier ditches. So we drowse, sun-dozed,
Littered with blossoms trickling where the blackbird
    fusses.
Is it that we are dying?

Slowly our ghosts drag home: glimpsing the sunk fires,
    glozed
With crusted dark-red jewels; crickets jingle there;
For hours the innocent mice rejoice: the house is theirs;
Shutters and doors, all closed: on us the doors are
    closed, –
We turn back to our dying.

Since we believe not otherwise can kind fires burn;
Nor ever suns smile true on child, or field, or fruit.
For God's invincible spring our love is made afraid;
Therefore, not loath, we lie out here; therefore were born,
For love of God seems dying.

Tonight, His frost will fasten on this mud and us,
Shrivelling many hands, puckering foreheads crisp.
The burying-party, picks and shovels in their shaking
     grasp,
Pause over half-known faces. All their eyes are ice,
But nothing happens.

Wilfred Owen

For the first four stanzas in this poem, Owen is mainly writing about the conditions suffered by the men in the trenches. There is no protection from the weather. How do they feel? Look at the line 'We only know war lasts, rain soaks and clouds sag stormy'. Apart from a few bullets passing over at dawn and the sound of distant guns, nothing is happening in the way of actual fighting. There is, therefore, boredom as well as discomfort. The growing light of dawn is described as an advancing army. The men feel flakes of snow on their faces. Notice how Owen uses the sound of the words to give an impression of the cold gentle flakes: 'fingering stealth', 'feeling for our faces'. Count how many times he uses words beginning with f and s. What is the pace and the mood of the poem so far? In the fifth stanza, lying in holes, the men seem to drift into day-dreams where they are lying in the grass in the summer, littered with blossoms and hearing the blackbird's song. The images created here and in the next two stanzas seem somewhat similar to those in Rupert Brooke's poem.

    Look carefully at what Owen is saying. In stanza six there is a picture of empty and deserted but peaceful houses with dying fires and mice playing. These soldiers are shut away from even this amount of cosy domestication 'on us the doors are closed'. Owen says, 'We turn back to our dying'. In stanza seven the argument which is put forward is that the men have to believe that they are fighting to preserve a worthwhile way of life: if they were not, 'kind fires' could not burn nor 'suns smile true' on 'child or field or fruit'. Because of this they have volunteered willingly to lie there as this seems to be the sacrifice which God requires.

    In the eighth stanza there seems to be an irony. They are not being killed in a fight but through the cold. It seems as if God, with the frost, will kill many of these soldiers from exposure. The living, almost as cold as the dead will have to suppress warm feelings for their comrades 'pause over half-known faces'. Ultimately, they will just have to stay there, waiting, because still 'nothing happens'.

    Finally what do you think Owen is saying here? What is the mood and tone of the poem. Compare this to the tone of 'The Soldier' by Rupert Brooke. Is there any similarity in what the two poets are saying?

Poem E, Night Duty

The pain and laughter of the day are done,
So strangely hushed and still the long ward seems,
Only the sister's candle softly beams.
Clear from the church near by the clock strikes 'one';
And all are wrapt away in secret sleep and dreams.

They bandied talk and jest from bed to bed;
Now sleep has touched them with a subtle change.
They lie here deep withdrawn, remote and strange;
A dimly outlined shape, a tumbled head.
Through what far lands do now their wand'ring spirits
    range?

Here one cries sudden on a sobbing breath,
Gripped in the clutch of some incarnate fear:
What terror through the darkness draweth near?
What memory of carnage and of death?
What vanished scenes of dread to his closed eyes appear?

And one laughs out with an exultant joy.
An athlete he – Maybe his young limbs strain
In some remembered game, and not in vain
To win his side the goal – Poor crippled boy,
Who in the waking world will never run again.

One murmurs soft and low a woman's name;
And here a vet'ran soldier, calm and still
As sculptured marble sleeps, and roams at will
Through eastern lands where sunbeams scorch like
    flame,
By rich bazaar and town, and wood-wrapt snow-
    crowned hill.

Through the wide open window one great star,
Swinging her lamp above the pear-tree high,
Looks in upon these dreaming forms that lie
So near in body, yet in soul so far
As those bright worlds thick strewn on that vast depth
    of sky.

Eva Dobell

What aspect of war is Dobell looking at here? This time the scene is not soldiers going off to war or suffering at the front. Here the injured soldiers are lying in the hospital ward and the poet looks at the changes caused by the war to their bodies and to their minds. How do they seem to behave during the day according to the second stanza? What happens at night? What do you think the final stanza is saying?

What attitude towards the conflict do you find here? What is the mood of this poem? Is it as strongly and forcefully written as those by Wilfred Owen? Does it successfully convey the poet's point of view?

ACTIVITY
4b

Coursework – Speaking and Listening

Discuss the five poems with a group of three or four other students.

What do you feel you learn about the poets' experience of war? Do you think all four writers had first-hand knowledge of it? Discuss the differences in what the poems are saying as well as how effectively the poets have communicated their thoughts and feelings. How did you feel when you read each one?

Try to decide what order you would rank the poems in in terms of how well the ideas are conveyed. Which one did you like best?

ACTIVITY

4c

Coursework – Writing in Response to Literature

Choose **one** of the following four suggestions for written coursework. Re-read the relevant poems before you start to write. Whichever option you choose, you should echo the words of the poems in your work but you should not copy out whole sentences. Use the ideas but put them into your own words, to a certain extent. For example, if you were writing a description of the soldiers' feet, don't put 'blood shod', the phrase used by Owen. Say that their bare feet were bleeding.

1   **Writing home**. Imagine that you are a young volunteer soldier. Write two letters home. The first one should be written early in the conflict (1914) soon after you have enlisted. You might be writing from a training camp behind the lines. Express the sort of happy optimism that is conveyed by the soldiers in the first two poems.

Add any details you like about your fellow soldiers to make the letter sound realistic.

The second letter is written later in the war (1916 or 1917). It should convey the reality of war now that you have been in the front line. Use the two poems by Wilfred Owen to provide material. Describe the effect of the weather, how you feel about the conflict and its purpose, the incident with the gas and so on.

Make the two letters express very different views about the war.

2   **A soldier's diary**. Use the poems to provide the basis for diary entries showing the experience of a young soldier.

Imagining you are the soldier, write at least four entries. The first ones should show the enthusiastic naivety of a new recruit as seen in the first two poems, later ones should show the real situation as seen in the poems by Wilfred Owen. The final entry could be written in hospital and you could use the fifth poem for inspiration.

3   **Female perspective**. Imagine that you are the wife or girlfriend of a soldier in the war. Write your diary. Use the same ideas as in (2) above but this time you are writing about the changing attitude of someone you love rather than about yourself.

The letters you receive would make you realise what the war was really like. You could assume that you are involved in nursing and use the last poem to provide material for one or more entries. Perhaps you might decide that your loved one did not survive. You could describe your feelings on receiving the telegram or letter informing you of his death from the commanding officer.

4   **Debate**. Imagine that Wilfred Owen and Rupert Brooke are discussing the war. Using material from their poems to provide the ideas

and examples, write a conversation between them, expressing their differing points of view. This could be written in the form of a play scene, set out appropriately (see Chapter 6, Unit 6) or using correctly punctuated direct speech (see Chapter 6 Unit 4). Put in descriptions of expressions, gestures and so on to enhance the dialogue.

Drafting and Revising

When you have finished the first draft of your coursework, read it through carefully. Have you used the poems to provide you with ideas and material? Have you lifted too much of the original wording without alteration? Try to get the balance right. Your tutor will advise you.

Have you written enough? The minimum length acceptable is about 500 words. Is your work too long? Again try to achieve a good balance between conciseness and detail.

When you are happy with the content, check the correctness of your work. Is your spelling and punctuation accurate? Revise and improve this as necessary. When you are satisfied that the standard is as good as possible, write out the final draft. Put your name, the date of writing and the appropriate title at the top plus 'work in response to poems written during the First World War'. You should then list the poems that you have used.

ACTIVITY

4d

Optional Further Coursework – Writing in Response to a Media Text

Obtain a videotape of the final episode of *Blackadder Goes Forth* (your local video rental firm should have it). Watch the programme carefully and then consider these points.

1 What picture does this programme give of conditions in the trenches? Does the programme use exaggeration? What conclusions about the War are likely to be reached by the viewer because of this?

2 Different attitudes towards the War are expressed by different people. What is the attitude of each of the following characters and **why** do they feel like this?

- General Melchet;
- Captain Darling;
- Baldrick;
- George;
- Blackadder.

Are any of these attitudes similar to those expressed in the poems?

- What is the viewer's likely opinion of the characters listed above? Do we approve of characters who are in favour of the War or those who are against it? Consider especially here what our reaction is to George's delight about being sent 'over the top'.

- What did you laugh at in the programme? How is humour used to make serious points about warfare.
- Consider the end of the programme. What final picture of the War is shown and what conclusion should be drawn from this?

Once you have thought about and made notes on these points, write about 500 words in answer to this question:

'What does the final episode of *Blackadder Goes Forth* say about war and how does it convey its message?'

In your answer you should write about all the points which you considered before: use of exaggeration, character, the opinion of the audience, humour and the ending. It is probably a good idea to discuss the points in this order. Your work should then move steadily towards a conclusion rather than hopping about from one aspect to another or going round in circles.

Drafting and Revising

As always, when you have written your first draft, check both the content and accuracy of your work. Make sure that you are answering the question. When you are satisfied, write your name, the date of writing, the title 'Blackadder' and the words 'work in response to a media text' as the heading for your final draft.

ACTIVITY

4e

Optional Further Reading and Research and Information Retrieval

Find out more about the First World War. Your local or college library will have information of various sorts and in various places.

To find more general facts and figures you might wish to consult an encyclopaedia. For more detailed information you can look in the history section where you will find books dealing with specific aspects of the War. There are also autobiographical accounts which you may find interesting such as Vera Brittain's *Testament of Youth* and Robert Graves' *Goodbye to All That*.

A novel such as Siegfried Sassoon's *Memoirs of an Infantry Officer* gives the writer's real experiences under the guise of fiction. The play *Journey's End* by R.C. Sherriff portrays life in the trenches; it has also been made into a film.

Review of Unit 4

- In Activity A you read, understood and analysed five poems (En 2.1, 4).
- Activity B was speaking and listening coursework in response to literature (En 1, En 2.1, 4).
- Activity C was written coursework in response to literature (En 2.1, 4 and En 3).
- Activity D was optional written coursework in response to a media text (En 2.2, 4 and En 3).
- Activity E was optional reading and research and information retrieval (En 2.3).

Making a Record

Write down the necessary information about the coursework in this unit. This was the group oral work in Activity B and the written work in Activity C and D. When you have done this, tick the relevant aspects of En 1, En 2 and En 3 on your Coursework Checklist.

What Should You Do Now?

You could choose another unit from this chapter, or turn to unit 1 of another chapter.

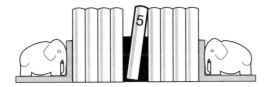

UNIT *Baby Beware*

In this unit you will be looking at six poems either about or addressed to very young (or even unborn) children warning them about what life has in store for them. By looking at these poems it is possible to draw some conclusions about the poets' own feelings about the world around them and what it has to offer.

You will either be able to write about several poems in one piece of coursework or you may wish to concentrate on one or two of them.

First, you need to read and understand the poems.

ACTIVITY

Reading, Understanding and Analysis

Read each poem carefully then look at the questions and comments about it. When you feel you understand the poem as fully as possible, move on to the next one.

Poem A, Infant Joy

"I have no name:
"I am but two days old."
What shall I call thee?
"I happy am,
"Joy is my name."
Sweet joy befall thee!

Pretty joy!
Sweet joy but two days old,
Sweet joy I call thee:
Thou dost smile,
I sing the while,
Sweet joy befall thee!

     Songs of Innocence and
Experience,   Willliam Blake

This poem is taken from a book called *Songs of Innocence*.

Explain why this poem seems to belong in a book with that title. Look at the words which the poet has chosen. Blake was writing in the late eighteenth century so there are some old-fashioned words but look how short most of the words are. Only 'happy' and 'befall' have more than one syllable. What is the effect of this on the sound of the poem?

What does the writer's attitude towards both the baby and life itself seem to be?

Do you like this poem?

Now look at the next poem. It is also by William Blake but this time it comes from a companion book called *Songs of Experience*.

Poem B, Infant Sorrow

My mother groan'd! my father wept.
Into the dangerous world I leapt:
Helpless, naked, piping loud:
Like a fiend hid in a cloud.

Struggling in my father's hands,
Striving against my swaddling bands,
Bound and weary, I thought best
To sulk upon my mother's breast.

> *Songs of Innocence and Experience,*
> William Blake

This time the attitude of the poet towards both life and the baby seems to be very different.

Birth is far from being a joyful occasion. Look at the parents' reactions in the first two lines. The birth seems to cause both pain and sorrow. The impression of the child becomes steadily more unpleasant: helpless and naked sound all right. When Blake says 'piping' he seems to mean crying. What sound do you imagine when the word 'piping' is used? The next line stops us having any favourable impression: this is a little devil in disguise. The baby itself seems to resent being there. Blake's choice of the word 'struggling' is interesting. He could have chosen a neutral word; 'moving' or 'kicking' might have suggested the natural exercise of the baby's limbs. 'Struggling' sounds as if it's trying to get away.

Babies in those days were bound up in a sort of cocoon by swaddling bands. You may previously have come across this in the Bible where Mary is described as putting the infant Jesus into such a wrapping. The effect is to restrict the baby's movements very severely. It was believed to be a way of helping the limbs to grow strong.

In the poem it sounds as if the child is being imprisoned in its swaddling bands and is fighting to get free. This perhaps reflects how it feels about being born at all. It finally seems to resign itself to its stay. The picture of the baby choosing to 'sulk' on its mother's breast is very different from the image of the loving bond that an infant at the breast might normally evoke.

In this poem, although the words are not complex, they are not as short and simple as in poem A. What is the difference in mood? If you were reading the poems aloud, what would be the difference in the tone of voice you would use? This difference is caused partly by the subject matter but also by the sound of the words which Blake uses. If you were to set them to music, what would be the difference between the melodies you would use?

How does Blake's attitude to life differ between the two poems? Which of these two poems do you find the more interesting? Which do you like best?

Poem C, The New Rose

The new rose
trembles with early beauty
The babe sees the beckoning carmine
the tiny hand
clutches the cruel stem.
The baby screams
The rose is silent –
Life is already telling lies.

> *Small Dreams of a Scorpion*,
> Spike Milligan

Most people would associate Spike Milligan with humorous writing. His poetry, however, is sometimes serious and thought-provoking. In this poem, the baby itself is not particularly being looked at except as an innocent being who does not yet know what life is like: that roses have thorns, for instance. What is Milligan saying about the world? The rose is shown to 'tremble with early beauty' and also its attractive red colour is described as 'beckoning carmine' almost as if it is tempting the child to reach out for it. When the baby does so, the rose says nothing. Of course, a rose cannot literally speak but it is as if Milligan is suggesting that it could have: either to warn or to apologise.

What does the final line mean? What attitude is Milligan expressing here? Which of poem A or B is this more like? Like the two poems by Blake, this poem is very short and simply worded. Do you think it conveys its message effectively?

Poem D, Unto Us . . .

Somewhere at sometime
They committed themselves to me
And so, I was!
Small, but I WAS.
Tiny in shape
Lusting to live
I hung in my pulsing cave.
Soon they knew of me
My mother – my father.
I had no say in my being
I lived on trust
And love
Tho' I couldn't think
Each part of me was saying
A silent 'Wait for me
'I will bring you love!'

I was taken
Blind, naked, defenceless
By the hand of one
Whose good name
Was graven on a brass plate
in Wimpole Street,
and dropped on the sterile floor
of a foot operated plastic waste bucket.
There was no Queen's Counsel
To take my brief.
The cot I might have warmed
Stood in Harrod's shop window.
When my passing was told
My father smiled.
No grief filled my empty space.
My death was celebrated
With two tickets to see Danny la Rue
Who was pretending to be a woman
Like my mother was.

Small Dreams of a Scorpion,
Spike Milligan

In this poem Milligan uses strong emotive arguments against the abortion of a foetus. Whatever your own personal views on the issue are, first of all let's see exactly what Milligan is saying and how he is saying it. You will have an opportunity to write either in agreement with or against his point of view in a later activity in this unit. The title of the poem is a quotation from the Bible. At Christ's birth these words are used; 'Unto us a child is born; unto us a son is given'. This suggests that Milligan views a child, or even conception, as a gift from God.

He makes an assumption in the first two lines that by having a sexual relationship with each other, the couple had made a commitment to the possibility of a child. He then stresses, in lines 3 and 4 that it had an existence of its own, however tiny. Because the poet is writing as the foetus he is able to attribute thoughts and feelings to it. What does 'lusting to live' mean? The 'pulsing cave' is the woman's womb. Is this an apt description?

By saying that the woman and man involved were 'mother' and 'father' Milligan is appealing for an emotional response from the reader. He is also doing this when he says that the foetus had 'no say' in its existence but that it 'lived on trust and love'. The argument here is that a foetus is not responsible for its parents' actions and all it can ask for is love. Milligan says 'I couldn't think' but then goes on to write as though the foetus could not only think but make an emotional demand – 'Wait for me, I will bring you love'.

Immediately after this there is a description of the abortion. The words 'blind, naked, defenceless' also have a strong appeal to the reader's emotions. It is implied that the people involved here are affluent financially. It sounds as if the operation takes place at an expensive private clinic. Notice that there are no capital letters at the beginning of the three lines after 'brass plate'. Why do you think this is? Does he want to give the impression of the whole thing being a routine matter, performed quickly? Notice that the disposal sounds both clinical and heartless: 'dropped on the floor', 'foot operated plastic waste bucket'.

By saying 'There was no Queen's Counsel' Milligan is implying that there should have been a top barrister because this was a serious crime, a murder, but there was not. Again he implies that the couple had plenty of money as the cot would have been bought from Harrods, an expensive and exclusive store. It sounds as if the cot is cold and would have been warmed by a child: perhaps it is more usual to think of this the other way round: for the cot to warm the child.

The parents' callousness is then stressed as the father's reaction is to smile and for the couple to then go to the theatre. The final two lines contain a very powerful concluding statement. Is Milligan implying that a woman who does not want a baby is not a real woman? Or that a woman who could have an abortion is not a true woman? This suggests that motherhood is a woman's principal role. In Chapter 5 you will find a unit which deals specifically with 'A Woman's Place'. Remember this poem when you are working on that unit.

If you feel that you would like to write about this poem now before reading the other poems presented in this activity, please turn to Activity C. You can then return to look at the other poems later.

Poem E, To An Unborn Pauper Child

Breathe not, hid heart: cease silently,
And though thy birth-hour beckons thee,
Sleep the long sleep:
The Doomsters heap
Travails and teens around us here,
And Time-wraiths turn our songsingings to fear.

Hark, how the peoples surge and sigh,
And laughters fail, and greetings die:
Hopes dwindle; yea,
Faiths waste away,
Affections and enthusiasms numb;
Thou canst not mend these things if though dost come.

Had I the ear of wombed souls
Ere their terrestrial chart unrolls,
And thou wert free
To cease, or be,
Then would I tell thee all I know,
And put it to thee: Wilt thou take life so?

Vain vow! No hint of mine may hence
To theeward fly: to thy locked sense
Explain none can
Life's pending plan:
Thou wilt thy ignorant entry make
Though skies spout fire and blood and nations quake.

Fain would I, dear, find some shut plot
Of earth's wide wold for thee, where not
One tear, one qualm,
Should break the calm.
But I am weak as thou and bare;
No man can change the common lot to rare.
Must come and bide. And such are we –
Unreasoning, sanguine, visionary –
That I can hope
Health, love, friends, scope
In full for thee; can dream thou'lt find
Joys seldom yet attained by humankind!

Collected Poems, Thomas Hardy

In this poem, instead of the poet taking on the identity of the unborn child, he is speaking to it. Let's look at the poem one stanza (verse) at a time to see exactly what is being said. Notice the title first of all. This is to an unborn pauper child. It is written in the late nineteenth century. Then the conditions which a child in a very poor family could expect to encounter would be awful. Food was scarce and disease rife with infant death rates extremely high. This influences what Hardy is saying in the poem. He knew about these conditions. In the first stanza he is telling the child not to be born; 'breathe not, hid heart'. It is hidden because it is still in the mother's womb. Hardy goes on to warn the unborn child that life has terrible things in store: the 'Doomsters' are the fates, your unchangeable future. 'Travails and teens' are troubles and pains. As time passes people stop behaving happily and become afraid; 'Time-wraiths turn our songsingings to fear'. Notice the s sounds of 'cease silently'; it's as if he's hushing the child.

In the first five lines of the second stanza he paints a gloomy picture of the world into which the child will be born. Notice the sound of the words: there is a sighing sound, reflecting the sense. The final line states that the child cannot do anything about any of this when it is born.

In stanza three, Hardy says that if he could speak to the unborn he would give them a choice 'to cease or be', after describing what life is like. The expected answer would seem to be that the child would choose not to be born.

In the next stanza Hardy says that there is no such choice. (Although even then abortions were not unknown.) The child will be born, whatever disaster is taking place 'though skies spout fire . . . ' etc.

In stanza five Hardy goes on to say that he wishes he could provide protection. Notice the tender tone produced by the word 'dear' and also by the sound of the words which are chosen such as 'shut plot', 'wide wold'. However, the poet himself is as weak and helpless as the child. No one can do anything. 'The common lot', i.e. what everyone gets, cannot be changed to something special or 'rare'. Notice how many of the words here have just one syllable.

However, in stanza six, to close the poem, Hardy introduces a more hopeful note. The child has got to come and stay. People are incurably optimistic, even if there is no good reason for it: 'unreasoning, sanguine (cheerful), visionary' (imagining unexpected good things), so Hardy can hope that the child will experience every happiness that life can offer; 'health, love, friends, scope in full for thee' and even extra special rare joys.

Ultimately, then, is this poem saying that the child should not be born? Does it say the child will suffer? What is Hardy's point of view? What effect and what tone is created through the use of 'thee' and 'thou' rather than 'you' throughout the poem? This wasn't how people spoke usually at the time Hardy was writing.

Poem F, Prayer Before Birth

I am not yet born; O hear me.
Let not the bloodsucking bat or the rat or the stoat or the club-
    footed ghoul come near me.

I am not yet born, console me.
I fear that the human race may with tall walls wall me,
    with strong drugs dope me, with wise lies lure me,
      on black racks rack me, in blood-baths roll me.

I am not yet born; provide me
With water to dandle me, grass to grow for me, trees to talk
    to me, sky to sing to me, birds and a white light
      in the back of my mind to guide me.

I am not yet born; forgive me
For the sins that in me the world shall commit, my words
    when they speak me, my thoughts when they think me,
      my treason engendered by traitors beyond me,
        my life when they murder by means of my
          hands, my death when they live me.

I am not yet born; rehearse me
In the parts I must play and the cues I must take when
    old men lecture me, bureaucrats hector me, mountains
      frown at me, lovers laugh at me, the white
        waves call me to folly and the desert calls
          me to doom and the beggar refuses
            my gift and my children curse me.

I am not yet born; O hear me
Let not the man who is beast or who thinks he is God
    come near me.

I am not yet born; O fill me
With strength against those who would freeze my
    humanity, would dragoon me into a lethal automaton,
      would make me a cog in a machine, a thing with
        one face, a thing, and against all those
          who would dissipate my entirety, would
            blow me like thistledown hither and
              thither or hither and thither
                like water held in the
                  hands would spill me.

Let them not make me a stone and let them not spill me.
Otherwise kill me.

Louis MacNeice *Poetry 1900–1975* (Edited by George MacBeth),

With this poem it's a matter of working out what particular fears MacNeice has for the unborn child. Again in this poem, the poet is speaking with voice of the unborn child. Look at each stanza – notice that they become longer and more impassioned as the poem continues.

In the first stanza he seems to be talking about the ingredients of horrific nightmares. In the second verse it seems to be society's threats which he is worried about. Work out what exactly you think he means by what he says. In the third stanza he is asking to be provided with the pleasures of nature. What do you think the white light is? He then goes on, in the next stanza, to talk about his future implication in crime and sin because he will be a member of the human race. In the fifth stanza he is asking for guidance in the roles he must play and the situations in which he may be placed. What do you think he means in stanza six by 'the man who is beast or who thinks he is God'? Do any historical figures come to your mind? What threat is posed by such people? What threats are discussed in the final, longest stanza? He seems to be pleading that identity and humanity are important. What could pose a threat to these? What do you think is meant by the last two lines?

Do you think MacNeice sees life as more threatening than it is potentially pleasurable?

ACTIVITY

5b

Coursework – Speaking and Listening

Discuss the six poems with a group of three or four other students.

What do you feel you learn about the poets' attitudes to life? Discuss the differences in what the poems are saying as well as how effectively the poets have communicated their thoughts and feelings. How did you feel when you read each one?

Try to decide what order you would rank the poems in terms of how well the ideas are conveyed. Which one did you like best?

ACTIVITY

5c

Coursework – Writing in Response to Literature

Choose **one** of the following four suggestions for written coursework. Re-read the relevant poems before you start to write.

1 'Baby Beware'. Discuss two or three of the poems you have read showing clearly what the poets are worried about in the world around them and what they value about it. Discuss the poets' attitudes and also how effectively you feel they convey their thoughts and feelings. Use short quotations (no more than about six words at a time) from the poems to illustrate the points you are making.

2 'Unto Us'. Write about your views on the subject of abortion. You may like to examine both sides of the issue, presenting arguments for and against. It would be a good idea to find out more about the law as it currently stands. You could write about specific situations where you feel abortion may be justified. Look at the extract from *Racing Demon* given in Activity E of 'Play For Today', Unit 4 of Chapter 2.

3 'Unto Us: the argument against'. Imagining you are the future mother or father, write a statement justifying the actions of the parents in aborting the foetus. You might find it useful to write one statement from each parent so that you can then differentiate their views. Make sure you keep to the situation as it is implied in the poem. You do not necessarily have to believe their actions were justified in order to write this. Present only their side of the argument, though.

4 'Baby Beware'. Write your own version. It could be a letter addressed to an unborn child or it could be a poem. Warn about the dangers as you see them and talk about what pleasures may be found. You can write on a personal level or include comments about the political situation in Britain and the world. Threats of nuclear war or to the environment could all be relevant here. You may paint a gloomy picture or an optimistic one, depending on your own attitude to life.

Drafting and Revising

When you have finished the first draft of your coursework, read it through carefully. Have you used the poems to provide you with ideas and material? Have you written enough? The minimum length acceptable is about 500 words. Is it too long? Try to achieve a good balance between conciseness and detail. When you are happy with the content, check the correctness of your work. Is your spelling and punctuation accurate? Revise and improve this as necessary. When you are satisfied that the standard is as good as possible, write out the final draft. Put your name, the date of writing and the appropriate title at the top plus 'work in response to literature'. You should then list the poems which you have used.

ACTIVITY
5d

Optional Further Reading

Obtain a copy of *The Unborn Dreams of Clara Riley* by Kathy Page. It is published by Virago and should be available through your local or college library. It is the story of a woman in the nineteenth century who resorts to abortion and is imprisoned for it.

Review of Unit 5

- Activity A was reading (En 2.1, 4).
- Activity B was speaking and listening coursework (En 1, En 2.1, 4).
- Activity C was written coursework in response to literature (En 2.1, 4 and En 3).
- Activity D was further reading (En 2.1).

Making a Record

Write down the necessary information about the coursework in this unit. This was the group oral work in Activity B and the written work in Activity C. When you have done this, tick the relevant aspects of En 1, En 2 and En 3 on your Coursework Checklist.

What Should You Do Now?

When you have finished these activities, turn to the first unit of another chapter.

4 Informing and Reporting

*T*HIS chapter looks at writing of a factual and transactional nature. You will not be concerned here with imaginative and expressive writing. You will be looking instead at ordering and presenting facts, in a variety of contexts, with precision and clarity.

This is what you will be working on:

- understanding, ordering and presenting facts;
- developing and demonstrating the ability to use language concisely;
- developing and demonstrating the ability to use language with clarity;
- showing understanding of other writers' use of factual language;
- comparing techniques used by different writers;
- assessing critically the effectiveness of factual writing of various types.

What Should You Work on Now?

You must complete Unit 1. It is strongly recommended that you then select at least one more unit from this chapter.

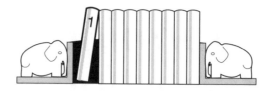

UNIT (**1**) *Do it Yourself*

This unit is about giving instructions and directions, both spoken and written. First of all let's look at instructions of the sort that you might come across any day.

ACTIVITY

(**1a**)

Reading and Evaluation

Passage A

These instructions for cooking Basmati rice appeared on the packet.

> Before Cooking – For Best Results – rinse rice thoroughly in a sieve under cold running water. For a softer grain, soak for 30 minutes in measured water. Choose any ONE of the cooking methods.
>
> If cooking Basmati for the first time we would suggest method one. 250g (8 oz) of uncooked rice will serve 4 generous portions. (Please follow either metric or imperial but do not mix the two.)
>
> **METHOD ONE** – OPEN PAN
> Put 250g (8 oz) rice in a large saucepan with about 1.25 litres (2 pints) boiling water. Return to a medium boil, stir and cook uncovered for 10 minutes. Drain and rinse in a sieve with more boiling water, then serve.
>
> **METHOD TWO** – COVERED PAN
> Put 250g (8 oz) rice in a medium saucepan with 450ml (1 pint) water. Bring to the boil, stir, cover with a tight lid, and simmer very gently without disturbing for 10 minutes, remove from heat and allow pan to stand for 5 minutes, then serve.
>
> **METHOD THREE** – MICROWAVE METHOD
> Put 250g (8 oz) rice in a deep microwave dish with 450ml (1 pint) water. Cover and cook on HIGH for 6 minutes, stir, then on DEFROST for 6 to 8 minutes. Stand for 5 minutes, then serve. Timings are for a 650 watt oven. Adjust ovens with different outputs according to manufacturers' instructions.
>
> Finally, after cooking, season lightly according to taste and fork through with a little melted butter or oil. (Applies to all cooking methods.)

Look at the instructions in Passage A carefully. First, let's consider where they are printed. Space is limited on the back of a packet of rice so it is important that the information is conveyed as concisely (i.e. in as few words as possible). The word 'of' is omitted when the quantities are given – of rice, of boiling water. The sense is clear without this word.

Second, consider the purpose of the instructions: the instructions are intended to allow you to cook the rice successfully. Is everything explained clearly? Would someone with little or no knowledge of cooking be able to follow them? Perhaps the only technical terms are 'medium boil' and 'simmer'. Do they need any further explanation, in your opinion?

How is this written? What is the tone? As you might expect, if you read it aloud it sounds rather abrupt – in other words, factual. The statements are generally quite short and so are most of the sentences. The words used are simple, short, everyday ones as they must be if anyone is to be able to cook the rice.

Is there anything about these instructions that you would like to change? There are a number of odd uses of capital letters and a few missed full stops. In method two, for instance, there should be a full stop after '10 minutes' with a new sentence starting 'Remove. . . '. The sentence 'Adjust ovens with different outputs according to manufacturers' instructions' doesn't make sense. The word 'for' needs to be inserted after 'adjust'.

Now let's look at another set of similar instructions to see how they compare.

Passage B

This recipe comes from the back of a packet of pavlova mix.

DIRECTIONS

1 Preheat oven to 150C (300F).
2 Place 150ml of warm water into a small mixing bowl.
3 Add pavlova mix and blend at low speed until mixed (approx. 15 seconds).
4 Mix on highest speed of electric mixer (not blender) for approx. 4–6 minutes, or until mixture is stiff and forms peaks.
5 On lowest speed, slowly add caster sugar (115g).
6 Return to highest speed for 1 minute.
7 Heap mixture into a high dome on centre of greased baking tray – DO NOT SPREAD (it will spread while cooking).
8 Bake for 40–45 minutes.
9 Turn oven off, open oven door and allow to cool.
10 Remove from oven. Decorate with whipped cream and sliced fruit as desired.

What are the similarities between the two sets of instructions? Again, space is limited. Occasionally here the word 'the' is omitted. Also abbreviations are used. All the numbers are put in figures as it takes up less space. Only metric measurements are given.

This time, because the process is a bit more complicated, it has been broken down into numbered steps. This is often very useful when giving instructions. It is much easier to understand and to follow. Are there any technical terms? Are there any grammatical errors?

Which set of instructions do you think is clearer? Try to explain why.

ACTIVITY

1b

Writing a Simple Set of Instructions

You are going to write instructions on how to make a cup of tea or a cup of coffee (you decide which) in a kitchen that you know well. These instructions are for a child who is just old enough to be allowed to handle a kettle. He or she does not know where the necessary articles are kept. You will have to explain. Make no assumptions: put in even the most apparently obvious steps like taking the milk out of the fridge and stirring the drink at the end. Make sure you explain how he or she will know when the kettle has boiled.

Number each step as in the recipe for pavlova mix. Use simple words which a child would understand. Keep your sentences short and to the point but write complete sentences. As you are not writing on the back of a packet you do not need to miss out 'of' or 'the'. Do not write 'Take mug from cupboard. Put in teaspoon coffee.' Instead, write 'Take a mug from the cupboard. Put in a teaspoon of coffee.'

When you have finished, read it carefully. Have you missed anything out? Are the steps in the right order? Have you assumed knowledge that a child would not have? Would you be prepared to drink the tea or coffee that would have been produced? Would the child have come through the experience safely without scalds or electric shocks?

Ask someone else to read your instructions through. It could be your tutor or it could be a friend. Ask this person to assess the quality of your instructions. Ask the questions you asked yourself about whether the tea or coffee produced would have been drinkable and the child uninjured.

You have now seen, perhaps, that there's more to even very simple instructions than you might have supposed.

You are now going to look at extracts from two more specialised sets of instructions. Again you will be assessing their quality and effectiveness.

ACTIVITY

1c

Reading and Evaluation

Extract A is taken from the instruction leaflet from a kit for assembling a model of the de Havilland Hornet F.MK.1 and F.MK.3.

Extract A

Wing and Nacelle Assembly

11 Assemble the upper and lower wing mouldings locating at the root end. Ensure that there is no gap in the front Nacelle area. The joint inboard of the ailerons is not a panel line.

12 Blend the outer contours of the radiator air intake and the carburettor intake slots in the leading edge. Remove blisters from the top surface of the wing and fill the wing folding joint lines.

13 Each pair of Nacelle halves are identified by marks on the inside rear. Support them on the wing attachment edges. Align the spinner face and bond the forward end, then the rear. Thin the edges of the U/C cut-out so that they are of uniform thickness and bond to the wing.

Remove flash from the inside of the Nacelle, but do not enlarge the exhaust slots.

14 The rear end will require slight blending and there will be a slight mis-match on the top of the Nacelle which should be corrected by removing plastic rather than building up with filler.

15 The Hornet F.1 carried no underwing stores, fill six holes under each outer wing.

Extract A is quite long enough to allow you to get the flavour of this set of instructions! It may be that you are an expert aircraft modeller. If so, the instructions would probably have been both understandable and interesting. If you are not knowledgeable in this subject area, most of the extract will have meant little to you.

The writer here knows exactly who will be reading the instructions: it will be someone who is trying to assemble this kit as well as possible. This person will already have a certain amount of skill and knowledge, so a vocabulary using technical terms is acceptable. Clearly the writer has already built the kit and is able to warn the reader about problems that might be encountered and can also give advice about how to deal with them. Supplementary facts are being given as well as directions, for example, 'The joint inboard of the ailerons is not a panel line'.

As in the earlier passages, the writer occasionally, omits words, 'Remove the flash . . . ' would be more correct than 'Remove flash . . . '. In item 15, the sentence would be improved by adding the word 'as' at the beginning or 'so' instead of the comma after stores, 'As the Hornet F.1 carried no underwing stores, fill six holes under each outer wing' or 'The Hornet F.1 carried no underwing stores so fill six holes under each outer wing'. Without those joining words, there ought to be a full stop after 'stores' and 'fill' should be the start of a new sentence.

Now look at part of another set of instructions. Extract B is taken from a book on container gardening and is about how to construct window boxes.

Extract B

The size of box you will choose will depend on the size of the windowsill, but it should not overhang the sill. Ideally it should be 2.5cm (1in) shallower than the depth of the sill, at least 20cm (8in) deep to provide adequate room for the plants' root systems, and long enough to fit comfortably within the space.

On casement type windows that open outwards, the box can be placed below the sill rather than resting on it, so it should only be half as wide again as the sill overhang. To have exactly the desired size of window box, it is easier to make your own.

Use any type of timber as long as it is 2.5cm (1in) thick. Teak, pine and split logs can be used; teak can be stained to give a rich effect, pine can be painted (but choose the colour carefully), and split logs give a rustic effect.

Use water resistant glue, and make sure screws and nails will not rust. The interior of the box must be treated to prevent rot, and there are wood preservatives available which will not harm plants. Don't forget to drill drainage holes in the base of the box.

Windowsills always slant forward to allow water to drain away. Therefore, you must put wedges under the front edge of the box to keep it level. This will also aid drainage. It is best if the wedges are fixed to the bottom of the box. If the box is to rest on an overhead sill it is essential for safety that it is fixed to the wall or secured to the sill. L-brackets fixed to the ends of the box and the wall are probably the easiest way of doing this.

Extract B is rather different from the other examples you have looked at. Here the writer is giving advice about how to make and site window boxes rather than giving step-by-step instructions. You would be unlikely to have this by your side when doing the construction; you would read it beforehand to prepare yourself but would not wish to consult it minutely as you were working.

The written text is accompanied by three pictures which show the steps involved in the construction. These, rather than the passage above, would be your guide on what to do. Pictures or diagrams are often useful in such situations. The instruction leaflet for a video recorder, for example, is likely to make extensive use of pictures which show the various buttons to be pressed and codes to be entered.

Precise information is given in Extract B – about the dimensions of the box, the thickness of wood to use, the necessity for drainage holes and treatment against rot – but as window boxes will vary according to the windows they are designed to fit, this is less specific. Because of this, there is no need for numbered steps or for 'minor' words to be omitted. The tone is factual. The language is everyday and simple because the target audience being catered for is wide. There is no technical language as such. Here, as with the model assembly instructions, a certain amount of interested commitment on the part of the reader can be assumed: the book has been deliberately purchased, it can be presumed, because of an interest in container gardening.

ACTIVITY

Coursework – Speaking and Listening

For this task you will need to work with another person, preferably someone who is not a close friend.

This is what you are going to do. You will give your partner directions from your house to a destination that you will choose. The journey can take place on foot, by public transport or by car. It can be as long and complicated as you like but you must be familiar with the route. Don't made it too short and simple or you will not have sufficient material.

Start off by reminding yourself of the route by travelling over it in your mind. You may make some notes of the key stages. Think of distinctive landmarks and tricky areas where you will have to give very precise and clear instructions. Your partner, meanwhile, will be making notes on his or her chosen route so that you can later play the role of the person receiving directions.

When each of you is ready, one will give the other directions. The person who is listening will write down the directions which you give. You can repeat what you say if your partner wishes you to and questions may be asked for clarification.

When you have finished giving your directions, your partner will repeat to you what has been written down. You can assess whether the correct destination would be reached. If it would not, the fault may lie in your directions or in your partner's comprehension and note-taking skills. Try to establish the cause of any difficulties.

Now change over. You will listen to your partner's directions in exactly the same way and repeat the information aloud once you have written it down. Assess how successful you have been this time.

Your tutor can assess this exercise by being present at the time. Alternatively you could record what you are doing on audio tape.

ACTIVITY

1e

Writing – Practising for the Examination

This type of writing is quite likely to appear in the written examination. You should spent between 45 minutes and an hour on **one** of the two activities which follows. In each case a situation is presented which requires you to tell someone what to do. Before you begin your chosen activity, read through the passage on drafting and revising.

Task 1

You have received the following letter. Decide what Jay is asking for and write your reply. Plan your answer carefully: think of the way you broke down the process of making tea or coffee into steps. What steps would be involved in taking up a hobby or going to college? If you are suggesting a hobby, write **in detail** about how to become involved with **one**, rather than a little bit about several. Obviously, choose something that you know about. You may like to start with a short paragraph in which you make some general remarks about Christmas and mutual friends.

Start a new paragraph each time you start to write about a new aspect of the subject: equipment, cost, skills, advantages. Use a friendly and informal tone.

16 Ballards Drive
Oldthorpe
Yorkshire
OT3 4BH

12 January

Dear (supply your name here),

I hope you had a good Christmas. I did. Lots of members of our family gathered at our house on Christmas Day. There were twenty-two of us for dinner. Mum cooked a huge turkey. Since I moved up here, away from you and all our other friends, I've really missed our little outings.

Anyway, the reason I thought I'd write to you is to get some advice. I've decided that my New Year's resolution is not to spend so much time sitting around watching television but to take up a hobby or activity instead. It also might be a good way of making new friends. I'd need to know what sort of person I should contact, and where – i.e. leisure centre, college or what – details of the equipment needed and how much roughly it would cost. Then, of course, I'd need to know what particular skills and talents I would need. You could also tell me what I'd get out of it too and why it's worthwhile.

I haven't got any really strong feelings about what I'd like to do. It could be a sport but I'll consider anything, even crochet!

I'm even considering going back to college for some further education so if you can't suggest an interesting hobby to take up my spare time and money, you could advise me how to go about applying for a course. As you know, I only gained a couple of GCSEs at school because of the accident.

I hope to hear from you really soon as I'm bored and you always come up with good ideas. Remember me to all our friends.

All the best for the year ahead.

Jay

Task 2

Your whole family is going abroad for July and August. While you are away an Australian family will be living in your house. You have never met these people (they are friends of friends) but have corresponded with them on a couple of occasions while you were arranging for their stay. You have also spoken to them on the telephone.

Make up the necessary details about the family: names, number and ages of children. Don't spend more than a few minutes on this as it's only background.

The letter you are going to write will be left in the house for them to read when they arrive. You should tell them all they need to know about using the equipment and facilities in the house, how to care for pets and plants which have been left behind by you and what to do in the event of disaster.

Base everything you say on a house which you know well. Do not cheat by saying 'I have left the instruction leaflets for the washing machine, video, etc., with this letter'. The whole idea is to write these directions. You can assume that the family is of reasonable intelligence and you don't have to cover everything.

Think of what they might need and what might be unfamiliar. You might want to include instructions on how to use the following: heating; hot water system; washing machine; video recorder.

You will not need to put an address at the top of your letter but should put the date and 'Dear . . .'. You may find it helpful to use headings and numbered steps. Don't forget to sign off at the end. The tone should be informal and friendly.

Drafting and Revising

In the restricted time you have available you are unlikely to have time to write more than one draft of your chosen letter. You should make some notes initially to plan the content and the order in which you will deal with points.

It is important that you put the correct headings at the top: think of a suitable title, put your name and the date. You will then set out your letter appropriately, according to which you are doing. The date in letter 1 will be one in January.

Write neatly and legibly. Do not use correcting fluid. When you have finished read your work through looking for errors in spelling and punctuation. If you wish to re-write a word, draw a neat line through it and write the replacement above. There is no need to block out the rejected word completely.

ACTIVITY

1f

Optional Coursework – Writing

If you are thoroughly involved in a particular hobby or activity or if you know a lot about one, you can write a longer, more detailed piece of work than was possible in Activity D. This could go into your coursework folder as 'personal writing'.

This writing could be about virtually any activity: amateur dramatics, woodwork, horse riding, plumbing, Morris dancing, fly-fishing: the list of possibilities is endless. You should only choose to do this, though, if you personally have the relevant information. You should not have to research the subject although you may check facts if necessary.

'The (your first or last name, depending on which sounds better) Guide to . . .' should be an appropriate title. For example, this book could be called either 'Diana's Guide to GCSE English' or 'The Wallsgrove Guide to GCSE English'. The second one sounds more formal and official, doesn't it?

What Should Your Guide Contain?

You can put in an introductory section with some background information – history, distribution through the UK, world, etc.

You can then talk about venues – clubs, courses or whatever. You can write about the equipment, recommending particular brands and giving estimated costs. You can describe the skills involved, advise the reader on how to get started, give a list of 'DOs' and 'DON'Ts'. You can have a section headed 'How to get the most from . . . ' and give advice on that. You can conclude with a summary of this activities' pleasures and advantages, whether physical, mental, personal or social.

It would be acceptable to include illustrations in a piece of work like this. These could be diagrams, photographs or what ever seems appropriate. For example, a drawing would help if you were explaining the dimensions of a badminton court and the rules about whether a section or line is in or out at a particular stage of the game. As this is an English course, artwork is not assessed as such but if it assists communication, put it in.

Think carefully about presentation in this piece of work. Have a look in a bookshop or a library to see how professionally-produced books like this are laid out. You could make a booklet, either binding together A4 sheets (you could staple them down the left-hand side or use a plastic spine) or by folding plain A4 paper to form an A5 booklet, stapled in the centre. A colourful cover with the title and an illustration would be a good idea. You might feel that typing this piece of work would be worthwhile. The GCSE syllabuses say that some work (usually 30 per cent) may be typed or word processed.

Drafting and Revising

Before you put the final draft together, check that you have included all the relevant information and that you have arranged it in a sensible order. Have you decided what illustrations you will use and where they will go? When you are happy with the content, check the accuracy. If there are any words which you are unsure how to spell, look them up in a dictionary before writing your final draft. When you write the 'neat' version, keep an eye on your punctuation and try to put in everything you need. Read through and check again before pasting in drawings, photographs and so on. If you are working on a word processor, you can easily get rid of errors even after you are satisfied with the content of your work.

Review of Unit 1

- Activity A and Activity C were reading non-literary material (En 2.2, 4).
- Activity B was writing (En 3).
- Activity D was speaking and listening coursework (En 1.1, 4).
- Activity E was examination practice.
- Activity F was optional written coursework (En 3).

Making a Record

Now find your Coursework Index Form and write down all the relevant information. Write down the number of the piece according to how many you have now done and put the chapter, unit and activity number for reference. Note the date and put a title or brief description, then list the ATs covered in the final column. The relevant activities here are the pairs' oral work in Activity D and the written work in Activity F.

When you have done that, tick the relevant aspects of En 1 and En 3 on your Coursework Checklist.

What Should You Do Now?

Choose another unit in this chapter or turn to Unit 1 of another chapter. It is a good idea to work through at least two units from every chapter. If you wish to move on to a different type of writing, returning to this chapter later, that is acceptable.

The other units in this chapter are as follows:

Unit 2 – Our Day Out

In this unit you will be making arrangements for a day trip. There will also be a letter of complaint and a short report.

Unit 3 – Job Search

This unit is about how to apply for jobs and present yourself effectively in order to be successful.

Unit 4 – Face the Facts

In this unit you will look at various pieces of writing, extracting facts and looking at the way the information has been presented. You have the opportunity to write a factual article on a subject of your choice.

Unit 5 – Sales Talk

This unit gives you some information about consumer rights, giving you the chance to investigate problems with the sale and purchase of goods. Later activities work on how to complain effectively.

Select the unit which appeals to you most.

UNIT (**2**) *Our Day Out*

In this unit you are going to look at several letters planning a day trip and then you are going to write some yourself. The written work in Activities E to I can be collected together to form a piece of coursework. You might be asked to write a letter in the examination so many of these activities are good practice for that. A report like the one in Activity I might also appear in the written examination. Finally there is an optional activity in response to literature.

ACTIVITY

(2a)

Reading and Evaluation

Paul, Sally, Geoff are on the Social Committee of the Monksworth Community Centre. They have decided to arrange a day trip for the over-sixties. Unknown to the others, each one has had an idea for an excursion and decides to write off to get further details. Here are their letters. Fortunately, they discuss the matter before any of the letters are posted.

Read the three letters. Decide what is good and bad about each. Consider how suitable the idea is and also how well each writer has communicated.

Jot down some notes about each one.

Letter 1

> Monksworth Community Centre
> College Road
> Oldthorpe
> Tel 897674

The Hiking and
 Mountaineering Centre
Central Peaks Park
Northshire

17th May 199X

Dear Sir/Madam
I am interested in arranging a day trip to your area on behalf of my local community centre. I am a keen walker and have some experience of mountaineering. I have all my own equipment but the others will not have. Can you hire out equipment on a daily basis? What are your rates? I have not visited your area before but I have got the necessary Ordinance

Survey maps. Can you recommend a circular walk of 15 to 20 miles? It would be better to avoid paths and tracks as we live in a built up area and therefore would appreciate being out in the open. Are camp fires allowed? My idea is that we would boil up water for refreshments and either eat sandwiches or have a barbecue at the half-way stage. I look forward to hearing from you soon.

Yours faithfully

Paul Smithson
Social Secretary

Letter 2

Monksworth Community Centre
College Road
Oldthorpe
Tel 897674

Shorefield Manor
Puckleton
Bucks

17th May 199X

Dear person in charge,

Hi! How're you going? Listen, I thought some of us would maybe come along to your place one day. What do you think? Let's see, we're quite a long way from you so we'd get a coach in the morning – but we'd need lunch, wouldn't we? So let's think. We'd leave Oldthorpe at about ten, then it would take, what, three, three 'n half hours to get down the road. But we'd need drinks – coffee 'n that on the way – and some of the old biddies would want the loo – so stop at half eleven, get going by twelve, have lunch somewhere about one thirty (better book that). That would be done by about half two, say three. Come along to you by about three thirty – what do you reckon? Have you got a gift shop?

Right, so you'll fill us in, yeah?
Cheers, all the best

Sally

Oh yeah, PS. There's two people in wheelchairs – is that okay?

Letter 3

To: Mackleton Fun Park
Little Lane End
Mackleton

17 May 199X

Dear Organiser

I would like to find out whether it's possible to get a group discount for a day at your Fun Park. There will be between 25 and 40 people, all adults. Is it possible to buy entrance tickets in advance rather than on the day? It is not necessary to pay for individual rides, is it?

What refreshment facilities do you have? Please send details plus sample menus. I would also like details of your main attractions. I have heard that you have a Major Mega Waltzer Wheel. Is that true? I understand they are fantastic, really hair raising.

What facilities do you have for the disabled? Some of our party will have a bit of difficulty with stairs etc. so I hope you have wheelchair ramps.

Please send all this information as soon as possible so that I can sort this trip out.

Yours sincerely

Geoff Rowley

ACTIVITY

2b

Coursework – Speaking and Listening

If possible, work in a group of four or five other students. Referring to your notes, discuss each letter thoroughly. Consider the ideas suggested for the excursion, bearing in mind the sort of people who will be going.

Next discuss the wording of each letter, identifying any problems of tone, phrasing, content (what the writer puts into the letter) and structure (the order in which the points are presented).

Decide whether any one is better or worse than the others, either because of the ideas or the way the letter is written.

ACTIVITY

2c

Planning – Research and Information Retrieval

You have been asked to arrange a day's excursion for a group of people. This time you are allowed to decide what the group is.

It could be:

- a group of students;
- a group of visitors (perhaps from overseas) who have come to your workplace;

- a group of colleagues from work;
- a social group, perhaps to do with a club or society;
- a group of people belonging to a particular organisation (as in Activity A, for example, a church or political party);
- a group of your own choice – check your choice with your tutor.

It is important to decide what the group is for two reasons. First, the destination and activities must be appropriate for it. Second, you are to use stationery which includes the group's address (as in Activity A) and possibly a logo.

Having decided the group's identity, you now have to choose an appropriate destination and activities. To make life a bit more interesting – or complicated – here are a few points which you must include.

1   You must travel there by coach but spend no more than two hours getting to your principal destination.
2   At least one person in your party is confined to a wheelchair.
3   You must make arrangements for a sit-down meal, either at lunch time or in the evening.
4   Some members of your party are vegetarian.
5   You must be away for no longer than twelve hours in total.

Go to your local tourist information centre. Look in the telephone directory to find out where this is. There will be information about local attractions and probably some about other parts of the country. Collect leaflets about possible destinations. Make a sensible decision, bearing in mind the nature of your group and the fact that one person is in a wheelchair.

ACTIVITY

2d

Coursework – Speaking and Listening

You are going to simulate a telephone call to obtain more information about the place you will be visiting. When you 'ring up', however, an answering machine replies.

Using a tape recorder, leave a message saying what you wish to know and where this information should be sent. Plan what you are going to ask beforehand. Do not write out a full script but note briefly what you wish to know about. You should end with your name, address and telephone number. Try to sound polite but friendly by including appropriate greetings.

If you wish to make this exercise seem more realistic, you could use a telephone handset and speak into the mouthpiece.

Be careful when you are making your recording. You must include **all** the necessary details if you are to receive the material you need. Speak very clearly and spell out any words which may be difficult for the listener to hear and understand. It is not necessary to repeat anything as your tape can be rewound by the listener.

When you have finished your recording, rewind and play it back to see if you have done it sufficiently well. If you are not satisfied and there is sufficient time available, record it again, improving on your first version.

Writing a Circular Letter

Now you are going to write a letter which gives the members of the group all the information that they need. This should include the following information:

- the day and date of the trip;
- departure and return times;
- details about where to meet;
- information about the cost. Give details of what will be included in the basic charge and what 'extras' will need to be paid for. Tell them who to pay and when;
- the itinerary, i.e. exactly where you are going, including meal stops;
- information about the attractions at the main destination. Include a short description.

You should try to keep all this as simple and clear as possible. It may be fairly long but try to avoid putting in anything unnecessary.

When you are describing the attractions of the place you will be visiting, you will probably find it helpful to use some of the information from the leaflet you have obtained. You will need to select only some of what it says and also you need to put it into your own words so that it fits in with the rest of the letter. You also need to make quite sure that what you say is easy to understand. To help you with this, look at the example below which is taken from a leaflet on Blenheim Palace.

Blenheim Palace

Blenheim Palace was built for John Churchill, 1st Duke of Marlborough in recognition of his great victory over the French at the battle of Blenheim, 1704. The Palace, designed by Sir John Vanburgh, is set in 2,100 acres of park land landscaped by Capability Brown and is one of the finest examples of English Baroque. The collection comprises tapestries, paintings, sculpture and fine furniture set in magnificent gilded state rooms. Of outstanding beauty is the long library containing over 10,000 volumes in a room 183 feet in length.

Blenheim's gardens are renowned for their beauty and range from the formal Water Terraces, Italian Gardens and Rose Garden to the natural charm of the Arboretum, Pleasure Grounds and Cascade.

The Churchill Exhibition

An exhibition of Churchilliana which includes manuscripts, paintings, personal belongings, books, photographs and letters (mainly to his father Lord Randolph Churchill). The Duke of Marlborough in association with Hallmark Greeting Cards Ltd. present 'Greetings from Sir Winston' a fine display of Antique greeting cards and prints with a unique photographic collage covering the whole period of Sir Winston's life.

The Marlborough Maze

> The Marlborough Maze which opened in 1991, The Year of the Maze, is the world's largest symbolic hedge maze and is a must for visitors. Along with the putting green, giant chess and draughts and the children's bouncy castle it is in the Walled Garden within the Garden Centre complex. Some 600 yards from the Palace, the Garden Centre also includes the Butterfly House, Garden Cafeteria, Adventure Play Area and shops.

If I were to write a paragraph about Blenheim Palace in a circular letter, this is what I might say (notice that I have rearranged the order of the information as well as re-wording it):

> When we arrive at Blenheim Palace there are many attractions. The Palace itself, built in the early eighteenth century, has some splendid rooms with fine furniture, tapestries, paintings and sculptures. There is also an exhibition of various letters, photographs, etc., connected with Sir Winston Churchill. If the weather is fine it is worth exploring the Marlborough Maze and the gardens, both formal and informal. In the Garden Centre complex there is a Butterfly House, an Adventure Play area, shops and a Cafeteria where you may wish to buy light refreshments.

Drafting and Revising

When you have worked out what you are going to say in your letter and in what order, write a first draft. At the moment concentrate on the main body of the letter. Do not worry about layout. You may wish to give the information in the order it appears in the list of what is to be included. Do not use numbers but start a new paragraph for each different aspect of what you are saying. You may find headings useful.

When you have written this once, read it through critically. Have you included all the specified information? Is it clear and easy to understand? Have you included anything unnecessary and irrelevant? Adjust the content and style as necessary. Check your spelling and punctuation.

Now think about how you are going to set the information out. You will wish to design a standard letterhead for your firm, club or whatever. If you wish to, design a logo (a symbol which identifies your organisation). See Chapter 6, Unit 6.

Also look in Chapter 6, Unit 6 to find what it says about circular letters. The main point to remember is that you are not going to include the address of the person the letter is going to and you will wish to think of a suitable collective noun to refer to the people who will be going on the excursion; for example, colleagues or members.

When you are ready to do so, write the letter neatly. If you have access to a word processor or typewriter you could type this letter and the others to do this trip which follow in Activities F to I. If you plan to put these together as one piece of coursework, check your syllabus's regulations about the proportion of typed work allowed.

ACTIVITY

2f

Writing Letters of Confirmation

Write a Letter Confirming a Coach Booking

Draft a letter confirming your coach booking. You have previously agreed the size, cost and times of departure and return in a telephone conversation. Mention these again in the letter along with any other special arrangements. Don't forget that you have at least one person (decide exactly how many) in a wheelchair.

Here is a suggested paragraph plan:

Paragraph 1. Say why you are writing and mention the date of your telephone conversation. Paragraph 2. State what they are going to supply you with including size of coach, departure and return times and cost. Paragraph 3. Mention any special arrangements, for example facilities on board, refreshment stops and so on. Paragraph 4. Close your letter politely saying, perhaps, that someone should contact you if there are any problems.

Drafting and Revising

Write the body of your letter in rough (remember the tone will be formal) and then check it through, adjusting both CONTENT and ACCURACY as necessary. Then look in Chapter 6, Unit 6 to see the layout recommended for a formal letter. You will need to invent the coach company's address. Start 'Dear Sir' and end 'Yours faithfully'. Use your organisation's headed paper.

Write a Letter Booking the Meal

You have agreed over the telephone that the restaurant will provide a set meal for an agreed price (in other words you have chosen the same dishes for everyone). Confirm the details of this. Remember to include a reminder of any special requirement (don't forget your vegetarians). Include, of course, details such as date and time.

Adapt the plan given for the letter confirming the coach booking. This time you will need to invent a name and address for the restaurant. Write your letter to the manager but address him as 'Dear Sir'. Again use the headed paper.

ACTIVITY

2g

Writing a Letter of Complaint

You have your day out and something goes wrong. Decide what it is. It could be that there were no facilities for a disabled person, that the coach was late and perhaps dirty or a problem with the meal in the restaurant. Make sure you think of something which you can make a valid complaint about. If you were held up in a traffic jam that is no one's fault – it would not, therefore, be a good choice of disaster.

Write a formal letter to whoever would have been responsible, making a complaint. You may wish to suggest that some action is taken for what has happened in the form of a refund or apology. The tone should be firm but polite.

Planning Your Letter

Work out a paragraph plan like the one given in Activity F. You need to give details about when you went on your trip, what exactly went wrong and the action which you are demanding.

Drafting and Revising

When you write the first draft try to make sure that the tone is firm but polite. You are angry but you must not sound rude or threatening. If you had to write a second letter having received no satisfactory response, that would be the time for a stronger tone. When you have written the main body of the letter, read it through carefully and adjust content and accuracy as necessary. The layout, when you come to write it out neatly, will be the same as in Activity F. The date will, of course, be after that of the trip.

ACTIVITY
2h

Writing an Informal Letter

Write to a friend or relative about what has happened. The purpose of this is to talk about the same situation but to use a totally different style. Here you can afford to express yourself in a much more colloquial way. You can perhaps make a joke about how awful it was and say how you felt about the whole thing.

Drafting and Revising

Plan your letter carefully nevertheless. Read it through to make sure you are including the right information expressed in the right way. Your letter must still be accurate although it's informal, so don't make sloppy spelling and punctuation errors.

Check the layout in Chapter 6. You will need to use a much more relaxed closing phrase – 'Yours sincerely' would be too formal.

ACTIVITY

2i

Writing a Short Report

Now that the trip is over, let's suppose that your boss or the social committee – whatever is appropriate for your own situation, wishes to know what happened. You are therefore going to write a short report including recommendations on how to ensure that a future excursion should be

trouble free. Your heading will be 'Report on One Day Excursion to . . . '
You should structure your paragraphs as set out below.

- **Paragraph one** – brief details about the date, destination and number of people who went. Give the name of the coach firm.
- **Paragraph two** – give a factual account of your excursion including refreshment stops and the meal as well as your visit to the main attraction. Give times of arrivals and departures for each.
- **Paragraph three** – state what was good and successful about the trip. Be factual.
- **Paragraph four** – state what the problems were and what you have done about them since the outing.
- **Paragraph five** – recommend ways of avoiding problems in future.

At the end, sign it (but don't use a letter style closing) and put a date later than that in the letter in Activity H.

Drafting and Revising

Write a first draft of your report. When you have finished this, check to see that you have included all the necessary information. Have you followed the paragraph plan? Have you included too much description? Have you put in material which is not factual? If you have, cut this out. Write it out again with any necessary revisions then check the accuracy of your work.

Make sure the final draft is as accurate as possible. Have you put the right heading and finished it off correctly?

Submitting the Results of Activities C to I as Coursework

If you are intending to submit this work as a piece of coursework, attach the individual items together with a staple in the top left-hand corner. It would be acceptable to omit one of the letters from Activity F and perhaps the informal one or the report. Put a general heading at the top, perhaps on a separate piece of paper, with the title 'Our Day Out', the date of completion and your name.

ACTIVITY

2j

Optional Coursework – Response to Literature

Obtain a copy of Willy Russell's play *Our Day Out*. It is published by Samuel French. The play is about a day's excursion to Wales by a group of fifteen-year-olds with two of their teachers, the sympathetic Mrs Kay and the starchy Mr Briggs. There are many difficulties and near disasters on the trip.

Read the play carefully. When you have done so, draft a report on the outing, either as Mrs Kay or as Mr Briggs, for the headmaster. You can follow the guidelines in Activity I but you will probably need to use more paragraphs.

Drafting and Revising

As always, when you have written a first draft, check the content and accuracy of your work. When you are satisfied and have written your neat version, put a heading similar to that in Activity I. You will also put your own name, the date and the words 'Work in response to *Our Day Out* by Willy Russell' at the top. At the end, you will put Mrs Kay's or Mr Briggs's supposed signature and an appropriate date.

Review of Unit 2

- Activity A was reading and evaluation (En 2.2, 4).
- Activity B was speaking and listening coursework (En 1.2, 3, 4).
- Activity C was preparatory work including research and information retrieval (En 2.2).
- Activity D was speaking and listening coursework (En 1.1, 4).
- Activities E to I were written coursework (En 3).
- Activity J was optional written coursework in response to literature (En 2.1 and En 3).

Making a Record

Write down the necessary information about the coursework in this unit. This was the group oral work in Activity B and the individual oral work in Activity D. Also record the details of the written work in Activities E to I and also Activity J if you did this. When you have done this, tick the relevant aspects of En 1, En 2 and En 3 on your Coursework Checklist.

What Should You Do Now?

Either turn to another unit in this chapter or turn to a unit in another chapter.

UNIT *Job Search*

This unit is about selecting and presenting facts for a particular purpose: to get your-self a new job. It is possible that for the examination you might have to write a let-ter of application, as yourself or as a fictional character. You could collect together Activities C to F as a unit of coursework. The work here may also be of general use to you.

First you will be looking at some advertisements in order to see what employers are asking for. You will then respond to advertisements in various ways and consider interview technique.

ACTIVITY

3a

Reading and Understanding

A first step towards getting a job could be seeing what vacancies are being advertised in your local paper. Let's look at some adverts and read 'between the lines' to see what the prospective employer requires.

Advert A

RSJ DIY require young ambitious Sales Personnel who wish to develop a career within our sales division selling DIY and garden products to well-established retail outlets. These opportunities will be based at our Wellfield branch and will combine inside sales work with outside field sales representation We are a market leader UK sales and distribution Company (plc subsidiary).

Apply in writing to Managing Director at:

3 Centre Court
Ford Street
Salford
Manchester M7 3YT

In Advert A quite a lot of detail is being given about the sort of person required and the nature of the job. Probably the company does not want to receive a large number of unsuitable applications. Let's look at some of the phrases used and see what they mean exactly.

The fourth word is 'young' – what does that mean? Almost certainly it rules out someone over forty. 'Ambitious' follows, implying that this job could lead to promotion and a good career. The word 'selling' may be off-putting but it then tells us that the customers are 'well established'. It is implied that there is more than one job but it is not clear how many: 'Sales Personnel', 'these opportunities'. There are then some phrases which may not be easily understood by someone without relevant experience – do you know what 'outside field sales representation' means? If you do, you would probably be a suitable applicant! Putting this in is a way of deterring unsuitable ones. The company then claims that it is an important one – in order to give prospective applicants confidence that they are dealing with a reputable organisation, I suppose. Notice that there is no information at all about pay and conditions. Presumably it would be possible to telephone for such details but you are not told to do so. You seem to be expected to apply first and find that out later. We can assume that they are confident that there will be sufficient applicants.

The next instruction given is that you should send an 'application in writing'. This leaves you to decide on the best way of doing this. Alternatives will be looked at later in this unit. Let's look at another example.

Advert B

SALES ASSISTANT
Our Wexford shop requires a versatile and lively self-starter. Good sales and telephone ability a necessity. Experience of office supplies and equipment a distinct advantage. Salary negotiable. Please send CV to:

The Manager
CEA EVERONG
144 James Avenue
Wexford, WD2 3PL

The precise nature of the job in Advert B is not entirely clear either. 'Sales Assistant' sounds as if it could be a shop job but then the statement about telephone ability and office supplies suggests something different.

As far as the applicant is concerned there is no mention of age or qualifications. What, though, is a 'lively self-starter'? It sounds a little like a reliable car engine, doesn't it? Presumably the successful applicant should have an outgoing personality and be capable of using his or her own initiative. It sounds as if experience in a similar job is pretty well essential. This would be the basis for the salary negotiation, one can assume. 'Salary' makes the position sound to have more status than if the word 'wages' had been used. The phrase 'salary negotiable' may mean that the company wishes to employ someone as cheaply as possible, however. This time you are told to send a CV. You are given no choice. No telephone number is given.

Advert C

HSM
PERSONNEL SERVICES
MUSIC SALES EXECUTIVE £12,000.
Very realistic OTE £25,000

Sierra type company car! Environmental music systems to restaurants, pubs, clubs, etc! Concept sales! Must be mega bubbly and able to make an instant impact! Music related background very useful! Excellent company reputation! Wonderful potential to develop!
Ring 0825 925925 now!

In Advert C the company name is not mentioned. A recruitment agent seems to have placed the advertisement. This is another sales job but here the applicant is being enticed by the suggestion that much more than the basic salary can be earned.

Most people probably would not know what 'OTE' stood for without thought – one assumes it means 'Over Time Earnings' – that implies a lot of evening and weekend work which might not sound attractive if actually mentioned in the advertisement. Look at the phrase 'Sierra type company car'. Surely it's either a Sierra or it isn't! Notice the number of exclamation marks. The advertiser seems to be trying to make every phrase exciting and dramatic. Some people might consider themselves to be 'MEGA bubbly' but this phrase might be off-putting to other readers. A selection process is going on: people who are attracted by the sort of language used here are more likely to be suited to this job. Having read the advert others might feel that they would wish to have nothing to do with it.

This time you are not asked to apply straightaway but to telephone. Responding by telephone will be dealt with a little later.

Advert D

MOBILE CLEANERS REQUIRED
For cleaning of railway stations in the Tewford–Thornleigh area. 39 hours per week, Monday to Saturday inclusive. 5.00–11.30 a.m. Transport will be provided. Clean full driving licence essential. For further details, please telephone 0734 123456

In Advert D the job title of 'Mobile Cleaners' is descriptive and perhaps attractive sounding. Later in the advert it says 'transport provided' but it also says that a full driving licence is essential. From those two statements it can be assumed that a vehicle is provided for the person to drive to work and also, perhaps from one station to another. The weekly hours are mentioned first and the times stated briefly. If you do this work you start at 5.00 a.m. six days a week. These are unusual and probably unattractive hours. No wage is mentioned in the advert.

Again this time initial contact is made by telephoning.

ACTIVITY

3b

_____

Coursework – Speaking and Listening

Find a job advert in your local paper which asks for initial contact to be made by telephone. It doesn't have to be for a job which would be suitable for you.

This activity can be done in two different ways: either working with a partner or on your own.

Working with a Partner

Each of you will have selected an advert. Photocopy your advertisements so that you each have a copy of both adverts. Your partner will invent details which were not supplied in your advert, trying to make them as realistic as possible. These should include wages, hours, holidays, what the job entails with regard to duties and so on. You will do the same with his or hers. You may have to be fairly inventive!

If you are doing this activity at college, if possible, use two telephone extensions. If that cannot be arranged, sit back to back so that you cannot see each other's faces and simulate a telephone conversation. If you can, use a real handset so that it seems more realistic.

Each of you in turn will play the role of the applicant and of the company advertising the job. When you are acting as the applicant you should 'telephone' the company and your partner should receive the call. Ask for any further details which you feel you require. Also ask to be sent an application form. Remember to give your address. Then swap over.

Working Alone

You should choose this method if it is impractical to work with a partner.

This time when you 'telephone' the company imagine you find that you are speaking to an answering machine. You therefore have to leave a message. You are going to do this by recording a message using an ordinary tape recorder. Holding a handset might make this seem more realistic than just addressing the machine. Sometimes it is impossible to leave a long message as the recording cuts off after a pre-set time limit. You therefore cannot ask a series of questions. You will just state that you wish to obtain additional information about the job advertised and suggest certain aspects in particular. You will also ask for an application form to be sent to you, leaving your address. Speak slowly and distinctly and spell out any unusual words. You do not need to repeat anything as your message can be re-wound and played frequently.

ACTIVITY

3c

Filling in an Application Form

By asking you to complete an application form, an employer is finding out particular information which he or she considers to be necessary. As everyone who applies for a job with that firm uses an identical form, particular items are easy to locate and easy to refer to when the forms are on file.

These are the areas that are usually covered:

- Personal details: these include items such as name, address and age.
- Education and training: you are asked to give details of schools and colleges you have attended and to put down your qualifications.
- Previous employment: here you are asked to list other jobs you have had and often to state why you left.
- Why you want this job: you may be invited to write a statement in support of your application. This is often done by deciding exactly what, according to the advert, the employer is looking for and trying to explain how you fulfil these requirements.

Look at the following form. Make out an application for the job using this as a template. You should use block capitals as far as possible and make sure that it looks really neat. It is often wise to fill in a form in pencil first.

Sometimes, if you call in to a firm to enquire about a job, you may be asked to complete a form there and then. This means that you should know, or carry a note of, the relevant details.

ELECTROPARTS APPLICATION FORM

Please complete this form in your own handwriting in black ink.

PERSONAL PARTICULARS
Surname
Forenames
Maiden Name
Title Mr, Mrs, Ms, Miss (delete as appropriate)
Address
Postcode

EDUCATION AND TRAINING
Schools attended since age 11
Further education
Qualifications

EMPLOYMENT HISTORY
Give details below of your present and any previous jobs, including dates
  of employment.
Present job (outline your duties and responsibilities)
Previous jobs (state reason for leaving)
Please state your reasons for wanting this job.
I promise to the best of my knowledge that the information I have given
  is correct.
Signature of applicant..Date ....

ACTIVITY

3d

Preparing a Curriculum Vitae

The Latin phrase 'Curriculum Vitae' means 'the course of your life', particularly referring to your career. This is like a form which you design yourself. You set out the necessary information in a clear and readable way. As you have seen in the adverts, sometimes an employer will specifically ask for this.

The main headings and some advice about each section appear below.

Name: your full name, in block capitals should appear here.
Address: put the full postal address.
Date of birth: put the day, month and year here.
Telephone: it's always worth including this.
Age: put this in years here.
Marital status: you can omit this if you like.
Education from age 11: put the dates (month and year) of attendance at schools and colleges plus their full names in this section.
Qualifications gained at school: list your exam results in order of merit. Put the month and year of the examination plus its level and the

examining board. For example, June 1978 'O' level Biology Grade C, History Grade D (Oxford).You could set this information out in a table.

You may wish to include non-academic achievements here such as a life saving badge, first aid qualification, grade exams in ballet or a musical instrument – anything for which you gained a proper certificate may be worth putting in.

Qualifications since leaving school: if you have obtained other qualifications, for example if you had an apprenticeship or did a training course at college, put the details here. There may also be non-academic items to add: full driving licence, for example. As before, include the date that you acquired the qualification and sufficient detail to explain to a prospective employer exactly what it is.

Employment: everyone's circumstances differ so it's difficult to give hard and fast rules. Basically in this section you should start with your present or most recent job. Give a fairly full description of your position and responsibilities. Give the date you began this job and, if appropriate, when you left. After that, give information on the other jobs you've had. If you've had a lot, you may not want to include them all. You don't want to leave suspicious gaps, however, as questions are bound to be raised in the reader's mind about what you were doing then. If you've had very little experience of employment but have had periods of work experience as part of your education, it's worth putting those in, particularly if they're directly relevant to a job you've applied for. Do make it clear, though, that it's work experience: to be employed by a firm for just three weeks gives a bad impression! Always give dates and say if the position was part time or full time.

Hobbies and interests: you should include a list of your main spare-time activities here. Make this sound as interesting as possible. In an interview, you might be asked about these so obviously you must be truthful but try to say something more exciting than 'reading' and 'meeting people'.

References: normally, when you apply for a job, you need to give the names and addresses of two people whom you are happy for the employer to contact to obtain a reference. Unless you left education a long time ago, one of these can usefully be a head teacher or college principal. The other one, usually, should be your present or most recent employer. It looks a bit odd if you don't put this person down although you may feel that their comments about you may not help your case. Apart from these obvious choices, put someone down who knows you but who is of good 'status' – a doctor, clergyman, senior business executive or some such. When a request is made for a reference it is likely that the person will be asked to say in what capacity they have known you and perhaps to indicate how honest and reliable you are. A part-time cleaner may be able to make a knowledgeable comment but is less likely to be regarded as a sound source of information than a local councillor.

Here is an example of a CV for further guidance:

Curriculum Vitae

Name: **Kay Aldridge**
Address: 28 Hatton Drive, Grantfield, Midshire
Date of Birth: 19–08–72
Age: 22
Marital Status: Single
Tel: 0111 222 333

Education from age 11:

September 1983 to June 1988: Francis Bacon School, Grantfield.

Qualifications Gained at School:

June 1988: M.E.G. (GCSE) English Language Grade D
Oral English 3
Geography D
Mathematics D
L.E.A.G. History E

Other Qualifications:

From June 1990: Full Driving Licence

Employment:

June 1992 to present: Oakwood College, Grantfield. Clerical Assistant. Full time. Duties include answering telephone enquiries, filing, typing, reprographics and leaflet distribution.
November 1991 to January 1992: Pasta Choice, Grantfield. Waitress. Full time.
April 1990 to September 1991: Clean – Bee, Grantfield. Full-time clerical assistant. Duties included telephone quotations, typing, filing, V.A.T. returns and staff wages.
November 1989 to April 1990: Pizza Express, Grantfield. Part-time coffee girl and waitress.

Hobbies and Interests:

Aerobics; jogging; travelling; going to the cinema; reading historical novels; meeting and working with people.

References:

Mrs P. Small
School of Arts and Sciences
Oakwood College Chequer Street
Grantfield

Mr D. Pepe
Pasta Choice
Grantfield

Writing your CV

Having armed yourself with the necessary information, draw up your CV. If a particular section doesn't apply to you, for example, qualifications since leaving school, omit it altogether. Similarly if you feel that your exam grades are too low to be useful, pretend they never happened. While you must, of course, be truthful, there is nothing to stop you missing out items which you feel might give a bad impression.

Drafting and Revising

Initially you will want to write it out by hand. Eventually, when you've checked that all the information is there and that you have made no spelling errors, it should be typed. The layout is important. Ideally you want it to occupy just one sheet of A4, using both sides if necessary. If you are using both sides, try to adjust the layout to fill the space nicely rather than ending half way down the second page.

This is a standard document and should be equally applicable whatever job you're applying for. If you are in the process of submitting a number of applications, there is the huge advantage that your CV can be photocopied, thus avoiding the lengthy process of writing out all the information in individual letters.

ACTIVITY

3e

Writing an Accompanying Letter

To emphasise relevant points and to expand on particular aspects of your CV, the normal practice is to write a letter to accompany it. The contents of the letter will obviously vary according to the job for which you are applying.

Find an advertisement in a local or national paper for a job which you would be qualified to apply for. If there is nothing suitable, invent one using a similar format to those you looked at in Activity A. Your letter will be a formal one so check the layout in Chapter 6, Unit 6, if you are unsure.

Before setting it out properly, you need to write a draft. This is a rough guide to the content of the paragraphs. A large number of short paragraphs tends to be more effective in a letter than a few long ones.

You will probably be writing to someone named in the advertisement or in the additional details for the job. If so write to them by name. Otherwise write 'Dear Sir or Madam'. Here is a suggested plan:

- **Paragraph one** – here you're going to say what job you are applying for and where you saw the advertisement (e.g. the *Lincoln Chronicle* of 27 March 1994).
- **Paragraph two to paragraph four/five** – refer to the enclosed CV and say that you wish to draw their attention to a few points. Select particularly relevant aspects of your career to expand upon. Possibilities would be specific experience in that or a related field and particular skills, whether personal or professional, which you possess. You need to be as positive as possible – having even a minor responsibility can be presented as evidence of initiative, reliability or trustworthiness. Start a

new paragraph for each new aspect.

- **Subsequent paragraphs** – if the advert asked for a particular sort of person: energetic, able to work without supervision, etc., make sure that you include a reference to this. Tell the employer, in other words, why it is YOU who should be employed – or at any rate interviewed – for this job.
- **Final paragraph** – express your willingness to supply further information and your availability for interview. Make it sound as if you're only too happy to put yourself out to accommodate them.
- **Close** – end with a formal sentence which expresses optimism, not 'See you soon', that's much too chatty; something like 'I look forward to meeting you in the near future' will do nicely.

If you have been writing to a named person end with 'Yours sincerely' and if not, with 'Yours faithfully'.

Drafting and Revising

Check the content and **accuracy** – nothing looks worse than spelling errors or ungrammatical sentences in a letter like this – then write the letter out on a plain piece of paper, correctly set out. It should be handwritten, not typed. Britain may not quite have reached the situation in the United States where handwriting experts are brought in to assess applicants' suitability for a job, but convention suggests that if your CV is typed, your letter should not be. Make quite sure that you make the correct choice between 'Yours faithfully' or 'Yours sincerely'. If the employer knows which it should be you'll cause irritation by getting it wrong – this is not a good idea!

ACTIVITY

3f

Letter of Application

As an alternative to using a CV and accompanying letter, you may wish to write one letter to cover everything. If an advert merely asks you for a written application (like advert A in Activity A) this would be acceptable. It will be fairly long as you need to include pretty well the same information as the CV. Here is a suggested plan for what you should put into each paragraph. The order can be varied, of course, but this is a reasonable guide:

- **Paragraph one** – exactly the same as in the accompanying letter, what you are applying for and where it was advertised.
- **Paragraph two** – your situation now. Say how old you are (if this is to your advantage) and why you wish to apply for the job at this particular time – e.g. you feel you can progress no further in your present post, you're completing a college course, or whatever.
- **Paragraph three** – education from age 11 and qualifications gained while of school age. You can use tabular form for your examination results, as in the CV.
- **Paragraph four** – further education and qualifications.
- **Paragraph five** – employment history. As with the CV, select how

many jobs or periods of work experience to write about and how much detail to give. This may occupy more than one paragraph.

- **Paragraph six** – draw the employer's attention, as you did in the accompanying letter, to your most relevant experience and strengths. Say why you should have the job.
- **Final paragraph** – as with the accompanying letter, express your willingness to supply further information and say you are available for interview.
- **Close** – 'I look forward to meeting you in the near future'.

Drafting and Revising

As always, write this letter in rough before attempting to do the final draft. Make sure you've stressed near the beginning as well as near the end that you are an ideal candidate. Have you included all the important facts? Once you are happy with the wording, check the accuracy of spelling and punctuation. Write it out using the correct layout for a formal letter. Include your telephone number after your address in case the firm wishes to contact you in a hurry. Probably even the final version of this should be handwritten but if your writing is especially illegible, typing it may be acceptable.

ACTIVITY

3g

Coursework – Speaking and Listening

If possible, do Part 1 and Part 2 of this activity. Suppose you are offered an interview for the job you have applied for. Using your previous experience and advice from friends or fellow students, draw up a list of ten questions which you think you might be asked. Also think of questions which you would like to ask about details not mentioned in the original advertisement.

Part 1

Discuss in a small group the right way to behave and present yourself in an interview. Talk about appropriate dress, the need for punctuality and so on. You can swap stories of personal experiences. This can be assessed as part of your oral coursework.

Part 2

Now find a partner, preferably a fellow student but a friend or relative would be an acceptable alternative. Brief this person on any necessary background details of the firm and particulars of the job. Now set up a mock interview. If you are not doing this in a classroom situation you will need to have it recorded on audio or even videotape. Videoing may be advisable anyway as you will be able to spot any less than positive answers and you will see any irritating mannerisms. If you are working

with a fellow student you can reverse the roles of interviewer and inter-
viewee after your interview is finished.

Review of Unit 3

- In Activity A you read four adverts, gaining an understanding of what each was asking for (En 2.2, 4).
- Activity B was speaking and listening coursework (En 1.1, 4).
- In Activities C to F you used various methods to apply for a job. These individual pieces could be grouped together as written coursework (En 3).
- Activity G was speaking and listening coursework (En 1.1, 2, 4).

Making a Record

Write down the necessary information about the coursework in this unit. This was the individual or pairs' oral work in Activity B and the group and pair oral work in Activity G. Also record the details of the written work in Activities C to F. When you have done this, tick the relevant aspects of En 1, En 2 and En 3 on your Coursework Checklist.

What Should You Do Now?

Either choose another unit in this chapter or turn to a unit in another chapter.

  Face the Facts

In this unit you will be looking at examples of factual writing from various sources in order to assess their effectiveness. You will then be writing a factual article and presenting factual information orally.

ACTIVITY

4a

Reading and Understanding – Finding Facts

As part of everyday life or when studying a subject other than English, people often have to read material in order to find out factual information.

Study the timetable below and answer the questions which follow. (The correct answers appear at the end of this unit of Chapter 4.) It is possible that reading information from a table could appear as an activity in your examination.

Questions

1   I live in London and have a meeting at 11.00 a.m. on Thursday in Liverpool. I want to travel first class and have a full cooked breakfast on the train. Which train should I catch?

2   I live in Watford, close to the station. Is there a train around six o'clock on a Saturday evening which will take me direct to Stafford?

3   When can I get directly from Nuneaton to Bangor on a weekday?

4   I am travelling on the 23.50 from London Euston to Crewe on a Tuesday evening. Do I need to book a seat?

5   I am getting a ferry from Holyhead on a weekday. I will have a lot of luggage and I want to catch a direct train there from Milton Keynes Central. I don't want to leave home later than six p.m. Is it possible?

ACTIVITY

4b

Coursework – Speaking and Listening

Telephone a British Rail recorded passenger information service. Listen carefully for a short while until you feel you have an awareness of the way information is being presented. When you put the 'phone down, make some notes about what was being said. Probably there was a polite but friendly introductory statement. The precise nature of the timetable being presented would probably have been given next: the voice will

6 London — Crewe — Chester — North Wales — Liverpool

London — Crewe — Chester — North Wales — Liverpool (page 57)

6 London — Crewe — Chester — North Wales — Liverpool

Full service London — Rugby, Table 4.

Saturdays

London Euston	0615	0715	0740	0815	0840	0855	0915	0940	0950	1040	
Watford Junction	0631u	0731u	0757u	0832u			0932u		1006u	1011	
Milton Keynes Central	0653		0820	0857	0915		0955			1049	
Rugby	0727				0950	1012		1046		1145	
Nuneaton	0741		0942					1100	1118		
Tamworth	0754									1222	
Stafford	0815	0914	0928	1049	1040		1119	1149		1246	
Crewe	0839	1008	0950	1031	1103	1126	1201			1324	
Chester	0924	1024	1024		1126	1234	1205	1149		1434	
Bangor	1034	1134	1201		1234	1312					
Holyhead	1101	1201	1014u	1101	1312					1305	
Hartford	0931	1034	1034	1102	1112			1208		1335	
Runcorn	0908	1014u	1502u	1125	1136	1609	1208	1233	1305	
Liverpool Lime Street	0931	1034	1034	1125	1136	1633	1233	1330	

Saturdays

London Euston	1115	1140	1240	1250	1315	1340	1350	1440	1450	1515	
Watford Junction	1149	1156u	1314	1331u	1406u		1411	1423	1549u	
Milton Keynes Central					1415			1524	
Rugby		1259		1432	1450	1533	1607	
Nuneaton								
Tamworth			1411		1549	1624	
Stafford	1314	1328	1420	1450	1519	1549	1533	1624	1714	
Crewe		1353	1457u	1524		1624	1648	1808	
Chester				1634				1928	
Bangor				1706					
Holyhead			1510			1609	1707	1739	
Hartford			1414	1502u	1816	1633	1732	1750	
Runcorn		1438	1522					1814	
Liverpool Lime Street									

Saturdays

London Euston	1540	1550	1640	1715	1740	1755	1815	1853	1910	1915
Watford Junction	1556u	1606u			1756u	1811u	1831u	1930u	1926u	1931u	1954u
Milton Keynes Central						1905	1923	2013	1949u	
Rugby	1705		1817		1905	1944		2047	2042	2047
Nuneaton		1731	1840	1915			2021	2106	2106	2058	2133
Tamworth	1744	1754		1920			2059	2129		
Stafford		1829	1925		1949		2216	2237	2128	2138
Crewe		1946			2004u		2251	2314	2138	2203
Chester		2021			2024		2053	2203		
Bangor	1824		1913			2106			
Holyhead	1803		1904u			2134			
Hartford	1827		1924						
Runcorn									
Liverpool Lime Street								*continued*	

continued

Notes for this and opposite page:
A Fridays only.
a Arrival time.
s Calls to set down only.
u Calls to pick up only.

On-Board Services (see page 1):
InterCity train with catering
First Class Pullman
Restaurant (First Class only)
Silver Standard
Seat reservations essential
(free of charge to ticket holders).
Seat reservations recommended.

Light printed timings indicate connecting service.

6 London — Crewe — Chester — North Wales — Liverpool (page 56)

Full service London — Rugby, Table 4.

Mondays to Fridays

London Euston	0625	0725	0750	0825	0850	0905	0925	0950	1000	1050
Watford Junction	0641u	0741u	0806u	0842u			0942u	1016u	1011	
Milton Keynes Central	0703			0907	0925	1005			1050	
Rugby	0727		0942	0950	1012		1046		1145	
Nuneaton	0741					1100	1118		
Tamworth	0754							1222	
Stafford	0815	0922	1031	1040	1119	1149		1246	
Crewe	0839	0946	1103	1126	1201		1324	
Chester	0924	1006	1024	1134	1312	1205	1324	
Bangor	1034	1134	1201		1434	
Holyhead	1101	1201		1501	
Hartford	1034	1102	1101	1208	1335	
Runcorn	0908	1010u	1112	1112	1233	1305	
Liverpool Lime Street	0931	1026	1125	1136	1330	

Mondays to Fridays

London Euston	1125	1150	1250	1300	1325	1350	1400	1450	1500	1525
Watford Junction	1111	1206u	1241	1341u	1416u	1441	1511	
Milton Keynes Central	1159	1241	1324	1425	1524	1534	1559u	
Rugby		1259	1432	1450	1607	
Nuneaton			1411	1534	1624	1714	
Tamworth					1622	1648	1800	
Stafford	1314	1328	1420	1450	1519	1549	1928	
Crewe		1353	1524	1624	
Chester			1634	1741	1739	
Bangor		1641	1816	1750	
Holyhead		1706	1814	
Hartford		1414	1502u	1609	1707	
Runcorn	1438	1522	1633	1732	
Liverpool Lime Street					

Mondays to Fridays

London Euston	1550	1650	1703	1725	1730	1745	1805	1830	1850	
Watford Junction	1606u	1629		1801u	1821u	1846u	1926u	
Milton Keynes Central	1616u	1656		1746	1832	
Rugby		1800	1830	1844	1902	1928	
Nuneaton	1705	1814			1944	
Tamworth						
Stafford	1731	1817	1903	1915	1921	2026	
Crewe	1744	1754	1840	1929	1950	1950	2059	
Chester		1946	2037	2020	2216	
Bangor		2114	2251	
Holyhead	1824	1913	1947	2053	
Hartford	1803	1904u	2002u	2106	
Runcorn	1827	1920	2022	2134	
Liverpool Lime Street					

Mondays to Fridays

London Euston	1903	1920	1925	2030	2100	2200	2330	0128	0209	
Watford Junction	1940u	1936u	1941u	2011	2216u	2216u	2346u	0154	
Milton Keynes Central		1959u	2004u	2105	2139	2238	2040	0005	
Rugby	2013	2139		2311	0050	
Nuneaton				2339	0038	
Tamworth				2337	0052	
Stafford	2042	2047	2238	0130	0147	
Crewe	2106	2058	2133	2303	0052	0224	
Chester	2129	2337	2330	
Bangor	2219	2322	
Holyhead	2237	2128	2347	
Hartford	2314	2138		
Runcorn		2203	0249	
Liverpool Lime Street					

Notes see opposite page.

have said which major station trains departed from and to what destination and on what days of the week. Times will then have been given with standard regular times (for example, 25 minutes past the hour) being grouped together from when they start to when they finish. At periods of the day with more frequent or varying times, each departure would be mentioned. Probably the message ended with an indication of the length of time the journey to the principal destination would take. A number to telephone for further enquiries may also have been given.

You are now going to make a similar 'talking timetable' using the information given in Activity A. You are going to do this for the Saturday service from London Euston to Liverpool Lime Street. Work out what you are going to say bearing in mind the example you have listened to earlier. When you have done this, record your message onto audio tape. State your name at the beginning or end so that your tutor can identify who is speaking. Remember to speak slowly but distinctly. Try to sound pleasant. When you have finished, rewind and listen to it. If your voice seems to sound odd, don't worry, everyone's does. If you feel that you have done this well enough, fine. The tape can now be assessed by your tutor. If you feel it could be improved, record it again.

ACTIVITY

4c

Reading and Evaluation

You are now going to read two written extracts. Identify the subject matter of each and think of a suitable title (this should be precise not general). Try to decide on the purpose of these pieces of writing.

Extract A

Rifleman (*Acanthisitta chloris*) 8cm. Found south of the northern third of the North Island, in the South Island, Stewart, Great and Little Barrier Islands, this bird's high pitched calls give its position away as it searches bark crevices for insects and spiders. Nests, in hollow branches or banks of old bush roads, are loosely woven and 4–5 white eggs laid. Males are often polygamous.

Bush Wren (*Xenicus longipes*) 9.5cm. This wren feeds largely on insects in the foliage and bobs its whole body vigorously when alighting. It makes subdued trills, rasping notes and loud cheeps. Three subspecies are known: North Island, South Island and Stead's Bush Wren, all of which are now extremely rare, if not actually extinct.

Rock Wren (*Xenicus gilviventris*) 9.5cm. Rock Wrens frequent open rock and talus slopes at altitudes of 750–2,500 m, mainly in the Southern Alps. Bobbing vigorously, they feed on insects, fruit, alpine plants and have a three-note call and a thin pipe. A globular nest of moss and lichen, lined with feathers, is built in a crevice and 1–5 white eggs are laid. Both parents feed the young.

Silvereye (*Zosterops lateralis*) 12cm. Silvereyes came over from Australia in 1856 and are now common up to 1,000 m in all types of settled habitat with tree cover including native forest and sub-alpine scrub. Aggressive birds with varied calls, they flock in autumn and winter.

Mainly insectivorous, they love nectar and are easily fed with fat, fruit and syrup. Their nests are of woven grass suspended from twigs 1–9 m. above the ground. Both birds incubate the 3–4 pale blue eggs.

Fantail (*Rhipidura fuliginosa*) 16cm. Common in forest, tree and scrub-covered settled districts. Fantails are insectivorous, inquisitive and lively, posturing with spread tails. Two colour phases occur: Black (very rare on North Island) and Pied. They have penetrating notes. The small cobweb-covered nests of fibre and moss are built, 3–4 spotted cream eggs incubated and young fed by both birds. Five broods have been recorded in one season (August–January).

Extract B

Geography

Spain shares the Iberian peninsula with Portugal and is separated from France by the Pyrenees. The Ballearic Islands (Mallorca, Menorca, Ibiza and Formentera) lie 120 miles south east of Barcelona. These belong to Spain as do the Canary Islands off the west coast of Africa. Spain also owns some territory on the African mainland. Its area is 504,682 sq. kms (194,858 sq. miles). It has a population of approximately 37,800,000 people. With the exception of Switzerland, Spain is the highest and most mountainous country in Europe. Much of the country receives between 400 and 600mm of rain annually. Most of the rain falls in the winter and the summers are hot and dry. The climate varies quite a lot depending on the region. The mainland regions are Northern Spain (Green Spain on the map) which consists of Galicia, Asturias and Cantabria; Castile in the centre; Andalucia in the South; Costa Blanca and Catalonia in the east.

History

The first signs of man living in Spain are found in caves in the south. These date back to 23,000 BC. In about 3000 BC Iberian tribes from north Africa moved to Spain. Coastal settlements were founded by the Phoenicians in 1100 BC, followed by Celts and Greek traders. The Romans conquered Spain in the second century BC. In the fifth century AD, at the break up of the Roman Empire, the Visogoths established a kingdom. By 565 AD the Moors had conquered part of Andalucia. By AD 750, all except Cantabria in the north was ruled by them. In the eleventh century the ruling Umayyads died out, replaced various petty emirates. Legendary crusaders like El Cid, along with the forces of the Kings of Castile and Leon, reconquered the central plateau. Toledo fell in 1085. Four centuries later the united forces of Ferdinand and Isabella, drove out the last Moors. Spain, in the shape of Columbus was involved in early voyages to the New World (1492). Charles V, who came to the throne in 1500, was one of the most powerful rulers in Christendom, only surpassed by his son Philip II who took the Spanish throne in 1556, adding that of Portugal in 1580. During this period the Conquistadores, such men as Magellan, Cortes and Pizarro discovered and annexed for Spain much of Middle America, then Peru. This brought great wealth and power. England was Spain's major rival, defeating the 'unbeatable' Armada in 1588. In 1704 Britain captured Gibraltar. In 1808 Napoleon Bonaparte invaded Spain, setting his brother Joseph up as King. The English during the Peninsula Wars, tried to drive him out. From 1814 the Spanish Colonies in America gradually became independent. The last were lost after a war with the USA which started in 1898 over Cuba, Puerto Rico and the Philippines. King Alfonso XIII left Spain after trouble with anarchist factions in 1931 after which a republic was formed. This lasted until 1936 when the Popular Front, a group of socialists, republicans and communists, brought down the government. At the same time General Franco led a military coup. The result was the Spanish Civil War, fought between 1936 and 1939. International Brigades of world communists fought with and supported the so called Loyalists. Fascist Germany and Italy aided Franco's Nationalists. Franco ruled Spain as a military dictator until his death in 1975.

The present tourist boom began in the 1950s. On Franco's death Juan Carlos became King and at once started to reintroduce democracy. The first general elections for forty-one years were held in 1977. The King helped to thwart a military coup in 1981. Spain entered the European Community in 1986. It currently has a socialist government.

How would you describe the way these two pieces are written? In both extracts the purpose seems to have been to inform the reader. There is no unnecessary description nor any comments intended to entertain. These pieces fulfil their intended purpose satisfactorily. They may be a little boring, however, if you do not specifically want the information which is being given.

ACTIVITY

4d

Finding the Facts

Sometimes you may find that factual information is presented in a more lively and entertaining way than in the extracts you have just read. If you wish to obtain facts from this sort of piece you need to sift through, deciding what is factual and what is not. The following is part of a magazine article about women's underwear.

Read it through and write down a list of the **facts** about underwear worn before the present day. Number each point and write as few words as possible. Make notes, i.e. do not write in full sentences and do use abbreviations. Ignore anecdotes, examples and opinions.

My grandmother always used to say that she had to be decent underneath in case she was involved in an accident and had to be taken to hospital. Women seem to vary between the extremes of those with a weakness for lovely silky undies and those who wear the grey stretched variety held together with safety pins. What unites most of us is that we buy our underwear originally from a certain famous High Street store familiarly referred to as M&S.

These days variety abounds. There are lots of different styles available from the more traditional and supporting, to garments you almost feel you could go out to dinner in! Cropped tops and minimum control emphasise comfort rather than providing a jacked-up outline. This was definitely not so for our ancestors whose undies seemed to rival instruments of torture.

The Elizabethans wore corsets made of steel and leather to create the fashionable outline. The discomfort must have been astounding. And of course this idea didn't die out then: corsets of similar design if made of rather friendlier materials continued to be worn by virtually all women, apart from a short phase in the early nineteenth century, right up to the First World War. The 'foundation' garment of today is its modern relation. The 'Liberty bodice', invented in 1908 was just that for the suffering females of the day! It seems positively masochistic for even young girls to attempt to produce waists of eighteen to twenty inches, let alone more mature women. It's no wonder ladies tended to faint and appeared delicate. Not surprisingly, in most times there was a fashion for loose 'undress' garments which were worn for at least part of the day. Apart from corsets or 'stays', the main item of underwear used was the chemise. Country schoolgirls this century may well have been taught to make such garments. It was essentially a bit like a long nightgown of white cotton or linen fabric but with a low, often frilled neckline, and in the seventeenth and eighteenth centuries with elbow length frilled sleeves which showed under the gown. It probably doubled as a nightdress in many eras. The corsets and umpteen petticoats were worn over the top of it. Stockings were worn but suspenders did not appear until the 1870s so these were held up with garters. Tights, although worn by men in medieval times were not introduced as a form of ladies' underwear until the 1960s, as many of us remember! Similarly, our most essential item, pants or 'knickers' did not appear until Victorian times, and even then in a very different form. The first long drawers to appear were cheats: they only existed from the knees down and were intended to prevent members of the male sex from receiving an exciting glimpse of ankle! Other styles consisted of two legs suspended from a waist band but leaving a gap in the middle. It was only the shortening of skirts in the twentieth century which made our version necessary, it seems.

In most eras long full skirts springing from a narrow waist has been the favoured style. Various fairly similar means have been adopted to create this fullness. For less prosperous ladies multiple layers of petticoats have done the job. The wealthy have been more inventive. The Elizabethan farthingale was a steel and leather cage. In the seventeenth and eighteenth centuries whalebone and metal hoops linked with tapes and tied on round the middle were used. 'Panniers' consisting of horsehair cushions tied onto the hips made the skirts so wide that a lady had to go through a door sideways. Most famous of all, the Victorian crinoline, again made of whalebone hoops, reached overall proportions surpassing all its predecessors. Its successor, the bustle, a cushion or wire framework sitting at the back had absurdities of its own: deliberately to increase the apparent size of that part of our anatomy which many of us would like to reduce would seem decidedly eccentric!

Look critically at your list of facts. Have you included anything which is more a guess or an opinion rather than something which could be found in a book about historical costume? If you have, cross that out. Probably you are not left with all that much.

In the first paragraph there are no facts; there are none in the second paragraph either. In paragraph three there are facts about what Elizabethan corsets were made of, about the continuation of corset-wearing, about the origin of the Liberty bodice and the wearing of 'undress' garments. Paragraph four gives facts about the chemise. Paragraph five has facts about stockings, drawers and the design of these. Paragraph six gives factual information about the way full skirts were supported at various times.

ACTIVITY

4e

Writing from Notes

When you are finding information on a particular subject from an article or a book, you select relevant facts as you did in Activity D, writing them down in note form, often in numbered points. If you then have to present this information in a piece of written work, it is necessary to write your notes as correct full sentences.

Working from the notes which you wrote in Activity D, write a paragraph containing the factual information found in the article. Do not write more that 150 words.

When you have finished, compare your factual paragraph to the original article. What is the difference? Probably yours sounds rather like Extract B in Activity C. It is just a list of information, probably in short rather abrupt statements. The article was trying to achieve a light-hearted tone and to amuse as well as interest the reader. Your new version is not.

ACTIVITY

4f

Reading – Research and Information Retrieval

Choose a subject in which you are interested and know something about. It can be anything: the history of a football club, all about a martial art, Flamenco dancing, the films of Alfred Hitchcock, Chinese cookery, the possibilities are endless. If you did Activity F of Unit 1 of this chapter, choose a different subject.

However much you know about the subject already, you are going to find out some more or refresh your memory.

Depending on the particular subject you have chosen, consult your local or college library and take out the books you need. Alternatively you can obtain pamphlets or specialist magazines to gain the necessary facts.

Make notes set out in numbered points like you did when analysing the article on underwear.

ACTIVITY

4g

Coursework – Speaking and Listening

This activity may be useful and possible, depending on your chosen subject. If it would be very difficult to arrange, do not do this activity.

Interview someone who is an expert on your chosen subject. For example, if you are researching a sport or martial art, you could speak to someone who teaches this.

You will need to contact the person beforehand and arrange a convenient time to meet. Prepare a list of questions. You are finding out more about the subject but some information about the expert's involvement with it and experience of it may be relevant. If the expert agrees, you could tape record the interview. This makes retrieval of the information easy as you can make notes as you replay the tape. If this is not possible or acceptable, leave gaps in writing down your questions so that you can note down the answers there and then.

ACTIVITY

4h

Coursework – Writing a Factual Article

If you chose to write the booklet in Activity F of Unit 1 of this chapter and are satisfied with the levels you achieved, you may not wish to do this activity. If you do wish to write the factual article, follow the advice given below.

Organise your notes into a sensible order so that one point naturally follows on from another. Now write a draft of your article. Suppose that this is going to be read by someone who knows little or nothing about the subject but would quite like to have some information. Bearing that in mind, you will want to make the piece easy to understand and also as interesting as possible. Use a lively and fairly informal style, adding comments and opinions where you think appropriate.

Drafting and Revising

Once the draft is written, read it through. Does it sound interesting or like a boring textbook? Check, as usual, both content and accuracy. Look up how to spell words which you're unsure of and check the punctuation.

When you're happy with all aspects, write it out neatly. You may feel that you wish to include photographs or illustrations – in a magazine you would often see these with such an article. You may wish to type it but check your GCSE syllabus regulations with regard to the proportion of typed or word-processed work which is permissible. Check the final draft for slips in punctuation and spelling. If you are using a word processor these are very easy to correct.

At the top put a suitable eye-catching title. On a separate sheet put your name and the date of writing.

Review of Unit 4

- Activity A was reading (En 2.2, 3, 4).
- Activity B was speaking and listening coursework (En 1.1, 4).
- Activities C and D were reading and evaluation (En 2.2, 4).
- Activity E was practice in note taking.
- Activity F was reading, research and information retrieval (En 2.3).

● Activity G was speaking and listening coursework (En 1.1, 2, 4).
● Activity H was written coursework (En 2.3; En 3).

Making a Record

Write down the necessary information about the coursework in this unit. This was the individual oral work in Activity B and the individual or pairs oral work in Activity G. Record also the details of the written work in Activity H if you chose to do this. When you have finished, tick the relevant aspects of En 1, En 2 and En 3 on your Coursework Checklist.

What Should You Do Now?

Either turn to another unit in this chapter or to a unit in another chapter.

Answers to the Questions in Activity A

1   07.50 from London Euston (arrives 10.26).
2   Yes, 18.11 from Watford (arrives 19.44).
3   10.12, 18.14, 20.13.
4   Yes.
5   No. The only direct train is at 19.40.

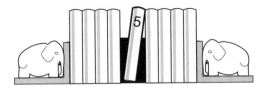

ACTIVITY

5a

UNIT **5** *Sales Talk*

In this unit you will be looking at various aspects of buying and selling. Some basic information about consumer law will be looked at and then you will be seeing how to complain effectively about faulty goods.

A letter of complaint or a reply to one could quite possibly appear in the written examination. The written work from Activities F and G could be collected together to form one piece of coursework. You will do some research into various retail establishments in your area, writing a short report about them. There will be an opportunity for a longer piece of writing which may be appropriate as coursework.

Reading and Understanding

Read the following information about consumer rights and answer the questions which follow.

Some Consumer Rights

A contract is made when one person buys goods from another. What is bought must conform to certain standards.

1   It must be fit for the purpose or purposes for which it is sold. It should be of 'merchantable quality'. A toaster which overheats, a hot water bottle which leaks, a dress with splits at the seams are examples of items which are not of merchantable quality.

If you have been sold faulty goods you may take them back to the shop and claim your money back. If you wish to, you may accept a credit note but you do not have to do so. You are entitled to the full cash price plus compensation for any inconvenience. Even if a shop displays a sign saying 'No refunds' this is not legally enforceable when you are within your rights. If the trader offers to repair the goods free of charge you do not have to agree to this. If you choose to, it does not affect your claim. You could ask the shop, meanwhile to provide you with a substitute or charge them for the cost of acquiring a temporary replacement. You should behave reasonably, however, and not incur undue expense for them on principle. If there are minor defects – little scratches, dirty marks or whatever, the seller may not be responsible for these. If they were pointed out to you at the time or you examined the goods carefully and should have noticed them, you cannot return the goods on this basis. You have to decide if the goods are of a standard which is 'reasonable to expect' and this is open to interpretation.

2   Goods must match the description given of them. Usually there will be a description of some sort applied even if it only refers to weight, size, quantity and colour. If you buy a 1300 cc car, the engine must be of that capacity. A shirt labelled 100 per cent cotton must not contain any nylon. Gouda cheese cannot be described as Edam. A shower-proof coat must be impervious to light rain. According to the Weights and Measures Act 1963, goods must not weigh less than the amount stated on the packaging or advertisement.

When you have bought goods which do not correspond to their description, you can claim a refund. If you have bought them from a trader then you may also report the matter to your Trading Standards Officer who may bring a prosecution against the trader.

If you buy an item from a private individual you are not protected under the Sale of Goods Act except that the goods must correspond to the description given of them. Buying from a mail order firm is covered by the Sale of Goods Act.

Questions

Answer the following questions using the information above to justify your answer.

1   I have bought a microwave oven with an automatic cooking pro-gramme. After a month, the other functions of the machine work, but not this one. What should I do?
2   I bought a dress in an expensive dress shop. When I got it home and tried it on, I decided that I didn't like the colour. What should I do?
3   I found a beetle in a tin of baked beans. What should I do?
4   I bought a bicycle from a Mr Roberts who had advertised in the local paper. The first time I rode it I found that the brakes didn't work. I only narrowly avoided being hit by a car. I fell off the bicycle and grazed my leg and shoulder. What should I do?
5   I bought a pair of high-heeled patent leather shoes. After owning them for three months, having missed the last bus, I had to walk home in them, a journey of four miles, the last part being on an unmade road. Two days later, the right heel came off. What should I do?

ACTIVITY

5b

Coursework – Speaking and Listening

Working with a group of other students, discuss your answers to the questions. Were you all agreed about the consumer's rights in each case?

Everyone in the group should think of examples of similar situations. Allow ten minutes for everyone to think of these. Each person in turn should then present his or her own experience to the group, saying what was done about the problem. Discuss with the other group members whether it was dealt with in the right way.

Reading and Analysis

Look at the letter which follows. Decide what is wrong with it (a) with regard to the consumer's knowledge of her rights and (b) with the way it is written.

A Letter Of Complaint

27 Mill Lane
Crossley Bridge
Midshire

Goodstuff Catalogues
Unit 4
Trading Estate
Sommerton

17 June 199X

Dear Sir/Madam
I am very unhappy about a dress which I received last week.

I ordered it from your catalogue. You described it there as a ladies floral print dress. I ordered it in size 20 and paid £14.99. The colour choices were lilac, coral or amber. I chose lilac.

First of all, it took a long time to come – nearly three weeks. This is ridiculous as Sommerton's only eight miles away. Then I found that it was just stuffed into a large brown envelope so it was ever so crumpled when I got it out. I really think you should pack goods up better than that as it might have been damaged. Next I thought the material was really poor – it's dreadfully thin and flimsy. Also, the pattern's only on one side. There aren't that many flowers either. The colour is a pale mauve, not my idea of lilac at all.

Lastly it's not the right size. I always take a size 20 but yours is too small. Your size 20s are obviously different so will you please send me a size 22 instead.

I am keeping this dress until you send me another, then I'll return it. I've filled in another order form so that you can see how I filled this one out.

I'm really disappointed as I was told your clothes were really nice.
Yours faithfully

Edith Bagshott (Mrs)

When you have read the letter through carefully at least twice, follow the instructions below.

1   On a piece of paper write 'justified complaints' as a heading. Find any aspects of the purchase which Mrs Bagshott was entitled to complain about and list them.

2   When you have done that put the heading 'unjustified complaints' and list any unfounded criticism which she makes.

3   Below that, put 'actions' as a heading. List everything which Mrs Bagshott has done in order to claim her rights. In each case decide whether she acted correctly or incorrectly.

4   Put a heading 'inappropriate style'. Under it write all the phrases from the letter which were out of place or inappropriate.

Is her complaint justified? What did you decide?

1   The only really acceptable complaint is that the dress is the wrong size. It could be that the firm has made an error. She may be justified in complaining about the packaging. The dress was not damaged, however, so she cannot demand any exchange or compensation on that basis.

2   Twenty-eight days should normally be allowed for delivery of goods. She has no grounds for complaint against the fabric. The dress was relatively inexpensive so the fabric might be expected to be thin and flimsy. 'Print' means that the pattern will be on one side only and the number of flowers is not specified. Mrs Bagshott is interpreting the word 'lilac' differently from the advertiser, but such a variation in view is not grounds for complaint. None of the colour descriptions are precise.

3   To write a letter is the correct action. To keep the dress, ask for a size 22 and to fill in a new order form are not correct actions.

4   The tone of the letter is much too informal. This sort of letter should sound polite but business like. Some examples of inappropriate phrases are 'just stuffed into', 'ever so', 'it's dreadfully', 'that many', 'really nice'.

Finally, Mrs Bagshott's opinion of the dress's quality can't be very low as she evidently still wishes to purchase it.

ACTIVITY

5d

Writing a Letter of Complaint

Now you are going to write Mrs Bagshott's letter as she should have written it. You are only going to include justified complaints and are going to use the right sort of style.

   Here is a suggested paragraph plan:

• **Paragraph one** – state exactly what you ordered.
• **Paragraph two** – state what is wrong with it.
• **Paragraph three** – state how you wish your complaint to be dealt with.
• **Paragraph four** – mention the packaging.

Don't worry if you feel that the paragraphs are very short. It is better, in a business letter, to have quite a lot of short paragraphs rather than just one or two long ones.

Drafting and Revising

Write out the main body of the letter. When you have finished it, check that you have only included justified complaints. Have you written in formal language? Check that you have avoided the sort of style used in the original. Check the accuracy of your work. Is your spelling and punctuation correct? When you're happy with the wording of the letter, write it out neatly using the addresses and close which were printed with the original.

ACTIVITY

5e

Coursework – Speaking and Listening

Imagine that you bought an item of electrical equipment from a specialist high street retailer. (Invent the shop's name – it is part of a chain.) Decide what this item was. It should be able to be carried with reasonable ease (it can't be something like a refrigerator or washing machine, therefore). It cost more than £40. This activity is going to be carried out working with a partner. One of you will be the purchaser. The other person will be the shop manager. Choose one of the two roles and prepare for your confrontation.

Purchaser

After a short period of time a fault has developed with your item of equipment. Decide precisely what the fault is. You put the item in a box and carry it to the shop. (Obtain a suitable box.) Once there you ask for the manager. You show your receipt (make one) and politely explain the situation. Ask for your money back. You do not consider anything else to be acceptable.

Manager

You have been told by the area manager to try to avoid cash refunds. You do not intend to give one in this situation. Offer alternatives: credit note, free repair, replacement item. Still retaining a polite and pleasant manner, try to convince the purchaser that he or she is not entitled to a money refund. (Make a sign to display on the counter.) Use every argument you can think of.

Role-play

Arrange the furniture to be as much like a shop counter as possible. Act out the conversation. Do not use a script, just make up what you say as you go along. Try to act in character.

If you are the purchaser you may wish to express anger. If you are the shop manager you must not. Eventually, after failing to obtain your refund, the purchaser walks out, leaving the item on the shop counter. This could be in disgust or the manager could find an excuse to bring the discussion to an end.

Your tutor should watch this in order to assess it. If the equipment is available, you could record this scene on video tape. If you are carrying out this activity in a larger group, you could then discuss how well the various 'purchasers' acted their parts and how well the 'managers' fulfilled their roles.

Writing Letters of Complaint

Following on from the role play in the previous activity, you are now going to write a letter to the retailer's head office. As this is your first letter you should keep your tone pleasant but firm. Write as if you expect everything to be put right as a result of this letter. Here is a suggested plan:

- **Paragraph one** – give the facts about the original purchase: what exactly you bought, when and where. Then state what fault developed and after how long.
- **Paragraph two** – describe, unemotionally, how you took the item back to the shop, requested a refund and how this was refused.
- **Paragraph three** – point out that you are aware of your rights as a consumer (refer to the information in Activity A). Ask for a refund.
- **Paragraph four** – put a final optimistic sentence, for instance: 'I am sure you will put everything right as soon as possible.'

Drafting and Revising

Write out a first draft of your letter. When you have finished check that you have included all the necessary information and left out anything irrelevant. Now think about your style: have you written like Mrs Bagshott? Make sure your phrasing is formal, correct, polite but firm. Write a second draft trying to be as accurate as possible. The layout will be similar to that used in Activity D in this unit. Check in Chapter 6, Unit 6 if you are unsure.

One Month Later

A month passes and you have heard nothing. In a real life situation of this nature, you could at this stage obtain advice from your local Citizen's Advice Bureau about how to proceed. Some local authorities have specialist centres for consumer problems. Your final course of action would be to take the firm to court. If the value of the goods is less than £500, the matter can be taken to the Small Claims Court which is much cheaper than the County Court. You do not need to be represented by a solicitor but can present the case yourself. This also makes it more affordable.

Write another letter. This time your tone will be sterner (but still be formal and polite). Here is a suggested plan:

- **Paragraph one** – refer to the date of your previous letter and to the fact that you have received no reply.
- **Paragraph two** – re-state the basic facts briefly.
- **Paragraph three** – demand action within a specified time limit.

Threaten legal action.
- **Paragraph four** – close with a stern and disappointed final sentence.

Drafting and Revising

As before, write a rough draft first and then read it through to see whether its contents are right. Adjust it as necessary. Is the tone appropriate? Even though you are angry, you must not be abusive. Re-write the letter as necessary, checking the accuracy of spelling and punctuation. You should set out the final version in the same way as in your first letter of complaint. The date will be one month later.

ACTIVITY
5g

Replying to a Letter of Complaint

Let's suppose that the firm has been taken over by another. Some of the managerial staff have been sacked. Your letter is now dealt with sympathetically by the new complaints manager, Roberta Dean. Write her letter. Here is the suggested structure.

- **Paragraph one** – refer to your previous letters and apologise for the fact that they have not been dealt with before.
- **Paragraph two** – give a brief statement about the company's problems.
- **Paragraph three** – refer to the enclosed refund and also compensation: this could be money off another purchase in one of their stores, a gift voucher or whatever you feel would be suitable. Don't offer too much: remember the firm wants to make money – but not lose customers.
- **Paragraph four** – end suitably apologetically.

Drafting and Revising

As usual, write a draft and then look at it critically. Is the content right? Is the tone appropriate – apologetic but not grovelling? Is your work accurate? Revise the letter as necessary. Look in Unit 6 of Chapter 6 to see how to set out a letter from a firm to an individual. Write out your final draft making sure you use a suitable date and that you sign it as Roberta Dean, not in your own name.

The work in Activities F and G can be grouped together as a piece of coursework.

ACTIVITY
5h

Coursework – Writing a Report

Decide on a particular type of shop. There should be at least three shops of this type in the area where you live. Any sort of shop is possible, but it would be best to choose one which you either use frequently or have an interest in the products on sale. For example, if you like sports you could choose shops selling sportswear and equipment; if you regularly buy food, you could look at a supermarket and perhaps two smaller food shops; if you like clothes, choose various clothing shops.

You are going to go to each shop and investigate various aspects of it. It is up to you whether you tell the shop keeper what you are doing. You will need to make notes and will probably wish to devise some means of recording quality – marks out of ten, 1–5 stars – decide on the best system for you. Here are some suggested aspects to look at; add to these as you like:

- size;
- location – high street, quiet back street, etc.;
- range of goods;
- quality of goods;
- quality of display – in the window and in the shop;
- service;
- prices.

When you are looking at prices, decide on a standard item (or items) likely to be found in each shop. For example, if you were comparing jeweller's, a 16 inch 9 carat gold chain should be available in each. When you write down the prices you will be comparing like with like. It's a bit more difficult with clothing shops, but do the best you can. You may want to look at the range of prices in that case. What is the cheapest skirt in each? What is the dearest? This will give you an idea of the differences between them.

When you have all the information on each shop you are going to present it as a report. These are the headings you should use and what should go into each section. Your written style should be formal and factual.

Introduction

Say what your report is about and how you obtained the information.

Findings

Here you are going to present all your facts. Use as headings the aspects which you looked at. It is acceptable to present tables, for example graphs or bar charts, but as this is an English assessment you will not be specifically assessed on these aspects. You must present the facts in words as well.

Try not to give opinions until you reach the conclusions section. 'The shop is approximately 20 feet by 12 feet' is a fact. 'The shop is small and cramped' is an opinion. 'Cooper's is smaller than Walsh's' is a fact. 'Cooper's is too small' is an opinion. This section of your report will probably be the longest.

Conclusions

Dealing with the aspects in the same order as in your findings above, now give your opinions about each aspect. When you have dealt with each of those, give your **overall conclusion** under a final heading. Here state which of the shops is the best in your opinion. If each is equally good (or bad) in different ways, give a final critical assessment of each one.

Signature and Date

At the end, sign it and put the date of completion.

Drafting and Revising

As always, write a first draft and then read it through. Have you included all your facts? Have you managed to avoid giving opinions too early? Have you used a formal, factual style? Revise your work as necessary, checking the punctuation and looking up words whose spelling you are uncertain about.

Write your final draft. If you are including tables, draw then neatly and present them attractively. You may wish to put a sheet at the front which contains the title 'Report on (name the type) shops in (put the name of your town or area).' List the shops which you have investigated. Put your name and the date of writing. This piece of work may be suitable for your coursework folder.

ACTIVITY

5i

Optional Reading – Research and Information Retrieval

Go to your library or Citizen's Advice Bureau and find out whether there have been any recent changes to consumers' rights.

Review of Unit 5

- Activity A was reading (En 2.3).
- Activity B was speaking and listening coursework (En 1, En 2.3).
- Activity C was reading (En 2.4).
- Activity D was writing (En 3).
- Activity E was speaking and listening coursework (En 1).
- Activities F and G were written coursework (En 3).
- Activity H was written coursework (En 3).
- Activity I was optional reading – research and information retrieval (En 2.3).

Making a Record

Write down the necessary information about the coursework in this unit. This was the group oral work in Activity B and oral work in a pair in Activity E. Record also the details of the written work in Activities F, G and H. When you have done this, tick the relevant aspects of En 1, En 2 and En 3 on your Coursework Checklist.

What Should You Do Now?

Turn to Unit 1 of another chapter. If you have studied the first unit of each chapter, select a later unit from the chapter of your choice.

5 Arguing and Persuading

*I*N this chapter we'll be looking at some of the tactics and techniques used in argument and persuasion. You will have opportunities to produce coursework for your folder and also to practise activities similar to those you may come across in the written examination.

This is what you'll be working on:

- recognising biased and emotive arguments;
- constructing a persuasive argument;
- presenting a strong argument on one side of an issue;
- considering both sides of an issue and reaching an informed conclusion;
- presenting an objective argument.

Where Should You Begin?

You must do all the activities in Unit 1. It is strongly recommended that you then choose another unit from this chapter. If you wish, when you have finished Unit 1, you may work on a unit from a different chapter, returning to Chapter 5 later in the course.

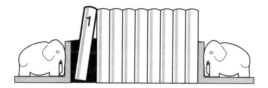

UNIT (**1**) *What the Papers Say*

In this unit you are going to carry out an investigation into British newspapers. You will look at the contents, the language used and the style and purpose of various daily papers. If you are following the LEAG syllabus, work from this unit would be suitable for your piece of coursework on language. In order to complete all the activities in this unit you will need to work in a group or a classroom situation.

ACTIVITY

(**1a**)

Reading – Research and Information Retrieval

Rule a piece of A4 paper into five columns. In the first column make a list of all the national daily newspapers currently published. In the second column fill in the price of each newspaper. In the third column note whether the paper is a broadsheet (printed on A2-size paper) or a tabloid newspaper (printed on A3-size and thus half the size). You can find out this information by visiting your local newsagents early in the day.

Now go to your local or college library. Find out who owns each of the newspapers and what the current readership number is for each one. If you are unsure where to look, the librarian will help you. Put this information in the fourth and fifth columns.

ACTIVITY

(**1b**)

Comparing the Content

For this activity you need to obtain three newspapers, one from each of the following groups:

Group A
The Times, the *Telegraph*, the *Guardian*, *The Independent*

Group B
The *Express*, the *Daily Mail*, *Today*

Group C
The *Daily Mirror*, the *Daily Star*, the *Sun*

They do not need to be today's newspapers but they do need to be from the same day as each other so that you can make a proper comparison. Try to avoid looking at a newspaper which you read on a regular basis. If, since the time this unit was written, a new paper has been started or one or more of these has closed down, make appropriate alterations to the list.

If you are working in a classroom situation, a group of you can work together on a selection of three newspapers. Others in the class can select a different one from each group, thus covering all the daily papers between you.

At the top of a piece of paper, write the word 'Contents' as a heading. **With each paper in turn, write down the following information**:

1   Number of pages (we will say that 1 broadsheet page is equal to 2 pages in a tabloid newspaper, so that, for example, 30 pages in *The Times* is equal to 60 pages in the *Sun*).
2   Work out the approximate space which the paper allows each of the following categories:
   a   home news
   b   foreign news
   c   sports
   d   entertainment – TV, theatre/film/concert guide, puzzles, games, etc.
   e   features – prominent articles **not** dealing with news or current affairs
   f   letters
   g   gossip (try to define a difference between this and features)
   h   adverts – either for products or for jobs
   i   others (if you think more categories are necessary, add your own).

You can give the space devoted to each category as the number of pages or fractions of a page (allowing for the size difference), percentage or any other useful method you can think of. Work this out in rough first. Then, on your contents sheet, put each category as a heading and then the information from each paper in turn, clearly labelled. Deal with the papers throughout in the same order. You may wish to tackle your Group A paper first, then B, then C.

Before you start decide what you mean by the word 'news'. The dictionary defines it as 'Tidings, new or interesting information, fresh events reported', so it can be broadly applied. Decide what **you** mean by 'news' and keep to this definition throughout.

Whichever method you are using to record the comparative amounts, try to ensure that the arithmetic is fairly accurate. You must not have a total of sixty pages for a paper which only had forty, nor must you have a total of 137 per cent or 75 per cent!

ACTIVITY

1c

Coursework – Speaking and Listening

When you have finished the analysis of the contents of the three newspapers you selected in Activity B, form a discussion group with students who have been working on different newspapers. Ideally, between you, you should have covered them all.

Present your findings about each paper to the group. Comment on anything which you thought was particularly interesting or surprising.

Discuss your own and the others' discoveries and consider their significance.

   Do not get rid of your papers when you have finished this activity, you will be needing them again later.

ACTIVITY

1d

The Front Page – Reading and Evaluating

You can learn quite a lot about a newspaper by looking at its front page. Here is some information about the front pages of four different newspapers published on Friday 7 May 1993. This was the day after a by-election in Newbury and the local council elections in England and Wales.

Financial Times

1   **Layout of front page**
    The page is divided up into six blocks, of a fairly similar size. There is a 'news in brief' column, with a small financial table at the foot of it; there are four articles and an advert for a venture capital company.

2   **Photographs**
    There is one very small photograph (3cm x 4cm) of a business consultant and a fairly large photograph (15cm x 17cm) of Asil Nadir, former chairman of Polly Peck who has just absconded to Cyprus. Nadir looks relaxed and smiling.

3   **Most prominent headline**
    At the top of the page, in the largest lettering apart from the paper's title, is the headline 'Voters deliver setback to Major'. This is a reference to Tory defeats in the by- and local council elections. Other prominent headlines on the page are 'Bosnian Serbs face Belgrade supply blockade' and 'Security row over looting of bombed City buildings'.

4   **Longest article**
    This is the article about the Government's performance in the previous day's elections.

The Guardian

1   **Layout of front page**
    The page is in seven sections. There is a large central block and then other smaller sections. A guide to the paper appears above the title, there is one advert, a 'news in brief' section and four articles.

2   **Photographs**
    There is a large central photograph (25cm x 16cm) of U.N. soldiers in Sarajevo. There are two small photographs (4cm x 4cm) in the 'guide' section of people who will appear later in the paper. There is a photograph of an appealing child in the advert and there is also a small cartoon.

3   **Most prominent headline**
    The most prominent by a long way is 'Belgrade cuts supply line'. Others, in order of prominence are 'Officers admit Nadir tip-off',

'Tory Councils wiped out' and 'Virgin starts court battle and threatens BA chiefs'.

4   **Longest article**
By far the longest article is the one which, accompanied by the large photograph, occupies the central block of the page. This is about the crisis in the former Yugoslavia.

Daily Mail

1   **Layout of front page**
This is divided in half horizontally. In the top half is a box about a competition and one banner headline (i.e. one which is very large and dominant). The bottom half has two articles, side by side.

2   **Photographs**
There are two. One (7cm x 5cm), of a thatched cottage, is in the box about the competition because it is the prize. The other (14cm x 11cm) is of a smiling Asil Nadir. Both photographs are in colour.

3   **Most prominent headline**
Even larger than the paper's title is the banner headline 'Major's night of disaster'. The others, in order of prominence are 'Nadir: why I jumped bail' (white writing on a black background) and, in colour 'Win this dream cottage'.

4   **Longest article**
The article about the Tory's defeat in the elections is just longer than that about Asil Nadir. The *Mail* boasts of an exclusive interview with him so this is given nearly as much space.

The Sun

1   **Layout of front page**
There is one large box with a slim column down the left hand-side of the page. There is also a small box inserted into the red band across the top where the paper's title is displayed.

2   **Photographs**
There are three, all in colour. The smallest (3cm x 5cm) is of Asil Nadir, smiling slightly grimly. There is one (10cm x 6cm) of the Queen, smiling happily, dressed in pale green and holding a posy of spring flowers. Almost the whole width of the paper immediately below the title is taken up by the third photograph (22cm x 9cm) of Buckingham Palace lit by bright sunshine.

3   **Most prominent headline**
'Sold Out', a white on black banner headline (larger than the paper's title) occupies the centre of the front page. This refers to the success of advance booking by the public to visit Buckingham Palace when it is opened to the public.

4   **Longest article**
The article about Asil Nadir which is in the column at the left of the page is just a little longer than the one about the Queen's successful fund-raising through the opening of the Palace. The *Sun's* article on the absconding businessman also claims to be an 'exclusive'.

When you have read about these front pages, consider these questions:

a   What are the main differences between the front pages described above?
b   What do these differences tell you about the papers' readers?

Now carry out the same analysis using the newspapers which you were looking at earlier. Deal with each one in turn, using these headings:

a   layout of front page
b   photographs
c   most prominent headline
d   longest article
e   approximate total number of words on the page.

ACTIVITY

1e

Coursework – Speaking and Listening

When you have finished Activity D you can again discuss your findings with a group of other students.

If you were using the *Guardian*, *Daily Mail* or the *Sun*, did you find that there were similarities between your edition and the one for 7 May 1993?

Discuss the main differences between the front pages which you and other members of the group have been looking at. Again think about the likely readers of each.

ACTIVITY

1f

Inside Pages – Reading and Evaluating

There are several other aspects of your chosen newspapers which need to be investigated.

Headlines

Turn to the inside pages of each of your newspapers in turn. Find **three** headlines from each one which you feel to be typical.

From the editions of 7 May, I might have chosen these from the *Guardian*:

● Heads spurn ploy to beat tests boycott
● Poverty link to unwanted pregnancies
● Watery grave foils Haynes

These from the *Daily Mail*:

● Brussels sprouts the curve-free cucumber
● What is Tony Bonnet's big secret?
● How Kyra tamed mighty Matador

And these from the *Sun*:

● Vodka hell of John, 8
● I love to drive rude men mad
● Kev's bugged off

Look carefully at the headlines above, and answer the questions below:

a   Could you tell, without knowing, which paper each came from? If so, how?
b   Do you know what the article would be about in each case?
c   How is the writer trying to persuade you to read on?

Look at the language used. Often the same first letter will be repeated, for example, 'beat . . . boycott', 'Curve . . . cucumber'. This makes it sound neat and catchy. Sometimes there may be a play on words, for example, 'Brussels spouts' or a word may be used which suggests something about the sort of article to follow, for example, 'big secret', 'vodka hell' give a hint of drama or scandal.

Now look at the headlines that you have chosen and answer questions a, b and c with reference to them.

Common News Items

Choose an item of news that is covered in the **inside** pages of each of the newspapers.

You are going to look at the way this article is written. Here is an example taken from the editions of 7 May. The articles are about Richard Branson's conflict with British Airways.

The Headline

The *Guardian*: 'BA spurns peace – so Branson goes to law'
Daily Mail: 'Virgin and BA battle flares up'
The *Sun*: 'Branson sues BA for "2 tricks"'

Content

Is it detailed, covered at length or what?

The *Guardian* gives half of page 15 to this article. Its length is about 1400 words. The background is fully explained and the current situation is discussed. It is both detailed and long.

The *Daily Mail* gives the article about one third of a column on page 54. It is about 140 words in length. The present situation is briefly explained and a statement from Branson is quoted. It is short, with little detail.

The *Sun* allocates the article about a quarter of a column at the bottom of page 2. Its length is about 100 words. There is a short statement about the dispute and a suggestion that BA attempted to buy Branson's silence. It is very short with virtually no detail.

Sentence Length

Quote the first sentence and count the number of words. For example, the *Guardian*: 'The row that has simmered between Virgin Atlantic and British Airways since January's High Court libel case boiled over yesterday.'(20 words)

Daily Mail: 'War has broken out again between Richard Branson's Virgin and British Airways.' (12 words)

The *Sun*: 'Airline boss Richard Branson yesterday said he is suing British Airways for its alleged "dirty tricks campaign".' (17 words)

Words Chosen

Look at the words in the sentences quoted and try to make some observations about them. Are they simple or complex, factual or dramatic, or what?

In the *Guardian's* sentence, the argument is described like a pan of water which has been simmering but is now boiling over. This livens up the statement. The words used are straightforward and familiar but references are made to the High Court and the libel case. The *Daily Mail's* short sentence is much more dramatic. Here the argument is described as 'war' and the word 'again' makes it clear that this is not new. It sounds very blunt. The language is very simple. The *Sun*, on the other hand, uses words that are emotive, i.e. which are intended to arouse the reader's feelings – 'suing', 'dirty tricks'. Branson is described as the airline's 'boss'. His statement is being quoted and thus the piece is personalised from the start. The words are simple but active – 'said', 'is suing'.

Other Words

Look at the words used elsewhere in the articles you have chosen. Are the words generally long (three or more syllables) or short?

In the *Guardian* story on Virgin and British Airways there was a high percentage of long but relatively familiar words, for example, 'infringement', 'confidential', 'documentary'.

The *Daily Mail* also used many of the same words plus 'regulatory' and 'jurisdiction'. As the whole article is so much shorter, the effect is rather different. There is no need to read hundreds of such words, just a few.

The *Sun* again used some of these words and frequently used strongly emotive words, for example, 'hacked' into computer records, 'poach' passengers, 'rivals', 'fallen out'.

Tone

If you read your chosen articles aloud, would you sound as if you were presenting factual information, or would you sound concerned, excited, outraged or what?

In the case of the *Guardian* of 7 May, the impression would be of factual information. The *Daily Mail's* tone is more excited and the *Sun's* is very dramatic and personal.

Response

How would someone feel who has read your chosen article? Would they feel that some action should be taken because of what is described?

If you had read the *Guardian's* article of 7 May you would probably feel you knew a lot about the situation and that you could give a good account to others. After reading the *Daily Mail's* and the *Sun's* account you might feel that something exciting had happened, but that you didn't quite understand what.

With the common news item that you have chosen, carry out the same analysis of how the three papers write about it. You should look at the following things:

- the headline;
- the content – is it detailed, covered at length or what?
- sentence length – quote the first sentence and count the number of words;
- the words chosen – look at the words in the sentence quoted and try to make some observations about them. Are they simple or complex, factual or dramatic, or what?
- the other words – look at the words used elsewhere in the article. Are the words generally long (three or more syllables) or short?
- response – how would someone feel who had read the article? Would they feel that some action should be taken, and if so, what action, and by whom?

Bias

Look generally through each newspaper and decide whether you think it supports one particular political party.

In order to come to a conclusion read articles concerned with government policies and decisions. Is the paper for or against? Also look at articles about opposition parties' politicians and policies. What is the paper's attitude to them? Is its attitude consistent throughout the paper?

Is the paper more interested in the personalities involved in politics than the policies themselves? Is it trying to tell the reader what to think? This could be obvious but it could be subtle, so look carefully.

Write down the conclusions you have come to in each case. Refer to and quote from the articles that are relevant.

ACTIVITY

1g

Coursework – Speaking and Listening

Choose one fairly short article (about 200 words) which you think is typical of each of your three newspapers. This time they do not have to be about the same subject.

You are going to read your article aloud, onto a tape, or to your tutor or to a small group of fellow students. You may decide which will be most convenient.

First read your chosen articles silently but think about their tone. You will need to read them aloud in a suitable way. Practise on your own until you feel that you are ready to read them aloud. You should make the differences between the newspapers obvious by the way you do this.

When you have read each one aloud, you could make a statement about what you were trying to achieve. If you are working in a group, you can discuss this at the end once all the articles have been read aloud.

ACTIVITY

1h

Coursework – Writing

The information that you have obtained can now be written up neatly as a piece of coursework.

This is your title: 'A Comparison of Three Newspapers'. You should then list the ones that you looked at. Use the headings that you have been using during the previous activities and under each, deal with **each paper in turn and in the same order**. You should cover:

- the content
- the front page
- inside pages, including headlines, written style of a common news item, bias, typical article (i.e. the one used in Activity G).

Also, you must come to an **overall conclusion** in which you suggest what sort of people might read each paper, what they read it for (for example, entertainment, education) and also whether you think it is good value for money.

Drafting and Revising

As always, make sure that you have included everything necessary. Refer closely to what the papers say, including short quotations to illustrate your points, especially when you are talking about written style. Revise the content of your work if necessary. Make sure that you are clearly showing the differences between the newspapers.

Make sure, too, that your work is accurate. Check your spelling and punctuation before you hand in a final draft. Put your name, the title and the date of writing at the top.

ACTIVITY

1i

Writing – Coursework or Examination Practice

The following pieces of written work may be done at your own pace with the option of drafting and revising as necessary. The work would then be suitable for your coursework folder.

Alternatively, if you wish to practise for the examination, you may write them in a restricted time. Allow yourself no more than one hour to do these (i.e. thirty minutes each).

Newspaper Articles

Write two newspaper articles of about 200 words each: one should be appropriate for the broadsheet newspaper that you have studied in

Activity B, the other should be suitable for the tabloid newspaper also studied in Activity B. Decide which of those two papers you are writing for.

You may write about the same subject in each, merely changing the style **or** you may write about two different news items. These can be real current topics or can be invented by you. Give each article a suitable headline.

The purpose is to demonstrate your understanding of and ability to use the language and tone typical of these newspapers.

Drafting and Revising

Coursework

If you are writing these pieces for coursework you should read your first drafts critically when you have written them. Check that the content of your articles is appropriate and that the way you have written them sounds authentic. If not, rewrite them until you are satisfied. Also look at the accuracy of your work. Improve spelling and punctuation as necessary.

When you have finished, attach the pieces together. Put a general title 'Newspaper Articles', your name and the date of writing at the top.

Examination Practice

If you are writing with a time limit it is obviously impossible to write more than one draft. You should have jotted down a few points before you started, to organise your thoughts. When you think you have finished, read your work carefully trying to get rid of any spelling and punctuation errors. Write 'Newspaper Articles', your name and the date at the top.

Review of Unit 1

- Activity A was reading, research and information retrieval (En 2, 3).
- Activities B and D were reading and evaluation (En 2.2, 4).
- Activities C, E and G were speaking and listening coursework using non-literary material (En 1 and En 2.2, 4).
- Activities H and I were written coursework in response to a non-literary text (En 2.2, 4 and En 3).

Making a Record

Now find your Coursework Index Form and write down all the relevant information. Write down the number and the piece according to how many you have done and put the chapter, unit and activity number for reference. In the next column write the date and put a title or brief description. Then, in the final column list the ATs covered. The relevant activities here are the individual and group oral work in Activities C, E and G and the written work in Activities H and I.

Then tick the relevant aspects of En 1, En 2 and En 3 on your Coursework Checklist.

What Should You Do Now?

The other units in this chapter are as follows.

Unit 2 – A Woman's Place

This looks at the role of women in British society. It examines traditional and alternative views through a variety of sources.

Unit 3 – A Worthwhile Cause?

In this unit two very different situations are looked at and various courses of action are assessed. One is about a listed building and the other about the conflict in the former Yugoslavia.

Unit 4 – Mix and Match

This unit asks you to examine the issue of marriages that involve class, cultural or racial differences, considering what is or is not a sound basis for a long term relationship.

Unit 5 – Save the Planet

The unit deals with two situations where the natural environment is being threatened. One looks at an English woodland, the other examines the issue of whale hunting.

Turn now to the one that sounds most interesting.

UNIT (**2**) **A Woman's Place?**

In this unit you should do Activities A to E. After that, you may complete all the rest of the activities or you may select one or two more which look particularly interesting. If you prefer, however, you may turn to another unit after completing Activity E.

Whatever your views about 'women's liberation' and the feminist cause, these days, in Britain, most people would regard the idea of a woman's place being just in the home as untrue – or would they?

ACTIVITY

(**2a**)

Writing a Questionnaire

Draw up a list of questions about housework.

Your first question should be about the age, sex, religion and ethnic background of the person who is answering. You should then include questions about who does the cooking, cleaning and child-care. It would be a good idea to include some questions about 'technical' jobs like fitting washers on taps, wiring plugs and perhaps gardening. You will need to think of about ten questions in total.

Make sure the wording is clear and easy to understand. Avoid asking biased and leading questions such as 'You think women should do all the cooking, don't you?' Try to ask specific questions related to the person you are questioning, about how things are done in that household, rather than questions of principle or belief. As a final question you may wish to ask 'Do **you** think a woman's place is in the home?'

It is much easier to analyse your results if you give various alternatives for answers (for example, 'How often do **you** vacuum the carpets: once a week? once a month? once a year? never?') rather than leaving questions open-ended.

You may wish to discuss with your tutor, or with other members of your group, the best possible wording and the most effective order for your questions. Once you're happy, start gathering answers – see below.

ACTIVITY

(**2b**)

Coursework – Speaking and Listening

Asking the Questions

If you are asking your questions in class, the tutor can assess this as part of your speaking and listening coursework.

If you are not limiting this to your English class, decide how many people you need to ask. Try to have an equal number of males and females, various ages and a mixture of ethnic backgrounds if this is possible. They can be friends, other students at college, or colleagues at work. You probably don't want to stop total strangers in the street. However if you do plan to do this you should work out what you will say before you start to ask your questions – for example, 'I am carrying out a survey on housework for my English course. Would you mind if I ask you some questions?'

When you have interviewed enough people, you need to look at your results. You certainly need to know the sex of the person who answered each question. You may also think other factors such as age and ethnic background may make a difference. Be careful, though, they may not. Perhaps a young male is just as likely to think his wife should do all the cleaning and child-care as an older one.

Follow up Discussion

Discuss your findings with a group of about four other people. A larger group makes it more difficult for everyone to give an opinion. In a group discussion you may wish to choose a 'group leader' whose job is to keep the discussion going.

In addition to the material you have gathered, you may also wish to discuss the following points:

- German housewives staged a day's strike a few years ago in support of their claim that the state should pay them for work in the home. Do you think that government should pay women to stay at home?
- Whichever partner is at home more of the time should do the majority of the housework. Do you agree?
- It has been said that, after money, housework is the most common cause of rows between couples. Does that surprise you?
- Two fifths of women questioned in a survey said that they did not want their husbands to do housework as they didn't do it properly. What is your opinion?

ACTIVITY

2c

Writing – Examination Practice

Choose one of the alternatives (1 or 2) below for a piece of written work. It is quite likely that you may come across activities like this in the written examination. Spend no more than **one hour** on the option you have chosen.

Option 1

Write two short articles (about 200–250 words each) for a newspaper or magazine. Each should use the title 'Grounds for Divorce?' but they should be from the opposite points of view.

Here is some specific guidance:

- One article should be from a female, one from a male viewpoint (this need not be the traditional one, however).
- The two should have opposite views on housework and consider the actions of the other person to be unreasonable.
- Each should express ONE line of argument really strongly. Obviously you are having, therefore, in one of the articles, to construct and express an argument which you yourself don't agree with.
- Try to make this sound realistic. Look in Chapter 6, Unit 5 for guidance on how to write newspaper articles.

Option 2

Use the same title as above but this time write a piece of dialogue. It could be set out like a play (see Chapter 6, Unit 6) or as a conversation written in direct speech (see Chapter 6, Unit 4).

It should be between two men or two women who hold opposing views on this subject. Try to make it realistic. You may use slang and dialect words in the characters' speeches but do make sure you still spell accurately. If you're a 'Smith and Jones' fan, you might think about Griff and Mel's 'head to head' discussions as a model for your work. It doesn't have to be humorous, of course.

Be especially careful about punctuation. Many students make punctuation errors when writing conversation – check and double check.

Drafting and Revising

When you feel you have finished, check your work through. You are unlikely to have time to write a second draft but correct any spelling and punctuation errors. Write the title 'Grounds for Divorce', your name and the date at the top.

ACTIVITY

2d

Examining Traditional Views

Divide a piece of A4 paper into two columns, one headed 'male' and the other 'female'.

1 List five toys in the 'male' column that would often be played with by boys and five in the 'female' column that would be played with by girls.
2 If a little girl was angry with her friend, what would she say and do? Think of three or four 'typical' ways of behaving and put them in the 'female' column. List what a boy would do in the same situation in the other column.
3 If a boy hurts himself and cries, what might be said to him? List the possibilities in the 'male' column. Put what would be said and done to a little girl in the 'female' one.
4 List five jobs traditionally associated with men in the 'male' column and five traditionally female ones in the other column.

Look critically at the columns. How far are the differences you have found because of real physical or mental differences between males and females? How far is it just tradition? Discuss your thoughts on this with other class members if this is possible.

Look at your answers to (4). By asking other people to make suggestions, increase the length of your list.

In each case, assess to what extent there is any justifiable reason for the job to be associated with only one sex. Try to think of examples of people who have been very successful in an area which is usually thought to be the preserve of the opposite sex – female prime ministers are an obvious example. Perhaps you know someone to whom this would apply. Again, discuss your thoughts on this with other people, friends if not class members.

Would it be better to break down traditional ideas and have a member of either sex doing any job? Think of plenty of reasons for your answer.

As with the Speaking and Listening coursework following your survey, this discussion may be assessed by your tutor.

ACTIVITY

2e

Reading and Response

Read the following extract from *Equal at Work?* by Anna Coote then complete the assignment which follows. This activity is similar to what might appear in the written examination at the end of your course. The article given below is longer than any you would be given in an examination, so if you are using this activity for examination practice take as long as you wish in reading the article but restrict yourself to the times given for answering the questions that follow it.

Equal at Work?
Barbara . . . might not have thought of engineering if she hadn't come across a newspaper report about a new scheme for training technician engineers. It was a four-year apprenticeship. [Most training schemes call for at least four 'O' levels, including Maths and a Science.] Barbara had all the necessary qualifications. [She had nothing to lose so she thought she would give it a try.] . . . 'I have the sort of brain that visualises things in pictures,' she said. 'I'm good with my hands. I've always done well at craft – I have my own loom and still do a lot of weaving. When my sister and I were young she was good at dismantling clocks and other gadgets, and I usually managed to put them back together in the right order.' The report listed seven companies which operated the new training scheme. Barbara wrote to them all. Three failed to reply. Three said they didn't take girls. [As this was before the Sex Discrimination Act of 1975 came into force.] Marconi, however, invited her to their Chelmsford factory for an interview and offered her an apprenticeship on the spot.

When her friends heard the news, they all fell about laughing. 'Typical,' they said. 'Trust Barbara.' Some of her teachers thought it gave the school an unfavourable image to have girls turning down university places. Her parents thought it a bit weird, but were used to surprises from

Barbara and allowed her to go her own way. [Her father remarked, 'I don't care what you do as long as you're happy – because you're going to make my life hell if you're not!']

At the time she had no idea how unusual it was for a girl to train as an engineer. The report had been written by a woman and referred to 'young people' not boys. She got quite a shock when she walked in on the first day. 'It was just a sea of male faces. Two hundred adolescent boys, all staring with open-mouthed astonishment and nudging each other – "What's she doing here?"'

In the first year the apprentices divided their time between the technical college in Chelmsford and the training centre at Marconi. At college they studied physics, the principles of electricity, maths, elementary mechanics – all the theoretical aspects of engineering. At the training centre they were taught the basic methods of machine operation – turning, grinding, welding, sheet metal work, wiring and assembly. 'I think,' says Barbara, 'if I were more domesticated I might get the same satisfaction out of making a cake. You take a lump of metal, put in on a machine and make it into something. You can take it home to your Mum and say, "Look what I did!" When I was on sheet metal work I made a little jug from scraps of copper and brass. My Mum keeps it on her mantelpiece. When I was doing engraving and welding I made my Dad a perpetual calendar, one of those cylindrical gadgets with a knob each end to adjust the date. He still has it on his desk in the office. '

She was living in digs in Chelmsford and going home to Colchester at the weekends. It was very cold that first winter, the machine work was sometimes backbreaking and her apprentice's wage was barely enough to live on. There were consolations, however. She was fascinated by what she was learning; her parents sent food parcels; and she had bumped into Trevor Stephens, who was following a student apprenticeship at another Chelmsford company. They started going out together and married the next summer. . . .

In the last three years of her apprenticeship, Barbara spent half of each academic year at college and the rest of the time at Marconi, moving about from one part of the factory to another. In each department she was posted with a supervisor who taught her to do one or more specific jobs. In the Development section, for instance, where they were constructing a large rig, Barbara had to make a technical drawing of one component for the rig, then go into the workshop next door and make it up on a lathe. At the same time she was encouraged to learn as much as possible about the work that was going on around her.

The men on the shop floor were wary of her at first. Some found it hard to believe that a girl could operate a lathe. Others were certain she'd complain as soon as she got her hands dirty. It took them a few days to adjust to the idea that she was just as competent as the average boy. Gradually she ceased to be a curiosity and became simply 'the apprentice'. But before that happened, there was one more hurdle to clear: the inevitable. 'Every time you go into a new workshop there's one bright spark who tries to pick you up. You can sense the danger signals – everybody pricks up their ears. Men on the shop floor have a tart and angel complex. You're either one or the other. You have to make it clear right from the beginning that you're there because you want to do the work, and you're not interested in other propositions. If you have even one or two mild flirtations they'll all think you're easy game, and things could get very awkward for you. It's grossly unfair, but it's something I've learnt to live with.'

At college she spent more time with her fellow apprentices. There she encountered a different kind of problem. [Having done A levels,] she was two years older than most of them and it wasn't easy to make friends. 'Boys of 16 and 17 have two main interests – football and food. There comes a point where you run out of things to talk about. It might have been better if I'd been to a mixed school. An all-girls school is no place to learn how to deal with teenage boys who don't want you around in the first place. Maybe it would have been easier if I'd known more about football, or if I'd been a dunce.'

Far from being a dunce, she was bright, articulate and always near the top of the class. The lecturers tended to pick her out to answer questions and the boys made their resentment clear. 'Sometimes when the atmosphere was bad I deliberately gave the wrong answer. It was easier that way.'

When she did well in the annual exams, the boys responded by sending her to Coventry for two or three days. 'In the second and third years I came top in workshop technology – that's the theory of machine work – THE male preserve. If it had been maths it wouldn't have been so bad, but this was beating them on their own ground. It was just like going out and scoring goals on their own football field!'

There were evenings when she went home vowing to give it all up. But by the following morning the prospect always seemed brighter. After all, she loved the work, especially her postings at the factory. She had plenty of support from the training officers at Marconi who were glad to have a girl on the course. 'I suppose they realised that a girl wouldn't go in for engineering unless she was really keen, whereas most boys are pushed into it just as girls are pushed into shorthand and typing.'

Barbara spent the last six months of her apprenticeship in Marconi's printed circuit board plant – a small self-contained unit where they manufacture the boards on which electronic circuits are mounted. The work is fairly specialised, involving high-precision drilling, photographic processes and silk screen printing. The plant is quieter and the work cleaner than in some other parts of the factory, and the atmosphere is friendly with everyone on first-name terms. As soon as Barbara finished her apprenticeship, she applied for a job there as Production Engineer – and she was still there when I met her four years later.

Equal at Work? Women in Men's Jobs, Anna Coote

Questions

Section A

Answer all these questions as fully as possible. Spend no more than 30 minutes on this.

a   What do you think is meant by 'tart and angel complex'?
b   What is the meaning of the phrase 'to send someone to Coventry'?

c   Why do you think Barbara applied for an apprenticeship in engineering in the first place? Find evidence from the passage.
d   What difficulties did she face and how did she overcome them?
e   What were her rewards?
f   What sort of job did Barbara eventually get at Marconi? Comment on
any aspects of this which you think may be significant.

Section B

Spend about 30 minutes on **each** of these questions.

a   Write Barbara's entry in her diary for one day during her apprenticeship.
b   Imagine that Barbara was going to give advice to a young woman
who was about to start a job in a traditionally male preserve. What
would she say? You may set out your answer as a speech given by
Barbara or as a dialogue, set out like a play script, between Barbara
and the other young woman.

Drafting and Revising

Because of the time limit you will only be able to write one draft of these
answers. You should read your work through carefully to check your
spelling and punctuation, however.

What Should You Do Now?

You may choose which further activities to complete from this unit. If you
prefer, you may turn to another unit now. Check at the end of this unit to
see what you have achieved. Keep a record of what you have done.

ACTIVITY

2f

Coursework – Writing in Response to a Media Text

Obtain a video-recording of the film *Thelma and Louise* and watch it carefully. When it is finished, answer the following questions:

1   What are the two women like at the beginning of the film? Write a
short description of each.
2   How does Darryl, Thelma's husband, behave towards his wife? What
does he expect of her?
3   How do the women change in the course of the film? Why?
4   List as many examples as you can remember of the women behaving
in a way that could be described as the opposite of the feminine
stereotype.
5   List examples of men behaving in a non-macho way; for example, by
showing emotions such as fear.
6   Write down your own feelings at the end of the film.

Choose **one** of the following for a piece of written coursework.

1   Diary. Choose to be either Thelma or Louise and write five or six
entries from her diary. Start at the beginning of the film or perhaps

just before that. Select significant episodes to write about which show how the characters change. If you are writing as Louise you can write about how Thelma is changing and vice versa.

2   Write Darryl's statement for the police where he describes his wife and their marriage.

3   Write the letter which Thelma might have written to Darryl just before the film's action ends.

4   Write a review of the film (see Chapter 3, Unit 3, Activity D).

Drafting and Revising

When you have written a first draft, read it through checking both the CONTENT and the ACCURACY. Revise your work as necessary then hand it in with your name, a title, 'response to a media text' and the date of writing at the top.

ACTIVITY

2g

Reading and Analysis

For this Activity I would like you to collect the lyrics of popular love songs. If you are working with a group of other students you will quickly collect quite a large set. You won't need entire lyrics. Just a few verses will do. Write out the lyrics you have chosen and then sort them into two groups: those where the singer is male and is addressing or describing a female love, and those where the singer is female and is addressing or describing a male love.

1   Draw up a table of two columns; one column headed 'descriptions of males', and the other 'descriptions of females'. Then note down all the words used in lyrics which indicate the gender of the person being described. For example 'peaches and cream' as a description of complexion is rather unlikely to appear in the list for males, and 'leader of the pack' is rather unlikely to appear in that for females.

2   Now look more closely at the lyrics. What do they say about the proper behaviour for male loved ones as described by females, and female loved ones as described by males. For example are the women supposed to be dependable and compliant, and the men supposed to be rugged and masterful ?

ACTIVITY

2h

Coursework – Writing in Response to Literature

The Ram

He jangles his keys in the rain
and I follow like a lamb
His house is as smokey as a dive.
We go straight downstairs to his room.
I lie on his bed and watch him
undress. His orange baseball jacket,

all the way from Ontario,
drops to the floor – THE RAMS, in felt
arched across the hunky back.
He un-zips his calf length
Star-walkers, his damp black Levi's,
and adjusts his loaded modelling-pouch:
he stands before me in his socks –
as white as bridesmaids,
little daisies, driven snow.
John Wain watches from the wall
beside a shelf-ful of pistols.
Well, he says, d'you like it?
All I can think of is Granny,
how she used to shake her head,
when I stood by her bed on Sundays,
so proud in my soap smelling
special frock, and say, Ah,
Bless your little cotton socks!

New British Poetry, Selima Hill

Read the poem 'The Ram' and answer the following questions:

a   What does 'downstairs' tell you?
b   Why 'The RAMS'? What is the associated image?
c   What impression do we get from the words 'bridesmaids', 'daisies', 'driven snow'?
d   What's the significance of John Wain and the pistols?
e   What effect will her comment have on him?

Now write about the poem making sure that you cover the following points as thoroughly as possible.

● What is actually happening in the poem? Give a brief account.
● What is he like? How does he want to be thought of by a girlfriend? Pick out particular words and phrases as 'evidence' for your answer.
● Is she behaving and reacting – traditionally? – as he wants her to?
● What do you think his reaction would be to what she says about his socks?
● Does the poem look at male and female roles in a conventional way?

Drafting and Revising

Write down your thoughts about the points above and then read your answer carefully. Have you tackled all the issues thoroughly? Have you referred to the poem to support your arguments? Have you expressed yourself clearly and written accurately?

Revise your work as necessary. When you are happy with it, write it out neatly and submit it for assessment. You should put your name, the date of writing and 'Work in response to literature – The Ram by Selima Hill' at the top.

Reading and Response

The National Curriculum specifies that students read material which was written earlier than this century. *Jane Eyre* by Charlotte Bronte was first published in 1847. She used the pseudonym 'Currer Bell' because men were more acceptable as novelists! Other female writers in the nineteenth century used male names. See if you can find out who they were.

Jane Eyre has had a strict and conventional upbringing and, as a poor, plain governess could easily be regarded as unimportant. Often, in the book, she is seen to possess remarkable courage in speaking up for herself. In this extract she believes that she must leave Thornfield as her employer, Mr Rochester, with whom she has fallen in love, is to marry the beautiful Blanche Ingram. Remember, in those days, women, like children, were supposed to be 'seen and not heard'!

Extract from *Jane Eyre* by Charlotte Bronte

The vehemence of emotion, stirred by grief and love within me, was claiming mastery, and struggling for full sway, and asserting a right to predominate, to overcome, to live, rise, and reign at last: yes – and to speak.

'I grieve to leave Thornfield: I love Thornfield: I love it, because I have lived in it a full and delightful life – momentarily at least. I have not been trampled on. I have not been petrified. I have not been buried with inferior minds, and excluded from every glimpse of communion with what is bright and energetic and high. I have talked, face to face, with what I reverence, with what I delight in – with an original, a vigorous, an expanded mind. I have known you, Mr. Rochester; and it strikes me with terror and anguish to feel I absolutely must be drawn from you for ever. I see the necessity of departure; and it is like looking on the necessity of death. '

'Where do you see the necessity?' he asked suddenly.

'Where? You, sir, have placed it before me.'

'In what shape?'

'In the shape of Miss Ingram; a noble and beautiful woman – your bride!'

'My bride! What bride? I have no bride!'

'But you will have.'

'Yes – I will! – I will!' He set his teeth.

'Then I must go – you have said it yourself.'

'No: you must stay! I swear it – and the oath shall be kept.'

'I tell you I must go!' I retorted, roused to something like passion. 'Do you think I can stay to become nothing to you? Do you think I am an automaton? – a machine without feelings? and can bear to have my morsel of bread snatched from my lips, and my drop of living water dashed from my cup? Do you think, because I am poor, obscure, plain, and little, I am soulless and heartless? You think wrong! – I have as much soul as you – and full as much heart! And if God had gifted me with some beauty and much wealth, I should have made it as hard for you to leave me, as it is now for me to leave you. I am not talking to you now through the medium of custom, conventionalities, nor even of mortal flesh: it is my spirit that addresses your spirit; just as if both had passed through the grave, and we stood at God's feet, equal – as we are!'

Having read the extract carefully, answer these questions.

a   Apart from her love for Mr Rochester, what else seems to have made Jane love Thornfield?

b   What arguments does Jane use in the final paragraph to say that she doesn't deserve to be treated cruelly by Mr Rochester? Would you describe these as 'feminist' arguments?

c   Read the last paragraph aloud with as much feeling as possible. How does Bronte's choice of words and sentence structure convey the strength of Jane's feelings? Look, for example at the length of sentences and the use of questions and exclamation marks.

ACTIVITY

2j

Optional Further Reading and Coursework in Response to Literature

To be acceptable as coursework, a piece of 'response to literature' should be written after reading the whole work, not just an extract. If you have time, read the novel *Jane Eyre*. You should be able to borrow it from your local library or buy it quite cheaply in paperback.

Here are some assignments which would be suitable for coursework. Attempt **one** of them.

1   Write an eye-witness account, as Georgiana Reed, Eliza Reed or one of the servants, of Jane's encounter with John Reed in Chapter 1. Try to convey the attitude of the onlooker – i.e., whose 'side' he or she would be on.

2   Write a magazine article, based on a supposed interview with Jane, about her life and the lessons she learnt from what happened to her. Try to convey an impression of her personality. Show how she changed as she grew up and matured.

3   In many ways, in chapters 37 and 38, there is a reversal of roles. You may wish to discuss this with your tutor. Write about this role reversal, discussing fully what effect it has on our perception of the characters involved and our sympathies for them.

Drafting and Revising

As always, read your work through carefully, checking both content and accuracy. When you are satisfied that your work is as good as possible, write it out neatly, put the date of writing, your name, work in response to *Jane Eyre* by Charlotte Bronte at the top. You may also wish to put a specific title depending which option you chose.

ACTIVITY

2k

Optional Further Reading – Research and Retrieval

In a library, see what else you can find out about gender and conditioning. Find out more about the most recent Sex Discrimination Act. Find out from your local college whether there are women on traditionally male training courses there and investigate whether women are doing 'masculine' jobs in local firms.

You may like to write a final piece discussing this subject generally. The unit title 'A Woman's Place?' would be suitable. Aim to write about 500 words in total.

Drafting and Revising

As always, read your work critically revising the content as necessary and checking that your work is accurate.

Review of Unit 2

- In Activity A you drew up a questionnaire.

- Activity B was speaking and listening coursework (En 1).
- Activity C was practice for the written examination (En 3).
- In Activity D you examined traditionally held beliefs.
- Activity E was examination practice in reading and response (En 2.2, En 3).
- Activity F was written coursework in response to a media text (En 2.2 and En 3).
- Activity G was reading and analysis (En 2.1, 2, 4).
- Activity H was written coursework response to literature (En 2.2, 4 and En 3).
- Activity I was reading and Activity J was optional written work both in response to literature (En 2.2, 4 and En 3).
- Activity K was optional research and information retrieval with a written follow up (En 2.3 and En 3).

Making a Record

Write down the necessary information about the coursework from this unit. This was the individual and group oral work in Activity B and the written work in Activities F, H and K. Tick the relevant aspects of En 1, En 2 and En 3 on your Coursework Checklist.

What Should You Do Now?

Turn to another unit which looks interesting.

UNIT (**3**) # A Worthwhile Cause?

In this unit two very different situations are presented for you to consider. You may wish to look at both of these, but if you wish you may choose to work on the activities in either Part 1 or Part 2.

Part 1 is about what should happen to a listed building in southern Scotland. Part 2 concerns the dilemma facing a Croatian family during the conflict in the former Yugoslavia.

ACTIVITY

(**3a**)

Part 1 – Denholm House

Reading and Understanding

Read the background information on Denholm House which will form the basis for later activities.

Background Information On Denholm House

Situated in the Border region of southern Scotland, approximately nine miles from the small town of Hawick, Denholm House was built in 1738 by the renowned architect William Adam. Part of an older building was incorporated into the structure. Other eminent architects, William Playfair, James Wardrop and Sir Robert Lorimer contributed to later alterations. The house was the principal seat of the Duke of Denholm. During the Second World War it was requisitioned as a hospital. It later became a girls' school. The school closed in 1966 because the building was said to be unfit for habitation and sufficient funds were not available for the necessary repairs. Attempts were made at this point to sell the house but no buyer could be found. The roof was removed so that rates need not be paid and the house has been uninhabited ever since. The building has category B listed status.

Current Proposals

The current proposals for the house's future are:

1   That the house should be fully restored to its original condition (the estimated cost is seven million pounds).
2   That the house should be gutted and turned into luxury flats. The cost would be undertaken by the developer and recouped when the flats were sold.

3   That the house should be dismantled and shipped to Japan to be re-erected as an example of Scottish culture. A buyer has expressed an interest in this.

4   That the house should be demolished as cheaply as possible and an alternative use found for the land.

ACTIVITY

3b

Assessing the Validity of an Argument

Strong feelings have been aroused about the future of Denholm House. The letters which follow appeared in the *Scottish Herald,* over a period of several months as the proposals listed above were in turn put forward.

Read each letter carefully then note down the answers to these questions:

1   Is the writer personally involved in the issue?
2   Is a biased argument being expressed?
3   Is the argument a reasonable one?

Letter A

Dear Sir,

As a former pupil of Mountcraig School, it was with disbelief that I read your article of 28 March concerning the proposed restoration of Denholm House.

When I was a pupil there in the 1960s the house was in an appalling condition. The wiring was archaic and giant fungi sprouted in the corners of the washrooms. It was freezing cold and draughts whistled through the badly fitting windows.

Certainly it was possible to see remnants of its original splendour. One or two rooms had wall coverings of silk damask in red or gold but this was split and tattered. The fine moulded plaster ceilings had been ruined by years of thoughtless girls flicking pats of butter at them – a popular pastime, as I remember. One dormitory had Japanese wallpaper which we delighted in drawing on or picking off. Having visited other stately homes subsequently I realise that this was probably extremely expensive handmade paper dating from the late eighteenth or early nineteenth century when it was fashionable.

In essence then, though this house was magnificent once, it was not in 1966 when Mountcraig closed down. I dread to think what nearly thirty years lying unoccupied has done. It is not worth spending a tenth of the sum proposed on trying to restore it.

Yours faithfully,

Bridget Thompson, Borthwick Farm, Peebles.

Letter B

Dear Sir,

I was horrified to read in your article of 14 August that a proposal to turn Denholm House into flats has been rejected.

Nicholas White is a most reputable architect and building restorer. The work which he undertook on Stansfield Park at Grange-over-Sands speaks for itself. The fire-damaged shell of that building was repaired and reconstructed with intelligence and skill using wholly appropriate materials and with an eye firmly on its classical simplicity. The same would doubtless have been possible here.

For Lord Denholm's architectural adviser to recommend rejection on the grounds of the project being incompatible with the building's status as a listed building is ludicrous. What does he think will happen to it now?

Not only would this have been a good way of preserving a fine piece of architecture, it would also have been a way of giving a much-needed boost to the local economy.

Yours faithfully,

J.G. Ballard, Builders' Merchant, Hawick.

Letter C

Dear Sir,

I refer to the news that Denholm House is to be dismantled and shipped to Japan. The original building is the work of Scotland's foremost architect. Other notable figures were also involved, not only with the house itself but with landscaping the grounds.

The Architectural Heritage Society of Scotland regrets that it is to be removed. According to your report today (23 November) a very substantial investment will be made in the building before it is shown to the Japanese nation as part of Scotland's social history. The interest thus being shown in Scottish architecture is very flattering.

However, as Denholm House is currently roofless and has lost most of its interiors, the building which will be constructed in Japan will be proportionally far more new than genuinely historic fabric.

The society would prefer to see a replica created from existing records on its present site rather than elsewhere. This would stand as a permanent memorial to the historic home of the Dukes of Denholm. It could then be appreciated in its true context – a designed and natural landscape of great value.

Yours faithfully,

Emily Baxter, Development Officer,
Architectural Heritage Society of Scotland, Edinburgh.

Letter D

Dear Sir,

I was disgusted by the news that a decision has been taken to demolish Denholm House. Too many fine buildings have been lost in the Border region over the years. This is just one more scandal.

I understand that the intention is to set the building on fire, burning the internal timbers in order to knock it down more easily. This seems terrible.

While I appreciate that the building is in poor condition, surely something could be done to save it. I believe an application has been made to change the building's status to category A instead of category B listing. I can only hope that this will be done in time.

It is disgraceful that so little concern is being shown by a peer of the realm for his own and our country's heritage!

Yours faithfully,

Sandy Macpherson, 14 Highcliff Road, London SW2.

If possible, discuss your answers to the questions about the letters with one or more other students.

ACTIVITY

3c

Constructing an Argument

Ideally this activity should be done in a group of at least four students. One person should choose or be assigned to one of the four proposals above. If there are more than four people, two or even three people could work together on a proposal. If you are working alone, choose one proposal.

1   Write down all the arguments you can think of **in favour of** the proposal which you are working on. You may invent supplementary information if you feel it would be helpful. You may use relevant material from any of the letters, not just the one which specifically referred to that proposal.
2   Now look at the other proposals. Write down as many arguments as possible **against** these. You will find it useful to put the proposal down in abbreviated form as a heading, for example '(2) conversion to flats', then list all the arguments against clearly underneath. You may wish to put each proposal on a separate piece of paper.
3   Looking back at each proposal and also at the information given in the letters, decide what Lord Denholm's attitude seems to be in each case. Which proposal do you think he would be most likely to favour? Which would he reject and why?

ACTIVITY

3d

Coursework – Speaking and Listening

This activity is only possible if you are working as part of a group of students.

There is now going to be a meeting to discuss the future of Denholm House. A final decision must be reached. One person should take the role of the Duke (or Duchess) of Denholm. This person will chair the meeting. One person may be the architectural adviser although this role is not essential.

This is how you will proceed: Denholm (the chairperson) will ask for each proposal in turn to be presented, starting with the first proposal given in the background details. All the arguments supporting each will be put forward by the person, or group, who have worked on it. There should be no discussion of the issues at present.

Once each proposal has been put forward, Denholm will open the meeting for discussion. Again, each proposal should be dealt with in turn but anyone can put forward arguments, either for or against. The person or team who is attempting to win Denholm's agreement should try to anticipate his or her objections. Denholm may ask questions but not express opinions yet.

When a full and fair discussion has taken place, Denholm should bring the meeting to a close. **Judging by the effectiveness of the arguments put forward**, Denholm should decide which proposal to accept and announce this to the meeting.

The discussion will be assessed by your tutor. If the equipment is available, you could video record the meeting. When you play it back you can assess how effectively you and the others involved presented your arguments both for and against the proposals.

ACTIVITY

3e

Writing – Coursework or Examination Practice

The following pieces of written work may be done at your own pace with the option of drafting and revising as necessary. The work is suitable for your coursework folder.

Alternatively, if you wish to practise for the examination, you may write just **one** of the letters and the newspaper article. Re-read the information presented in Activities A and B before you start to write. Allow yourself no more than one hour to do these (thirty minutes each).

1   **Letter in support of Denholm's decision**
    Write a letter to the editor of the *Scottish Herald* saying how pleased you are about what has been decided. Do not write as yourself but as someone who has reason to be pleased. Put forward your argument on that basis. Put an appropriate name and brief details of who you are at the end of the letter.

2   **Write a letter against the decision**
    Write a letter to the editor of the *Scottish Herald* expressing your disgust at the decision which has been taken. Put forward forceful arguments from the point of view of someone who would be likely to think this way. If you like you may propose an alternative – either one of the other options which was debated or a new idea of your own. Put an appropriate name and brief details of who you are at the end of the letter.

3   **Write a newspaper report**
    Write an article which would be suitable for a broadsheet newspaper reporting the decision that has been made about Denholm House. You should write in an objective (unbiased) way. You may talk about the meeting which was held and the alternatives which were put forward. Use an appropriate tone and style. Put a suitable headline at the top.

Drafting and Revising

Coursework

If you are writing these pieces for your coursework folder you should read your first drafts critically when you have written them. Check that the arguments in the letters are forceful and are expressed appropriately. Make sure that the newspaper article is written in a different way. Check back in Unit 1 if you can't remember how it should sound. Also look at the accuracy of your work. Improve spelling and punctuation as necessary.

When you have finished, attach the pieces together. Put a general title 'Denholm House', your name and the date of writing at the top.

Examination Practice

If you are writing with a time limit it is obviously impossible to write more than one draft. You should have jotted down a few points before you started, to organise your thoughts. When you think you have finished, read your work carefully trying to get rid of any spelling and punctuation errors. Write 'Denholm House', your name and the date at the top.

What Should You Do Next?

If you do not intend to work on Part 2 of this unit, turn now to page 239 of the unit where you will find a final activity and a statement of what you have achieved so that you can keep an appropriate record.

Part 2 – Letter From Dubrovnik

ACTIVITY

3a

Examination Practice – Reading and Understanding

Read the background information and the letter carefully and then answer the questions which follow the letter. Spend about 45 minutes on this in total.

Background Information

The Socialist Federal Republic of Yugoslavia, established immediately after the Second World War under the leadership of President Tito, consisted of six republics (Serbia, Croatia, Slovenia, Bosnia-Herzagovina, Montenegro and Macedonia). The capital city, Belgrade, was also the capital of Serbia, the largest of the republics.

During the 1970s and increasingly after the death of President Tito in 1980, much of the political power previously shared by all the republics gradually came to be centralised in Belgrade, so that many people believed that the federation was dominated by the Serbs. The Yugoslav National Army, 70 per cent of whose officers were Serbs, played a powerful part in Yugoslav life.

At the end of 1990 Croatia, the second largest republic, approached the Belgrade government, requesting constitutional changes enabling more self-determination for the individual republics; in other words Croatia wanted a greater degree of home rule. The Belgrade government refused to discuss the matter.

In the spring of 1991, for the first time since the formation of the modern Yugoslavia, Croatia held free elections in which the Croatian Democratic Party defeated the Communists. In the summer of 1991 Croatia declared itself an independent democracy, and requested international recognition as such. Within weeks, the Yugoslav National Army and Navy besieged the ancient walled city of Dubrovnik on the Adriatic, the pride of Croatia and one of the glories of Europe. Its inhabitants were unarmed and unprepared. Schools, houses, hospitals, churches and ancient monuments were systematically bombed from land and sea.

Radica's Letter

The following letter from a teacher living in Dubrovnik to her English friend records the experiences of one family.

My dear friend,

I hardly know how to write to you. Certainly you cannot imagine what life is like here in our beloved Dubrovnik.

We have been without water and electricity for the last seventy days. Can you imagine that – no heating, no light, no refrigeration? We are managing to cook spaghetti in sea water over a little wood fire, but coffee made with sea water tastes horrible!

Dubrovnik is cold, dark, desolate and hellish. To think that we used to call it the pearl of the Adriatic! The hospitals and hotels, now crammed full of refugees, are targeted night and day by our enemy. All but one of the hotels have been partially or completely bombed out, and the poor refugees from the surrounding villages shelter inside as best they can, shocked and bewildered by having no animals to care for or crops to harvest.

St. Blaise's Church, the Franciscan and Dominican monasteries, my school, the beautiful palaces on Stradun as well as thousands of ordinary houses have been either badly damaged or totally destroyed. Our house has had all its windows blown out by the shelling, and the front gate and steps are no more. Every night from the hill above the house I hear our enemies hurling down threats and insults. Several times we have been terrorised by anonymous threatening phone calls from the enemy who vow to come and cut our throats. Every night they open fire, both from the surrounding hillside above and from the sea below. Heavy artillery is positioned at the airport, trained on us. The nights seem never-ending and our fear then is stronger than our determination to survive.

You remember my nephew Pero, don't you? He lived just a few miles along the coast at Cavtat, which is under enemy occupation. He along with the rest of the men and boys from Cavtat, has been taken prisoner and sent to Montenegro. God knows what tortures they suffer!

As if all this is not enough, my friend, I have another terrible fear. My son Davor, as you know, has so far escaped this war because of his musical engagements in Italy and Germany. His band has been very successful and has been offered an extended tour. Davor says that his duty is to break the tour and to return to Dubrovnik to fight for our city. Fifteen-year-old boys in jeans and T-shirts have been called up to defend Dubrovnik and without artillery cannot succeed in holding out for much longer. Already many have been killed, blinded and maimed. A seventeen-year-old friend of Ivana, a gifted violinist, had his right hand shot off last week. She went to the hospital to see him and he wept and asked her how should he live for the rest of his life, unable to play. She was grief-stricken. Now my son wants to come back to become another casualty, and I cannot bear that he should return to lose his life and youth. Davor says why should he leave it to others to defend us – that Dubrovnik has no right to beg the United Nations for help, if its own young men shirk from defending it as best they can. Is he right, or am I?

It's so sad that today we must live like captives, waiting to be injured or slaughtered. Really we are paying a very high price to realise our desire for liberty and independence. I can only hope that this cruel war will end and that one day we shall all meet again and remember the good times. God help us and don't forget us!

We send you our love,

Radica

Once you have read the material thoroughly (at least twice), answer the following questions as fully as possible. You will probably be asked to do something similar in the examination.

a   What are the physical discomforts suffered by Radica and other inhabitants of Dubrovnik?

b   What are the psychological pressures on Radica?
c   Does Radica seem to be a strong supporter of Croatia's fight for independence? Give reasons for your answer.

ACTIVITY
3b

Constructing an Argument

You are going to concentrate now on the dilemma of whether it is right or wrong for Davor to come back to Dubrovnik and fight.

Rule a line down the centre of a piece of paper so that you have two columns. Put a heading at the top of each – on one side 'To Fight' and on the other 'Not to Fight'. Under each heading think of as many different arguments as you possibly can. Do not restrict yourself to what you personally believe, but also think of arguments which might be put forward by others – politicians, priests, teachers, pacifists, committed nationalists, etc.

ACTIVITY
3c

Coursework – Speaking and Listening

When you have thought of as many arguments on each side as you can, and if you are working in a classroom situation, discover by a show of hands, which side of the argument people support. If there is a fairly even split, find a partner who holds the opposite view to yours. If a large majority supports one side of the argument, each partner will have to agree which side he or she will represent.

One of you is going to argue on one side, one on the other. Decide who is going to present which case. It is not necessary for you to believe what you are saying but this activity would be easier if you and your partner have a genuine difference of opinion.

Debate the issue. Probably it will be best if one of you starts by presenting the arguments in favour of Davor returning to fight. Then the opposite view can be presented. After that you can discuss the issue freely, presenting as many points each as you can.

Your tutor can listen in order to assess this or it can be recorded on audio tape and assessed later. Make sure you each state your names at the beginning of the tape so that the tutor knows your identity.

ACTIVITY
3d

Writing – Coursework or Examination Practice

The following pieces of written work may be done at your own pace with the option of drafting and revising as necessary. The work would then be suitable for your coursework folder.

Alternatively, if you wish to practise for the examination, you may write the pieces in a restricted time. Re-read the information presented in Activity A **before** you start to write. Allow yourself no more than one hour to do these (thirty minutes each).

Written Work

1 Imagine that you are a reporter who has gone to Dubrovnik to gain factual information about conditions there. You have interviewed Radica. Write an objective (unbiased) newspaper or magazine article using material from her letter. You may refer to your interview, describe how she looked and behaved and quote her actual words briefly if you wish. Make this sound as realistic as possibly, both in terms of its content and also the style in which you are writing.

2 Imagine that you are Radica's English friend. Reply to Radica's letter, giving **your opinion** about what Davor should do. You may also comment on and respond to any other parts of her letter. Use an appropriate style and tone.

Drafting and Revising

Coursework

If you are writing these pieces for coursework you should read your first drafts critically when you have written them. Check with Radica's letter that the information in the article is accurate and expressed appropriately. Look back at Unit 1 if you can't remember how it should sound. Make sure that the letter sounds believable. Also look at the accuracy of your work. Improve spelling and punctuation as necessary.

When you have finished, attach the two pieces together. Put a general title 'Letter from Dubrovnik', your name and the date of writing at the top.

Examination Practice

If you are writing with a time limit it is obviously impossible to write more than one draft. You should have jotted down a few points before you started, to organise your thoughts. When you think you have finished, read your work carefully trying to get rid of any spelling and punctuation errors. Write 'Letter from Dubrovnik', your name and the date at the top.

ACTIVITY

3e

Optional Coursework – Writing

Whether you have worked on Part 1 or Part 2, you may now wish to do a final activity in this unit.

Open Space

There may be a cause which you feel strongly about, one that you think is worth fighting for, either in the military sense or through forceful argument and action. This is your opportunity to write about it.

This will be a fairly long (at least 500 words), detailed and persuasive piece of writing, the intention of which is to make the reader give support to the cause. Below is a suggested structure whatever subject you choose – and almost anything is possible from nuclear disarmament to tunnels for badgers under motorways.

Suggested Structure

1 **Present the facts.** Give detailed information about this particular cause which makes it clear that it is something worth fighting for. If necessary, research the subject in order to present as much information as possible. Put in real life examples to strengthen your case.
2 **Outline the present campaign.** Say what is being done at present in support of this cause. If it is not adequate, say so, giving reasons.
3 **Plan the future campaign.** Say what should be done in the future.

Drafting and Revising

Write a first draft and then read it through. It may be that you have written in a way which is intended to appeal to the reader's emotions. Have you distorted the facts when you were doing this? If you have, re-write this so that your information is accurate. It is easier for an opponent to counter an argument if it is not a truthful statement.

When you have adjusted this, if it was necessary, consider whether you have been sufficiently forceful and persuasive. Ask a friend to read what you have written. Would this person support your cause because of what you wrote? Again, adjust your work if necessary.

When you are satisfied with the content, make sure that you have written in correct English. Do not ignore punctuation and spelling because of the strength of your feelings. Check your work carefully.

When your final draft is neatly and accurately written, put 'Open Space' then an appropriate individual title at the top. Also put your name and the date of writing.

Review of Unit 3

In Part 1:
- Activity A was reading and understanding.
- In Activity B you assessed the validity of arguments presented in four letters (En 2.2, 4).
- In Activity C you constructed various arguments.
- Activity D was speaking and listening coursework (En 1).
- Activity E was either written coursework or examination practice (En 3).

In Part 2:
- Activity A was examination practice in reading and understanding (En 2.2, 4).
- In Activity B you compiled arguments on both sides of a question.
- Activity C was speaking and listening coursework (En 1.1, 2, 4.).
- Activity D was either written coursework or examination practice (En 3).

- Optional Activity E (relevant to Part 1 or Part 2) was written coursework (En 3) which may have involved research and information retrieval (En 2.3).

Making a Record

Write down the necessary information about the coursework from this unit on your Coursework Index Form. If you worked on Part 1 this was the individual/group oral work in Activity D and the written work in Activity E – unless you did this as practice for the examination. If you worked on Part 2, write down the information about the individual oral work in Activity C and the written work in Activity D, unless you did the latter for the examination.

If you did the optional Activity E record the information about that also. When you have done this, tick the relevant aspects of En 1, En 2 and En 3 on your Coursework Checklist.

What Should You Do Now?

Turn to another unit in this chapter or to a unit in another chapter.

UNIT

UNIT **4** *Mix and Match*

This unit is about marriage. There is some material about relationships which mix culture and religion and you will be asked to look at various case studies. You will think about differences in the ways in which different cultures view marriage and also consider different methods of finding a marriage partner.

ACTIVITY

4a

Examination Practice

This activity is similar to one which you may meet in the written examination. Spend no more than 45 minutes on it.
Read extracts A and B and then answer the questions which follow.

Extract A

I'm in love. It's the most wonderful feeling and I'm ecstatic with happiness. I never thought I'd meet someone who could cope with all my foibles and idiosyncrasies – but I did. And for once he's not the wimp who wants to give up his own life and do everything for me. He has his own career and his own mind – and expects me to have mine too. It's sickeningly fairy-tale, coated in sugar and surrounded with a Barbara Cartland haze of pink and squidgy euphoria.

You know there's a but coming up. No, he's not married. Yes, he's faithful and so am I. Neither of us is an illegal alien, registered insane or a member of the clergy.

But he is Muslim and I am Sikh. That's that. It should never have happened. If we had been thinking, we would have left each other after our first date and remained friends. Instead we became lovers and now we don't know what to do.

Neither I nor my partner believes that religion is a barrier. We are both happy with the way we are. But as one of my friends remarked, 'Your family would rather you shacked up with a baboon than married a Muslim.' He's right.

In Extract B Judith talks about the horrified reaction when she tells her Jewish family that she intends to marry Alex, a Catholic. The first Passover after she meets him is made intolerable by the unspoken reproach of her family. Alex, as a non-Jew, was not invited to the family party.

Extract B

By the time Passover came round again I was finding it almost impossible to hold a conversation with my family without breaking off in helpless, furious tears. I simply couldn't face the thought of another Seder night, so I stayed home. Soon after, my mother rang to say she missed me and wanted to see me. A turning point had been reached and the pressure slowly started to lift. Perhaps my parents felt that they really would 'lose a daughter' if they did not take some positive steps towards restoring our damaged relationship. They slowly started to take an interest in Alex. Our parents met and the meeting was polite and dignified. After three hours, a real friendship seemed to develop and the talk became relaxed, sprinkled with laughter.

We're getting married next year and most of the family will be coming. We won't need separate tables for the Jews and the Catholics, they won't be brandishing candlesticks or rosaries. Whether we have fish on Fridays or salt beef on Sundays is yet to be decided but, whatever we choose to do, it will be our decision.

When you have read the extracts carefully (at least twice) answer these questions.

a The writer of Extract A gives a number of reasons for her belief that she and her partner are well suited. List them.

b In Extract B, how does the parents' attitude change and why?

c What possible problems may arise for these two couples in the future?

d In your opinion, is one of these relationships more likely to be successful than the other? Give reasons for your answer.

ACTIVITY

4b

Reading and Understanding

Read case studies A, B and C.

Case A

Daljit's parents moved to England from Lucknow in central India in 1967. They belong to the Hindu religion. Daljit, their only child, was born here. Her father owns a chain of small supermarkets and has been very successful. She attended the local comprehensive, acquired a good range of GCSEs then opted, with her parents' full support, to study for A levels at the college nearby. There she met Ahmed who was also studying for A levels. He was also born and bred in Britain but his parents originate from Pakistan and he is a Muslim. Doing two of the same subjects, Daljit and Ahmed became friends and then fell in love. Their relationship was kept secret from both sets of parents. Daljit's parents suspected that something of this sort was happening and her father asked his brother in Lucknow to find a suitable husband. Rajiv, aged 23, a qualified accountant and son of a lawyer cousin was proposed as a possibility. A trip to India was arranged for December in the second year of Daljit's A level studies. The wedding would take place in January if both families were satisfied with the arrangements. Two days before the departure date, Daljit discovered what was planned. She and Ahmed ran away together.

Case B

Three years ago, at a party, Amanda met Vick. He was born in the Philippines and his family (Roman Catholics) moved to Britain when he was eight. He lives with his widowed mother and his five brothers and sisters in a council house; his mother works as a cleaner in a local hospital. He is a trainee technician with British Aerospace. Amanda's family are prosperous upper middle class. Her father is a History Professor at a London university, her mother a part-time interior designer. They live in a large detached house. No one in the family follows any particular religion, both parents openly declaring themselves atheists. At school, Amanda gained grade As in ten GCSEs and one A and two B grades at A level. She is now studying Archaeology at Sussex University and is in her second year. Despite her frequent absences, her relationship with Vick has continued during each of her holidays and Vick has frequently travelled down to Sussex to visit her. He says he dislikes her student friends as they are 'stuck up'. Under strong pressure from Vick, Amanda has agreed that they should get engaged, with the intention of marrying next July, as soon as her degree course has finished.

Case C

Clive is in his early forties. He is the only son of parents who were in their late thirties when he was born. They have very traditional, even old-fashioned views about life. Clive's first marriage ended in divorce and he has two children who live with their mother, who has a successful florist business. His parents were very fond of Clive's first wife, considering her to have been the perfect wife and ideal daughter-in-law. They frequently reproach Clive for the breakdown of the marriage. He lives in a small flat nearby. Despite their differences in outlook, Clive is very fond of his parents and is extremely conscious of the fact that they have no other family to look after them. His father suffered a heart attack last year and his mother is a diabetic. Six months ago he met Patricia; they have recently started living together and Clive is keen for them to marry, perhaps in a year's time. She is Afro-Caribbean and was born in Jamaica. She is a class teacher in a junior school and is currently looking out for a job as deputy headmistress. Although Clive has told his parents that he has a new girlfriend, they have not met her yet.

When you have read the extracts, make **notes** on the following:

a What information is given in each case study about the reasons for the couple being attracted to each other? If little information is given, suggest possibilities.
b What is the likely reaction of the parents on both sides in each case?
c What problems do you think each couple may face in the future?

ACTIVITY

Coursework – Speaking and Listening

In this activity you need to work with one other person who has made notes on the case studies.

Discuss your answers to the questions in Activity B. Did you come to the same conclusions? What do you think the prospects are for the long-term happiness of each couple? Are all the relationships likely to survive the pressures on them? If you think that a couple should split up, decide why. Which couple do you think is most likely to stay together? Which couple do you think is least likely to stay together? Explain why.

If your tutor can't be present while you discuss this, tape record what you say so that it can be assessed later.

ACTIVITY

4d

Writing – Coursework or Examination Practice

The following may be done at your own pace, drafted and revised and submitted as coursework. Alternatively if you have already produced a piece of coursework from 'Letter Line', (Chapter 2, Unit 2), or if you prefer, spend no more than a total of one hour and do the work under examination conditions – that is without consultation. You should re-read the relevant case study before you begin to write. If you are opting for exam practice the reading should be done within the hour allowed.

1   **Letter 1.** Choose the case study which you find most interesting. Imagine that you are either one of the couples involved or a parent. Write a letter to the 'agony aunt' in a magazine or newspaper (there's no need to specify which one) outlining the situation, explaining how you feel and asking for advice.
2   **Letter 2.** Write the reply, giving sound practical advice. You may give alternative suggestions for differing courses of action if you like. Consider the person's feelings but don't be afraid of being frank.

Drafting and Revising

Each letter should be about 250 words in length. One may be slightly longer than the other. Set them out properly so that they look like letters. In Letter 1 try to put yourself in that person's situation so that what you say sounds realistic. Try to weigh up all the courses of action possible and make sensible suggestions in Letter 2. Put the title 'Problem Page' with a reference to the relevant case study as a title. Also put your name and the date of writing at the top.

Coursework

You will almost certainly wish to write a first draft of each letter. You will then read it through carefully before making any adjustments which you feel are necessary. Think carefully about style and tone as well as accuracy. Check your spelling and punctuation. When you have written the final draft, check again.

Examination Practice

It is unlikely that you will be able to write more than one draft so try to get the content right first time. Work out a paragraph plan for each letter and think about the appropriate phrasing before you begin. If you make errors or are unhappy with a phrase, cross it through neatly and write the alternative above it. When you have finished, read your work through and check your spelling and punctuation.

Reading – Research and Information Retrieval

So far you have been looking at the prospects for relationships or marriages which cross cultural, religious or class boundaries. Let's look now at the way a relationship may start.

1   By consulting books in the library or by talking to people with personal experience, find out as much as you can about marriage customs in a culture other than your own. What is the acceptable basis for a marriage? Who proposes the marriage and whose permission must be sought? Is there a dowry? If so, who is it paid by and to whom? Look at what is done before the wedding itself and also what the ceremony consists of. What gifts are customary? What is worn by those attending?

2   Find out as much as you can about marriage arrangements among the upper classes in this country before the twentieth century. What were the most important considerations? Is everything completely different today? Find out what is meant by the term 'breach of promise'.

3   Draw up a questionnaire about marriage and ask up to twenty married friends or relations to help you by answering your questions. Here are some of the questions which you might wish to ask: How did you first meet your husband/wife? For how long did you know each other before you married? How old were you when you got married? What qualities are important in a wife/husband? Is financial security important? What is good/bad about being married?

   Think of a total of six to eight questions. Try to arrange them so that the ones which are easiest to answer are at the beginning and the harder ones are at the end. If you can offer various alternatives as answers (for example 'How did you meet – at a social event, at work, through your family?') this will make it easier for you when you look at the answers – they won't be quite as widely different from each other.

4   Draw up another questionnaire to find out about the attitudes towards marriage of your unmarried friends, relations or fellow students. Again think of between six and eight questions. You might like to ask whether they intend to marry, what age they think is best, what qualities are important in a marriage partner. Ask the same number of people to answer your questions as you asked in (4).

5   Find out the current statistics concerning marriages and divorce in this country. Among other sources you will find the annual publication called *Social Trends* very useful. You will find it in most large libraries.

Coursework – Speaking and Listening

If it is practicable, work in a group with three other students.

Each of you should choose **one** of the areas you have been researching in Activity E and present your findings to the group. After each part there can be discussion. If others in the group have found additional or different information (differences are especially likely in 3 and 4 then this can be considered. Compare your findings in 5 and consider their significance).

Coursework – Writing

A Good Marriage?

Using your research in Activity E and your discussion in Activity F to provide the information, write about how a good marriage may be achieved.

You may wish to discuss whether marriages arranged by parents are more or less likely to be successful than those based on personal attraction between the individuals involved. You may write about the qualities which seem to be most important in making a marriage successful and about the pressures which might cause it to fail. You may comment on what seems to you to be the best age for getting married and whether children are more or less likely to help to strengthen a relationship. Put in examples from your own or friends' experience to illustrate the points you are making.

Before you start to write, you should list the aspects of this subject which you intend to consider. When you have a list, decide whether some items on it belong together and naturally follow on from one another. Re-arrange the order of your items if necessary.

Now write an opening paragraph making some general statements about marriage. You may wish to refer to the statistics on the annual number of marriages and the percentage which end in divorce or to describe very briefly some of the different customs practised in different cultures. At the end of this paragraph (write no more than eight to ten lines) write a sentence which leads into the first of the points you listed above.

Go on then to present each of your points in turn, discussing them fully and giving specific examples from real marriages which you know about. Tick each point on your list when you have written about it. This will prevent you from repeating yourself.

When you have covered all the points in your list, read what you have written. Now write a final paragraph where you say how, in your opinion, a good marriage can be achieved today. Say what you think is most important and what its basis should be. Again write about eight to ten lines.

The total length should be about 500 words or two sides of A4 paper in average handwriting.

Drafting and Revising

If you have planned carefully, you should not need to revise the content radically. Perhaps your work is too short. If that is the case you perhaps should have put more aspects into your original list or you have not discussed or illustrated your points fully enough. Decide what the problem is and adjust what you have written accordingly. If your work is much longer than 500 words this may not matter provided your discussion of the subject is interesting and relevant. If you feel that it rambles and becomes tedious or perhaps moves away from the main question, you may wish to cover fewer aspects or in less detail.

As well as content, you must also check the accuracy of your work. Is your spelling correct? Have you used appropriate punctuation throughout? Look carefully at what you have written. If necessary, write your work out again. Check it through for errors. Write the title 'A Good Marriage?' at the top along with your name and the date of writing.

What Should You Do Now ?

If you wish, you may turn now to Activity I which is optional further reading. After that, look at what you have achieved. You can then make a record of it.

A further activity on this topic now follows should you wish to continue.

ACTIVITY

4h

Optional Written Coursework – Reading and Response

If you are looking for a marriage partner when you are older or if you find it difficult to meet people and form relationships, there are various ways of trying to overcome your difficulties.

Read the extract from a short story called 'The Singles Club'.

The Singles Club

When I first moved to Hertfordshire, I decided that the way to meet people and make friends was to join things. Being unattached, what I was actually looking for, if I'm completely honest, was an attractive man aged between twenty-five and fifty-five who would make me feel that there was more to life than looking forward to the state pension.

Country dancing with the Colne Folk Basket (Tuesdays at St Paul's Church Hall) yielded only two possible candidates. Both were divorced, lonely and rather plump and neither exactly made my pulses race, however energetically they 'swung their partner'.

At first sight, badminton at the Grasshill Club (they meet on Wednesdays above Fineways Supermarket), seemed more promising. There were plenty of lithe, sparsely clad males exhibiting rippling muscles and neat firm buttocks (through their snowy white shorts and expensive tracksuits, of course!). As they introduced me to their wives and told me about their girlfriends, my hopes faded. I resigned myself to concentrating on chasing the shuttlecock.

In desperation I began to scan the Lonely Hearts column in the local paper.

'Handsome male, late thirties, seeks sincere outgoing female for friendship/romance.' If he was so handsome, why did he need to advertise?

'Librarian, 29, unattached, non-smoker seeks female aged 20–40 with an interest in bird watching and classical music.' I could just picture him!

I was just closing the paper when I spotted the advert for 'Asterisk'.

'Was I,' it asked, 'interested in meeting single professional people, aged between 20 and 35, in Herts, Bucks and Beds?'

What could I say! I telephoned at once and allowed myself to be persuaded by a charming sounding individual called Simon, to come along to an introductory meeting at a nearby Sports Centre.

As the club had been founded very recently, there were not, as I had pictured, throngs of fun-seeking people, all longing to make my acquaintance. In fact, as one member had already decided to leave, there were five of us and only two were male. Never being the type to give up easily, I decided still to give the club a try and, over the weeks, its membership steadily increased – well it couldn't have got much smaller, could it? We met on Thursdays in a pub called The Golden Flagon. We went out for meals, went ice-skating, ten pin bowling and even, once, to see a ballet in The Big Top, Milton Keynes. We had company and culture. But I was no nearer finding 'Mr Right' and I was starting to get fed up. After all, I hadn't really joined Asterisk to meet lots of lively, extrovert **women**, had I?

When you have read the extract, choose one of the following as a piece of written coursework.

1   Carry on from the end of the extract. What happens is entirely up to you. The character may find a suitable partner or decide to give up altogether. It would probably be a good idea to describe an Asterisk social event where she met a man who seemed attractive. You can then decide what happened next. Work out all the details before you begin. Write at least 400 words. Try to use the same style of writing as in the original story.

2   Look at the personal or Lonely Hearts column in a local or national newspaper. Pick an advert where someone who sounds interesting appears to be looking for someone a bit like you. Write a story in which you, or a character like you, replies to the advert. You would probably include something about your initial contact with the person by letter or telephone and then describe a meeting. You must work out all the details such as where the meeting took place, how you recognised each other and what happened, both at the meeting and after it.

Drafting and Revising

You may wish to remind yourself about constructing a plot by looking back at Unit 1 of Chapter 2. Plan carefully and make your story interesting. You will almost certainly include conversation so be careful to punctuate this correctly. Check in Chapter 6, Unit 4 if you are at all unsure.

When you have finished the first draft, read it through, considering both **content** and **accuracy**. Revise as necessary. Check spelling and punctuation in the final draft before you hand it in. At the top put the title, 'The Singles Club' if you chose 1 or 'Lonely Hearts' if you chose 2. Also put your name and the date of writing.

ACTIVITY

4i

Optional Further Reading

There are so many books about marriage that a long list of titles could be suggested. Here are three which you may find interesting:

- *Pride and Prejudice* by Jane Austen (written in 1813 and readily available in a library).
- *The Bride Price* by Buchi Emecheta published in paperback by Fontana – you may find you need to order this in the library. It should be on sale in a good bookshop.
- *The French Lieutenant's Woman* by John Fowles – published in 1969 but about Victorian times. This should be readily available in a library and there are various inexpensive paperback editions available.

Review of Unit 4

- Activity A was examination practice (En 2.2 and En 3).
- Activity B was reading and understanding (En 2.2).
- Activity C was speaking and listening coursework (En 1).
- Activity D was written coursework or examination practice (En 3).
- Activity E was reading, research and information retrieval (En 2.3).
- Activity F was speaking and listening coursework (En 1).
- Activity G was written coursework (En 3).
- Activity H was optional written coursework (En 3).
- Activity I was optional further reading.

Making a Record

Write down the necessary information about the coursework from this unit on your Coursework Index Form. This was the oral work in pairs in Activity C and the individual or group oral work in Activity F. Then there was the written work in Activity D, unless you did this as examination practice – and the written work in Activities G and H.

Tick the relevant aspects of En 1, En 2 and En 3 on your Coursework Checklist.

What Should You Do Now?

Turn to another unit which looks interesting.

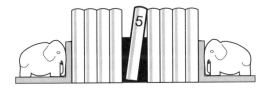

UNIT **(5)** *Save the Planet*

This unit presents two different environmental situations for you to consider. You may wish to look at both of these, but if you wish you may choose to work on the activities in either Part 1 or Part 2.

Part 1 is about a stretch of English woodland which is threatened by plans to widen a motorway. Part 2 is about the issue of whale hunting.

Part 1 – Piggotts Wood

ACTIVITY

5a

Reading and Understanding

Read the background information on Piggotts Wood.

Background Information on Piggotts Wood

Over the last ten years, the volume of traffic using the M34 motorway between Newbury and London has increased dramatically. Originally planned as a two lane road, parts of it were widened to three lanes immediately after its completion in 1974. Some parts still have only two lanes. This causes severe congestion at peak traffic hours and in the event of accidents, jams occur, resulting in long delays. The ten mile stretch between junction 10 (with the A523) and junction 11 (A578) is extremely prone to fog in the winter because of the proximity of the River Deepen which flows parallel to the motorway, two miles to the north. There are frequent accidents in this section, the worst being a multiple pile up last February in dense fog, in which nine people, including a six-month-old baby, lost their lives. A proposal to widen the road to three lanes between these junctions has been approved by the Government. Work will start in June.

To the south of the M34 in this region lies Piggotts Wood. It is a twenty square mile stretch of ancient woodland, containing mainly beech and oak trees. Records of it date back to the Doomsday Book and Henry VII had a favourite hunting lodge at Kingsbourne nearby. It is the home today of many species of flora and fauna. Badgers, deer, and owls can be found, as well as the very rare Tawny-fronted Woodpecker, Purple Fritillary (Britain's largest butterfly) and Striped Moss Beetle. In May the woods contain a profusion of bluebells. In the late summer the sharp-eyed rambler might spot the Gommbard orchid, celebrated by the poet Shelley and now found nowhere else in Britain.

When you have read this information, complete the following.

a Using the facts supplied, and adding any detail which you feel might be useful, draw a map of the area. You can assume that the M34 runs east–west and that the roads at junction 10 and 11 run roughly north–south. Make sure you include everything which is mentioned.

b List (in note form) all the arguments you can think of **in favour of** widening the road. Use all the arguments suggested in the background information. Add any further points you can think of such as the possible increase in local employment, improved efficiency in travelling to work or anything else which occurs to you.

c Now rewrite the points above into order of priority, the most important being first, the least important last.

d List (in note form) all the arguments you can think of **against** the road being widened. As with (b) add to what is provided by the background information by using your imagination – for example, consider recreational activities provided by the woodland and pollution created by the road.

e As with (c) put the arguments into order of importance.

ACTIVITY

5b

Coursework – Speaking and Listening

A public meeting about the issue is planned.

If you are working in a group with other students, the meeting can be held in class. One person should chair the meeting. This person's job is to ensure that everyone is allowed to present his or her views. The discussion must continue without it developing into a row. When everyone has had a chance to speak, and the issue has been thoroughly discussed, the chairperson should ask for a vote to see whether there is a majority in favour of the scheme to widen the road or not.

You should decide before the meeting which side you support and present the arguments which support your point of view. If it is not practical to have a meeting, prepare a statement supporting your point of view. Do not write this down and then read it out. Just make a few notes if you wish to. You can then state your views, either directly to your tutor or onto audio tape.

ACTIVITY

5c

Coursework – Writing

The following pieces of work should be collected together to form one unit of coursework: a newspaper article; a letter to the editor; materials for a campaign.

Newspaper Article

Write a factual, unbiased article for the local newspaper the *Kingsbourne Chronicle*, giving all the information about the situation. Make sure that you represent both points of view and quote statements from people involved on each side. It should not exceed 200 words.

Letter to the Editor

As a local resident, write a letter to the newspaper, responding to the newspaper article. Express, as forcefully as possible, one point of view, either for **or** against the road widening scheme. You do not have to take the same side as you did in Activity B. You may find it more interesting if you do not. Before you start to write decide exactly who you are and why you care so passionately about this issue. Write no more than 150 words.

Campaign to Save Piggotts Wood

On behalf of a local environment conservation society (give it a name), produce the following to publicise the campaign to save the Wood and drum up local support:

1 a design for a badge (use only one colour);
2 a poster (use no more than two colours);
3 a single page A4 leaflet to be distributed to households in the area (one colour only). Say what action people should take. Include the society's address;
4 proposals for action which will attract media attention. This should take the form of a letter to the secretary of the society.

Drafting and Revising

In each part of Activity C you should make your written style as effective and authentic as possible. When you are working on the campaign materials (1–3), make sure that you think about visual impact. Use pictures and different sizes of lettering to make the most important words stand out. Remember, in the leaflet, that all local residents may not find this issue equally interesting – you will need to capture their attention and tell them why it should matter to them.

Write a first draft of each then read it through carefully and critically, revising the content, structure and style as necessary. Check your spelling. Make sure place names are spelt the same as in the background information. When you are satisfied, write the final drafts of each one. Check one last time then attach the work together, with a cover sheet on top. On this write the title, 'Piggotts Wood', the date of writing and your name.

What Should You Do Now?

If you do not intend to work on Part 2 of this unit, turn now to the last page of this unit where you will find a final activity (D) and a statement of what you have achieved so that you can keep an appropriate record.

Part 2 – Whale Hunting

Reading and Understanding

Read the background information on whaling

Background Information on Whaling

At one time whaling was a massive worldwide industry, with many items such as jewellery, corsets and oil being produced. A century ago whale stocks started to decline. At the same time large factory ships were developed which could process the carcasses in mid-ocean while the boats continued to hunt for more whales. Hundreds of thousands of animals were killed every year. By the 1930s some species of whale were in danger of extinction. In 1946 an international agreement was drawn up which attempted to regulate hunting. The maximum number allowed to be killed in each species was limited by quota. However, quotas were set too high and whales were being killed faster than calves could be born to replace them. In the 1970s, a complete ban was placed on killing the blue whale as there were virtually none left. In 1900, the estimated population of this, the largest species, was 250,000; the estimate in 1993 was 500. The numbers in the other large species have also declined sharply. This has led to increased hunting of the minke whale, previously considered too small. In the 1985/86 season a moratorium (temporary ban) was declared until stocks recovered. A small number could be killed for 'scientific purposes'. The Norwegians, Icelandics and Japanese pressed for quotas for harvesting to be re-introduced.

Arguments in Favour of Whale Hunting

The countries in favour of whaling say that the number of whales is increasing. In 1993 the number of minke whales in the North-Eastern Atlantic were 86,000 with 600,000 in the Southern Ocean. One per cent per year could be killed without affecting the viability of the species. Some whales eat fish, thus competing with fishermen. Some communities in Norway depend on the fishing industry but the stocks of cod and capelin are being reduced by the whales. Quotas are set for cod fishing which severely restricts the income of some communities; whaling is necessary to allow these to survive. It is stated that the minke whales is a threat to the larger species. Food supplies are being eaten by the minkes whose population is increasing to fill the gap left by the absence of the larger types. This prevents the recovery of these larger species. Killing the minkes would therefore be beneficial to whales generally. Whales are no more intelligent than other animals and are not a special case. If the killing of whales is wrong, so, logically, is the killing of other animals too. Whaling is part of the cultural heritage of Norway and Japan. Eating whale meat has particular religious and cultural significance to the Japanese.

Arguments Against Whale Hunting

Countries against whaling question the assertions that fish stocks are being affected and that culling minkes would assist other whale species. There is little money to be made nowadays from killing whales but watching whales is a growing and popular part of the tourist industry. Few people are employed in whale hunting although Japan has specialist whale meat restaurants. The life span of a whale is naturally longer than that of a human being. They are intelligent and sophisticated creatures living in family groups. The part of the brain dealing with emotions is highly developed. Death by harpoon is not instant; it can take thirty minutes for the animal to die. Other members of the family group nearby exhibit signs of distress. Whales move extensively around the oceans therefore they cannot be considered to be the resource of one particular nation. Protection must be worldwide otherwise animals protected in one area may be killed when they migrate to another. Killing hundreds of individuals for 'scientific' purposes seems unjustified as whales are slow to mature and little can be learned about population growth by culling individuals. Other practices such as dog and cock fighting have been banned despite these having been part of a country's cultural heritage. Inhumane acts should not be condoned however traditional they may be.

When you have read the information on whaling carefully at least twice, follow these instructions.

1   Write down as fully as possible why, according to the background information, whale numbers have declined.
2   Rule a vertical line down the centre of a piece of paper. Head the left hand column 'Arguments For'. Using as few words as possible and numbering each point, write down in note form, all the arguments presented supporting whaling. Start a new line for each argument and leave a line or two in between that and the next one.
3   Head the right hand column 'Arguments Against'. Find the corresponding arguments from the passage against whaling and place each alongside the supporting one. You should now have all the arguments written on one sheet so that you can easily see them and compare them.
4   Trying to put aside whatever opinions you had about whaling before you started this unit, decide which side has presented stronger, more convincing arguments.

ACTIVITY

5b

Coursework – Speaking and Listening

Imagine that there is a radio phone-in programme on the subject of whaling.

Using arguments which you have identified in the previous activity, tape record two speeches, one supporting whaling and one against.

Rather than simply speaking as yourself, you probably want to invent a suitable character to be in each case. In the speech supporting whaling, you might speak as a Japanese person (though in English!).

Imagine that you have been asked to speak for one to two minutes in each case. You do not have to state all the arguments but should focus on the one or two which you think are strongest on each side. Do not write your speech out. Work from headings or brief notes. You may wish to make a recording, listen to it and then do it again if you are not satisfied. State your real name at the beginning or the end so your tutor can identify you. The tape should be handed in for assessment.

ACTIVITY

5c

Writing – Coursework or Examination Practice

The following pieces of written work may be done at your own pace with the option of drafting and revising as necessary. The work would then be suitable for your coursework folder.

Alternatively, if you wish to practise for the examination, you may write the pieces in a restricted time. Re-read the information presented in Activity A before you start to write. Allow yourself no more than one hour to do these (thirty minutes each).

1   The International Whaling Commission is meeting next week to decide whether to renew its ban on hunting. Write a letter to the British representative urging him to present a strong case. You may either argue **for** or **against** the whale-hunting ban, depending on your own personal point of view.

Set your letter out correctly. You will need to invent a name and address for the British representative to whom your letter is being sent. Use a polite formal style but express the arguments as effectively as possible. Do not feel you have to include them all. You should write between 200 and 250 words.

2   Write an article to be published in a women's magazine (mainly read by 16 to 25 year olds) in which you try to persuade the readers to be **against** whale hunting. Use strong arguments which will have maximum impact.

You should not write more than 250 words. Give your article an appropriate headline. If you wish, you could indicate space for a photograph, giving a brief description of what it should contain.

Drafting and Revising

Coursework

If you are writing these pieces for coursework you should read your first drafts critically when you have written them. Make sure that both pieces are expressed appropriately. Does the letter have the right tone? You do not know this person so you must not address him or her familiarly. Also look at the accuracy of your work. Are the pieces set out correctly? Is the spelling and punctuation as it should be? Improve all of these aspects as necessary. When you have finished, attach the two pieces together. Put a general title 'Whaling', your name and the date of writing at the top.

Examination Practice

If you are writing with a time limit it is obviously impossible to write more than one draft. You should have jotted down a few points before you started, to organise your thoughts. When you think you have finished, read your work carefully trying to get rid of any spelling and punctuation errors. Write 'Whaling', your name and the date at the top.

Further Information

You may wish to write more on this topic by making it your chosen issue in the final optional activity (Activity D) There are a number of organisations from whom further information can be obtained:

The Whale and Dolphin Conservation Society,
19a James Street West,
Bath,
Avon.
BA1 2BT

Dept WDEC, ICCE Services,
Greenfield House,
Guiting Power,
Cheltenham,
Gloucester.
GL54 5TZ

The Norwegian Embassy,
25 Belgrave Square,
London.
SW 1X 8QD

The Japanese Embassy,
101 Picadilly,
London W1

You should find out what the current situation is and what agreement has been reached for the following year at the time that you are writing.

What Should You Do Now?

Whether you have worked on Part 1 or Part 2, you may now wish to do a final activity in this unit.

ACTIVITY

5d

Optional Coursework – Reading, Research and Information Retrieval, and Writing

Think of an environmental issue which you find interesting and which you consider to be important. It could be a local matter, concerning a particular feature being damaged by development or pollution. Alternatively it could be of international and planet-wide importance such as the destruction of the ozone layer or global warming.

Complete the following then attach the work together as one piece of coursework.

1 Go to your local or college library and find out as much as possible about this issue. You may wish to contact any organisation which is involved in this issue, asking them to send you further information. Once you have the necessary material, write a fact sheet stating the exact situation in unbiased and objective language. You may wish to give background information as well as projected future developments. This should be no more than ONE side of A4 paper. Organise what you write carefully, using several sub-headings.

2 Imagine that you have been asked to speak about this subject to a group of local sixth formers (years 12 and 13). Plan the speech that you would give. Remember that you need to capture and sustain their interest throughout, so think about their age, intelligence and likely attitude to life. Your purpose here is not just to give factual information but to warn them about what is happening and to persuade them to give their support. Write down what you would say. If you were actually giving the talk, you would not do this; you would work from brief notes. As this is a written assessment, this time write down the exact words that you would use, correctly punctuated.

3 Design an eye-catching leaflet to be widely distributed through the post. You should use a single sheet of plain A4 paper and may fold it in any way which helps to convey your message. Use different sizes and styles of lettering to emphasise important points. Do not use more than two colours. Persuade readers to make a financial contribution and/or to give active personal support.

Drafting and Revising

Write a first draft of each then read it through carefully and critically, revising the content, structure and style as necessary. Check your spelling. When you are satisfied, write the final drafts of each one. Check one last time then attach the work together, with a cover sheet on top. On this write a suitable title, the date of writing and your name.

Review of Unit 5

In Part 1
- Activity A was reading and understanding.
- Activity B was speaking and listening coursework (En 1).
- Activity C was written coursework (En 3).

In Part 2
- Activity A was reading and understanding.
- Activity B was speaking and listening coursework (En 1).

- Activity C was either written coursework or examination practice (En 3).

- Activity D was optional reading, research and information retrieval (En 2.3) and written coursework (En 3).

Making a Record

Write down the necessary information about the coursework from this unit. If you worked on Part 1 this was the individual or group oral work in Activity B and the written work in Activity C. If you worked on Part 2, write down the information about the individual oral work in Activity B and the written work in Activity C – unless you used this for examination practice. If you did the final Activity D, record the information about this also.

When you have done this, tick the relevant aspects of En 1, En 2 and En 3 on your Coursework Checklist.

What Should You Do Now?

Turn to another unit which looks interesting.

6 Writing Accurately

*T*HIS chapter is different from the earlier ones. Here you're not concerned with producing coursework. Instead the units deal with the more technical aspects of English, covering accuracy, register, layout and presentation.

This chapter is for you to refer to and consult whenever it is necessary. You will have found references in earlier chapters to what is covered here. Don't try to work your way through everything; rather, when you are working on an activity elsewhere, and you are unsure of a technical matter, consult the relevant unit.

You may find it useful to work through the exercises here when your coursework is finished and you are preparing for the written examination.

This chapter is not intended to be a comprehensive guide to English grammar. If that is what you feel you need, consult a bookshop and find a text that meets your requirements. What we are dealing with here are problem areas that have adversely affected the examination results achieved by students studying English at GCSE.

Here is a summary of what is included:

Unit 1 – Writing Correct Sentences

This covers making complete sense, where to put full stops and commas with advice on the use of colons, semicolons, exclamation and question marks.

Unit 2 – Problems with Spelling

Here we cover forming plurals, double letters, words that are confused because they have similar sounds, and other common misspellings.

Unit 3 – Agreement

This unit deals with problems in making words agree according to person, number and tense.

Unit 4 – Speech Punctuation and Use of the Apostrophe

Here the rules for punctuating direct speech are explained and the correct uses of the apostrophe are discussed.

Unit 5 – Choosing the Right Words

Differences between certain styles of writing (registers) are looked at and advice given on what is appropriate for particular situations. Such aspects as informal writing, formal writing, jargon, officialese, and journalese are discussed.

Unit 6 – Presentation and Layout

General advice on presenting work is given here. The appropriate layouts for particular sorts of writing are also shown and discussed, for example: plays, various types of letter, reports and newspaper articles.

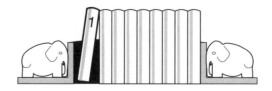

UNIT *Writing Correct Sentences*

For easy reference here is a list of what you will be looking at in this unit:

1 what is a sentence?
2 incomplete sentences;
3 writing longer sentences;
4 using a comma where a full stop is needed;
5 when to use commas: pairs of commas; a single comma; a series of commas;
6 using a colon (:);
7 using a semicolon (;);
8 using question marks and exclamation marks.

1. What is a Sentence?

The first thing that needs to be decided is what exactly we mean by a sentence.

A sentence is a group of words that begins with a capital letter and ends with a full stop and which makes complete sense.

Let's look at this definition for a moment.

Below finger smash ballooning a joining marshmallow.

Above is a group of seven words, with a capital letter at the beginning and a full stop at the end, but the words chosen are totally random and make no sense at all. No doubt a psychiatrist could find something deeply meaningful in this but, for the purposes of writing clear meaningful English, it gets us nowhere.

It is now obvious that the second part of the definition 'which makes complete sense', is the important part.

How do you make sure that your sentence **does** make sense?

The most important ingredient in a correct sentence is the **verb**. A verb is a 'doing' word. Don't forget, though, 'to be' is a sort of doing: is, are, was, were, have been, am. These are all verbs. As you can see by 'have been' above, sometimes the verb consists of more than one word.

Look at the following sentences and identify the verb. Ask yourself the questions: 'What is being done?' and 'What action is there?'

a   The girl is sitting on the bus.
b   I have driven down from Manchester.
c   The book was on the shelf.
d   Henry will be in charge on Tuesday.

In sentence (**a**), then, what is the girl doing? She 'is sitting'; 'is sitting' is the verb.

In (**b**) what is the action? We are told that I 'have driven'; that is the verb.

In (**c**) we are using the verb 'to be'; 'was' is the verb.

Again in (**d**) 'to be' is being used, this time in the future tense; 'will be' is the verb.

Notice also, in each case, there had to be someone or something doing whatever it was (technically this is called the 'subject' of the sentence – this has nothing to do with 'subject' meaning topic or what it's about). In sentence (**a**) it's the girl, in (**b**) it's I, in (**c**) it's the book and in (**d**) it's Henry.

Look what happens if either of those elements is removed. Sentence (**a**) could either read

Is sitting on the bus.

or

The girl on the bus.

Neither of these makes sense. Neither is a sentence. Carry out the same process on (**b**), (**c**) and (**d**).

You will see, now, that both a verb and a subject are necessary for a sentence to make complete sense.

2. Incomplete Sentences

The sun shining

Is this a sentence?

It has a subject, 'the sun'. It has a verb 'shining'. What is the problem? 'shining' is only part of the verb. What is needed is another word to complete it: is shining; was shining; will be shining.

When writing descriptive pieces there is an unfortunate tendency for students to use non-sentences. You know the sort of thing:

It was lovely in the park. The birds singing, the swans building their nests, the grass blowing in the gentle breeze.

Unfortunately this is not correctly written; in each case the appropriate form of 'to be' would need to be added to make it accurate.

Look at the following examples. Which of them are sentences and which of them are not?

a   The man was kicking his lawnmower.
b   Flowing swiftly to the sea.
c   I like you.
d   She walked along the beach.
e   Idly swung his bag.

The answer is that (**b**) and (**e**) are **not** sentences. As you will have noticed (**b**) lacks a complete verb **and** a subject. It would be necessary to add something like 'The stream was' in order to correct it. In (**e**) the subject is lacking. A male name or something like 'The boy' needs to be added to correct it.

3. Writing Longer Sentences

All the sentences you have looked at so far have been very simple ones. Often you will tend to write longer sentences than these. Look at the following examples which show how the examples used previously can be extended.

a   The man was kicking his lawnmower because it would not start.
b   Flowing swiftly to the sea, the stream glistened in the sunlight.
c   Despite your obvious faults, I like you.
d   She walked along the beach and watched the tide starting to cover the rocks.
e   Kevin idly swung his bag but stopped in alarm when he saw his mother.

In (**a**) a reason for the man's behaviour has been given. The joining word 'because' has been used to link the two parts together.

In (**b**) no joining word has been used but the original part of the sentence has become a supplementary piece of information. The main statement now is 'the stream glistened in the sunlight'; the first part just tells us where it is doing this. The comma is needed to divide these two statements. If you read the sentence aloud you will naturally pause there, possibly taking a breath. The comma marks that pause.

Something similar is happening in (**c**) but the other way round. This time extra information has been added at the beginning of the sentence but 'I like you' remains the main statement. Again the comma marks the pause.

In (**d**) another action is simply added to the first. She is watching the tide at the same time as walking; a joining word, 'and' links the two.

The same is found in (**e**). This time his second action, to stop swinging his bag idly, is linked to the first by one joining word 'but' and then another statement explaining why is added on, using another joining word 'when'. The appearance of his mother is the reason for his second action.

These sentences are now much longer but they are still correct.

4. Using a Comma Where a Full Stop is Needed

When looking at incorrect sentence structure, the error which teachers and examiners come across most frequently is where the writer used a comma, or sometimes a whole series of commas, where a full stop was needed.

A sentence, even a longer sentence, **must contain only one idea**.
Look at these examples:

a   The man was kicking his lawnmower, Arsenal had won the cup.
b   The stream was flowing swiftly to the sea, Reginald had his boots on.
c   I like you, I am going to have egg and chips for supper.
d   She walked along the beach, she had been to Scotland a week ago.
e   The boy idly swung his bag, he was going to see his friend Bob after school.

It is possible, I suppose, that there could be a link between the man kicking his lawnmower and Arsenal having won but it seems unlikely. This should therefore be two sentences, not one. The same is true of all the other examples. But, you might say, in (**c**), (**d**) and (**e**), both statements are about the same person. This is true but in each case the second statement is a **new idea** not directly linked with the first except by being associated with the same person. Therefore, the correct punctuation is a full stop and a new start with a capital letter.

Look at the examples below and decide, in each case, whether there should be one or two sentences. If you decide it should be one sentence, choose a joining word (for example, 'and', 'because', 'therefore') to link the statements.

a   Jean is a secretary, she lives in a fourth floor flat in Brighton.
b   Janet works at Reynolds Engineering, it's only a mile from where she lives.
c   Polly is always left out at parties, she suffers from bad breath.
d   Kevin is always left out at parties, his father works for British Home Stores.

In each of these cases the comma must go.

If you are unsure whether to put a full stop or a comma at the end of a statement it is safer to choose the full stop **as long as the statement makes sense on its own.**

5. When to Use Commas

People often use far too many commas. 'If in doubt, leave it out' may be good advice. Let's look at the correct uses, though.

Pairs of Commas

It is possible to use commas like brackets to separate additional information which is placed in the middle of an already complete sentence. Here are some examples:

a   The tanker, having run aground on the rocks, was towed away by the tug-boat.
b   Caroline, looking in the mirror, was worried about her acne.
c   The children, having eaten all the food, ran races in the field.
d   The Sociology examinations, I'm sorry to say, will be very difficult.

In each case extra information is inserted into the sentence. What is added is **not** a sentence but, without it, the rest still would be. Look back at the sentences above to prove this to yourself.

If you insert the word 'however' into a sentence, it is always treated like this. So is the name of someone you are addressing in a speech. Here are some examples:

a   The westerly gales, however, will continue to affect Wales.
b   I wouldn't do that, John, if I were you.

A Single Comma

If the additional information is added to the beginning of a sentence, a single comma divides it from the rest. This has already been seen in examples (**b**) and (**c**) of the lengthened sentences in section 3. It also applies if you put the name of the person you are addressing at the beginning. Here are some examples:

a   Robert, pick that up off the floor.
b   Now that it had started to rain, the air was much cooler.
c   Whether we like it or not, the profits are falling.
d   Sir, I thought you wanted to see me.

Notice that if you omitted a comma from some sentences, the sense would change.

'Wake up, Anne' and 'Wake up Anne' are different. In the first, Anne is being addressed directly. In the second another person is being told to wake her.

A Series of Commas

If you are writing a list, each item is separated from the rest by a comma. This applies up to the second from the end where the joining word 'and' is used to link on the final item. You don't need both a comma and a joining word. Here are some examples:

a   I am studying History, Geography, Technical Drawing and Music.
b   Please add peppers, tomatoes, aubergines and courgettes to the shopping list.
c   The man shuffled his papers, cleared his throat, looked at his watch and then finally began to speak.
d   I want Jenny, Rachel, Samantha and Rosie to come with me.

Although the list in (c) may not be so obvious, it is one nevertheless. Each of his actions could have been written as a separate sentence:

The man shuffled his papers. He cleared his throat. He looked at his watch. Eventually he began to speak.

This is equally correct. The **effect** is different.

6. Using a Colon (:)

This is quite simple. It is used, sometimes with the addition of a dash (:-) to **introduce** something: often a list, an explanation or a piece of supplementary information. For example:

a   Here is my address: 43 Willow Drive, Bletchley.
b   This is what I require: some butter, some eggs, a pint of milk and a tub of cream.
c   Here is the answer: the truck travels at 45 m.p.h.
d   I knew why he was late: he had slept through his alarm clock.

7. Using a Semicolon (;)

Unless you're very confident, don't bother using the semicolon!

This mark indicates a longer pause than a comma and a shorter one than a full stop. The two parts of the sentence should be closely linked and each one should be a complete sentence on its own. You can avoid using a semicolon by putting a full stop. Alternatively, you could rephrase the sentence to emphasise the link between the two parts.

Here are some examples of its correct usage:

a   I want Jenny, Rachel, Samantha and Rosie to come with me; Nick, John, Simon and Paul go with Mr Stevens.
b   Vera is very generous; she supports all the local charities.
c   As I went into the house the phone rang; it was my husband.
d   The woman hadn't eaten properly for weeks; she looked thin and gaunt.

8. Using Question Marks and Exclamation Marks

Using a Question Mark

Whenever you write a direct question, a question mark must follow. Is that clear? Except sometimes in direct speech (see Unit 4), a question mark is followed by a capital letter. For example:

a   What is it? It's a food mixer.
b   Didn't I tell you? I've got a new job.
c   Where are you going? Can I come too?
d   Are you finding it difficult? Don't worry, it's okay once you're used to it.

You don't put a question mark at the end of an indirect question, i.e. a sentence where someone is talking about a previously asked question. For example:

a   John asked how you were.
b   She enquired when the decorating would be finished.
c   The police constable asked whether it was my car.
d   I asked her whether she would wait for me.

None of the sentences above needs a question mark.

Using an Exclamation Mark

If there is an exclamation, this is the mark to use.

Goodness me! Wow! What a shame!

If you want to emphasise the extraordinary, you also might use this mark.

In his first year of trading he made three million pounds!

Don't overdo it. It loses its effect if every other sentence ends this way.

As with the question mark, except for a few specific instances in direct speech (see Unit 4), it is treated like a full stop and so is followed by a capital letter.

Exercise

Cover the correct version in the box below and punctuate the following correctly.

> there were four of us there Joan Sally Dorothy and me as it was a fine day we decided to go out on the lake Dorothy because she'd had lots of experience took the rudder Sally and I took turns to row we hadn't gone far when the wind got stronger black clouds scudded by they looked very threatening what do you think happened next yes bother it we overturned there we were all four of us clinging to the upturned boat luckily a fishing boat happening to come past picked us up and took us back to dry land we all agreed never again.

Correct Version

There were four of us there: Joan, Sally, Dorothy and me. As it was a fine day, we decided to go out on the lake. Dorothy, because she'd had lots of experience, took the rudder. Sally and I took turns to row. We hadn't gone far when the wind got stronger. Black clouds scudded by; they looked very threatening. What do you think happened next? Yes, bother it! We overturned. There we were, all four of us, clinging to the upturned boat. Luckily a fishing boat, happening to come past, picked us up and took us back to dry land. We all agreed, never again!

If you chose to put a full stop after 'by', starting again with a capital T for 'they', that's fine. So is inserting the word 'which' at that point, thus avoiding the need for a semicolon.

If you made two errors or fewer, award yourself a gold star and put into practice everything that you have learned here. If you have doubts when you're writing, check the appropriate section again.

UNIT **②** *Problems with Spelling*

Correct spelling is a vital aspect of accurate writing. You should own a dictionary and use it whenever you are uncertain about how to spell a word. A good one to use is the *Collins Paperback Dictionary.* If you are told that you have spelt something incorrectly, look it up and put it right. You may wish to build up your own personal dictionary in a notebook with an alphabetical index. You can keep a list there of words that you know you find it difficult to spell correctly.

Dyslexia

If you have **very severe** problems with spelling it is possible that you may be dyslexic. This is a specific learning difficulty that needs to be treated in a special way if your spelling is going to improve. If you think this might be the case and you have not previously been tested, you should find out where such a service is available in your area. Testing is usually carried out by an educational psychologist and some education authorities have units specifically for learning difficulties. Your local college may run one or may know of such a unit. If the college is unable to help, telephone your local education authority to find out. Probably you yourself will have to pay a fee for testing. If the test shows that you are dyslexic, you will receive a certificate. A copy of this should be included with your examination entry for forwarding to the board. You should be entitled to extra time and some extra marks (usually five per cent) as compensation. There may also be special tuition available in your area to help you overcome this difficulty.

Most people have some difficulties with spelling but are not dyslexic. There may be various reasons for this. Perhaps you are unsure of the rules. Perhaps you don't read very much and so see few words in print on a regular basis. Perhaps you are a bit lazy and put the word down on paper without thinking too much about whether it's correct or not. This often happens with pairs of easily confused words.

In this unit the aspects of spelling which will be discussed are:

1 plurals;
2 prefixes and suffixes;
3 doubling;
4 frequently confused words.

1. Plurals

Many English words form their plurals simply by adding 's'.

For example:

chicken – chickens
pan – pans.

There are exceptions, however:

Some words add 'es'. Often these are words which end in 's', 'ch', 'sh', 'z', 'x', 'o'. Here are some examples:

dress – dresses
beach – beaches
splash – splashes
waltz – waltzes
fox – foxes
tomato – tomatoes.

Words ending in 'y' change the 'y' to an 'i' and add 'es'. This rule is often ignored, probably through carelessness. Here are some examples:

penny – pennies
country – countries
cry – cries.

Words that have a vowel (a, e, i, o, u) before 'y', simply add 's'. For example:

toy – toys
way – ways
donkey – donkeys.

Some words ending in 'f' change this to 'ves' in the plural. For example:

scarf – scarves
loaf – loaves.

But some don't, for example:

roof –roofs.

Some words have unusual plurals. For example:

man – men
child – children
goose – geese
mouse – mice.

Some foreign words used in English keep their original plurals. For example:

bureau – bureaux
stimulus – stimuli
formula – formulae
medium – media.

Some words stay the same in the plural. For example:

deer – deer
sheep – sheep
salmon – salmon.

Some words are always plural. For example:

scissors

trousers
mumps.

Exercise

Form the correct plurals of the following words: peach, boss, monkey, lady, potato, witch, half, batch, county, woman.

Check your answers. You probably got all these right. Try to remember these guidelines when you are doing your written work.

2. Prefixes and Suffixes

Prefixes

A prefix is something we add to the beginning of a word. When you do this, you do not change the spelling of the original word.

Here are some examples:

un + usual – unusual
un + necessary – unnecessary
dis + appear – disappear
dis + appointment – disappointment.

Suffixes

A suffix is something we add to the end of a word.

Adding -ly

Adding -ly is very straightforward. The suffix is just put onto the end of the existing word without altering the spelling.

For example:

sincere – sincerely
extreme – extremely
live – lively
principal – principally
fundamental – fundamentally.

Adding -ing

The suffix –ing is added straight onto the end of the original word **except** if the word ends in 'e'. If it does, the 'e' is dropped. (There are a few exceptions to this rule, but don't worry about these here!)

For example:

ring – ringing
drink – drinking
jump – jumping
move – moving

bounce – bouncing
freeze – freezing.

Adding -ness

This is straightforward **except** when the word ends in 'y'. Usually this changes to 'i'

lovely – loveliness
happy – happiness.

Adding -able/-ible

In the case of adding -able and -ible there is no rule and which suffix is the correct one simply has to be learned. For example, comprehensible, unavoidable, commendable, gullible.

Exercise

a   Form the opposite of these words by adding a prefix:
     obtainable; disputable; approachable; noble; decorated.
b   Add -ly to the following words:
     beautiful; sole; like; critical; soft.
c   Add -ing to the following words:
     scrape; establish; cringe; investigate; organise.

Check your answers in a dictionary. Were all twenty correct?

3. Doubling

When -ing is added to words which end with a vowel and then one consonant, that consonant is usually doubled.

For example:

tap – tapping
pin – pinning
jog – jogging
run – running.

A useful general rule is that a single vowel before a double letter consonant is usually a short sound – as in the examples given above. When the vowel sound is long, there is usually only a single consonant.

For example:

dine – dining
write – writing.

Look at the differences here:

scrapping – scraping
filling – filing
mopping – moping.

When in doubt, read it out!

   When adding -fill, -till or -full onto a word, they lose one -l.

For example:

   full added to fill = fulfil
   un added to till = until
   beauty added to full = beautiful (notice the -y also changes to -i)
   awe added to full = awful (the -e is also dropped).

On the end of a word it is always -ful:

   meaningful, useful, harmful.

Exercise

Put the correct -ing spelling of the verb in brackets into the space. For example:

   The student is (drop) Mathematics.
   The student is dropping Mathematics.

a   I am thinking of (tile) the bathroom.
b   He is (hope) to get a letter tomorrow.
c   Shall we eat in the (dine) room?
d   The child was (hop) down the street.
e   The recession is (hit) those who make a living from (write).

Check your answers with the rules we have outlined above. Congratulate yourself if they were all correct.

4. Frequently Confused Words

I Before E

Although there are exceptions to it, this is a useful rule to remember:

-i before -e except after -c

This will solve any problems you might have with 'friend', 'believe', 'receive': words which are frequently misspelt.

Homophones

Homophones are words which **sound the same** but are spelt differently and have different meanings. You must know what the difference is and learn when to use each.

   Here are some examples. Identify the meaning in each case:

   threw – through
   course – coarse
   draft – draught
   council – counsel

passed – past
principal – principle
stationary – stationery
complement – compliment
there – their – they're
whose – who's
knew – new
no – know.

If you use some of these words frequently, you may wish to invent a way of remembering which is which. For example, stationary means standing; both contain an 'a'. Stationery includes such items as envelopes: it has an 'e'.

They're means they are; if you are unsure whether this is the right version, try writing *they* are in full. Similarly *who's* means who is. By putting this into the sentence in full you will see if this is the correct version.

'Who's Uncle Walter?' means 'who is Uncle Walter?'.

'Whose Uncle Walter?' means 'To whom does Uncle Walter belong?'

Similar Words

Some words are pronounced slightly differently by most people but are still similar enough to be confused. Here are some examples:

weather – whether
were – where
quite – quiet
advice – advise
lie – lay
lose – loose
to – too
precede – proceed.

As with homophones, you must learn what each means and use it in the correct context. If you pronounce the words slightly differently it is easier to sort them out. Sounding the -h in whether, for example, helps you to get it right. 'Should have' wouldn't be written mistakenly as 'should of' if the words were pronounced more distinctly.

Exercise

Choose five pairs of words from the examples of homophones and a further five words from the list of similar words. For each word make up a sentence using it correctly. You will compose twenty sentences in all.

For example, I might have chosen 'threw – through' from the homophones.

The boy threw his cap over the wall. The brick crashed through the window.

I might have chosen 'weather – whether' from the similar words.

As usual, the weather over the Bank Holiday was wet. He asked whether I had finished my essay.

When making your selection try to choose words which you might confuse. Look up each one in a dictionary before you write your sentence. Use this as a way of clarifying the words. Ask your tutor to check whether you have used the words correctly.

Extra C, Extra N

Some words have 'c' where you might not expect there to be one. It generally appears before 'q' in such words as acquire, acquiesce, racquet. Some words contain an almost silent 'n' which often catches people out, for example government, environment.

Perennial Horrors

There are some words which always cause problems: it's just a question of learning how to spell them correctly. Here is a list:

accessible	accommodation
address	analysis
appalling	argument
beneficial	changeable
committed	conscious
conscience	definite
desperate	develop
embarrass	grateful
humorous	necessary
noticeable	occasion
occurred	psychology
recommend	separate
technical	temporary
tragedy	woollen

Exercise

Learn the correct spelling of the words in this list. When you think you know them, try to write each in a sentence. Check in the list to see if you were right or wrong. If you can't remember the words, ask someone to read them out to you. If you make mistakes, keep practising until you get them right. Try to remember how to spell these words when you use them in your written work.

When it comes to spelling, you must try hard to learn from your mistakes. Carry a pocket-sized dictionary around with you and use it whenever necessary. Remember the golden rule:

IF IN DOUBT, CHECK IT OUT!

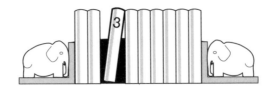

UNIT **3**   *Agreement*

This unit is all about being consistent – about continuing something in the same way as you started. For the sake of clarity, this will be considered under three headings:

1   person;
2   number;
3   tense.

1. Agreement of Person

If **you** start writing a sentence like this **you** have to continue in the same way or **you** will be making a mistake.

The best way to explain the sort of confusion that often arises is to demonstrate it. It occurs when a long sentence is being written and the end is thus some distance from the beginning. It is easy in this situation to forget how you started. Here is the same sentence which was printed above but this time the writer has become confused:

If **I** start writing a sentence like this **one** has to continue in the same way or **you** will be making a mistake.

This time instead of correctly using 'you' all the way through, the writer has started with 'I', changed to 'one' and then finished off with 'you'. This is an illustration of a sentence where there is no agreement of person.

Sometimes, in a sentence, there will be a correct and deliberate change of person. For example:

If I explain something badly you will become confused.

If you disrupt the filing system he will be the one who has to sort it out.

It is necessary to be aware of how you begin in order to remain consistent. If you are discussing a particular subject over several sentences it may be necessary to continue throughout using the same person. This can start to sound clumsy, though, especially if you are using 'one'. This is probably best avoided or left for the use of royalty! See the following example.

If one lives on a council estate one may encounter many problems due to the local authorities being reluctant to carry out maintenance of one's property. One therefore has to put up with inconvenience and discomfort or carry out repairs at one's own expense.

This may be grammatically correct but it sounds awful. You may feel that putting in 'you' instead gives the wrong tone, making it sound too personal. It may be better to rewrite it altogether, for example:

Council tenants may encounter many problems due to the Local Authorities being reluctant to carry out maintenance of property. It may be necessary for them to put up with inconvenience and discomfort or carry out repairs at their own expense.

Exercise

Add to these sentences in a consistent way:

a   If one is the Prince of Wales . . .
b   I will be looking at some of the problems . . .
c   It is generally believed that gardening, as a hobby . . .
d   When you are cooking highly spiced dishes . . .

2. Agreement of Number

This is an area where students encounter many problems.

Following Through

One of the most common problems is again because of someone's failure to notice how a sentence began, thus following it through inconsistently. For example:

When the author introduces a character into a book he really brings them to life.

This is incorrect.' A character' was introduced.' A character' is singular and therefore 'them' cannot be correct. For 'them' to be correct, characters, plural, must be used. A singular character might be referred to as 'him' or 'her'.

Here are several examples where you might make a mistake, especially if you went on to add further sentences written in the same way.

a   People who live in a city have to be careful about crime.
b   A child growing up with older parents looks at the issue differently.
c   A basket of apples is being delivered today.
d   Families with only one child often choose to travel together.

In all of these examples the verb is closer to a noun with a different number to the subject of the verb – the originator of the action.

In (**a**) 'People' is the subject and 'have' is the plural verb. Don't be distracted by the singular 'city' next to it.

In (**b**) the singular subject is 'child' with the singular verb 'looks'. 'Parents', a plural word, is not relevant.

In (**c**), 'basket' not 'apples' is the subject, so 'is' rather than 'are' is correct.

In (**d**), 'Families'. . . 'choose'.

Singular Words

Problems often occur when one of the following singular words is used in a sentence:

anyone, anybody; everyone, everybody; no one, nobody, someone, somebody; either, neither.

'Everybody' causes problems because it seems to refer to lots of people. For example:

Everybody has their own ideas about it.
This is **wrong**. It has to read:
Everybody has his (or her) own ideas about it.
Similarly, it is necessary to say:
Neither Jenny nor Vera **is** able to do anything about the problem.
Each one is being considered separately.

Exercise

Put in the correct form of the word:

a   Everyone should be allowed to make their/his own choice.
b   Either Geography or History are/is compulsory for pupils in that year.
c   Everybody in town knows/know Fred Dawson.
d   A container of heavy crates has/have been dumped by the motorway.

Alternatives

When giving alternatives in a sentence you have to be especially careful. Here is some further advice about sentences which contain these words: either . . . or; neither . . . nor; whether . . . or.
   These are the rules:

1   If all the subjects are singular, the verb is singular, for example:
    Either the elephant or the whale **is** the largest.
2   If one of the subjects is plural then the verb is plural, for example:
    It doesn't matter whether Hannah or her sisters go.
3   If pronouns (he, she, you, I, they, etc.,) are used, the verb agrees with the pronoun it's nearest to, for example:
    Neither she nor I am capable of such stupidity.

Collective Nouns

These are usually singular, for example: flock, herd, staff, government, and so on. But it is possible to see them as plurals if you are talking about the members as individuals. For example:

1   The committee were divided over the decision.
2   The crowd argued among themselves.
3   The team train separately.

   It is a question of deciding what you mean and constructing your sentence accordingly.

3. Tense

When you are writing you should always make a deliberate decision about which tense is appropriate.

Describing

If you are writing a description you may wish to use the present tense:

The lake is shining in the sun. The grass is green.

If you choose to do this, you must **not** suddenly and accidentally change to the past tense.

The grass is green. The geese were building their nests on the island.

You must only do that if you are talking about a previous occasion:

Last time I was here it was raining and the birds were hiding in the shelter.

Narrating

Usually if you are writing a story, you will use the past tense.

He walked down the street. There was a noise behind him . . .

Responding to Literature

When you are discussing a piece of literature it is usual to write in the present tense as if the characters exist now: 'Jane Eyre falls in love with Mr Rochester.' The same is true of films: 'Flash Gordon saves the world with moments to spare.'

Informing and Reporting

When you are writing instructions or factual pieces about a current situation it is quite likely that you will wish to use the present. For example: 'the weather in Tunisia is very hot' or 'place the flour in a large mixing bowl'.

Arguing and Persuading

In discursive writing, especially if you are comparing a previous state of affairs with the situation now and also suggesting possible future developments, you will almost certainly have to make frequent changes of tense. For example:

In the past, this situation was tolerated but worries are increasing and some action will have to be taken before it is too late.

Exercise

Write **two** more sentences in the same tense as each of the 'starters' below:

1 I went to the coast last week.
2 She is feeling depressed today.
3 There will be a number of different jobs to be done.
4 It was getting dark.

Remember these three rules, whatever you're writing:

1 **think about what you are saying**
2 **be consistent**
3 **check your work carefully.**

UNIT **4** *Punctuating Direct Speech and Using the Apostrophe*

This unit is divided into two sections: Section A looks at punctuating direct speech; Section B explains how to use the apostrophe correctly

Section A – Punctuating Direct Speech

There are some rules that you must follow if you are going to punctuate speech accurately, these are outlined for you below.

1   Most people already know that the **words which are spoken** must be enclosed by speech marks or inverted commas '. . . '.

'I am going to be sick,' he said.
    The words he actually says are 'I am going to be sick' so these are enclosed in speech marks.
    What are the words actually spoken in this example?
    Anyway she said brightly looking out of the window it's going to be a lovely day.
    What she says is, 'Anyway it's going to be a lovely day'. The rest of the sentence tells us who spoke and how the words were said. The spoken words, then, wherever they are in the sentence, have to be **enclosed** in inverted commas – like this:
    'Anyway,' she said brightly looking out of the window, 'it's going to be a lovely day.'

2   The **first** word which is **spoken**, wherever it is in the sentence, must be given a capital letter.

In the examples above the first words were 'I' and 'Anyway'; 'I' referring to oneself is, of course, always a capital letter. 'Anyway' starts the sentence so could be assumed to be a capital because of that. Let's look at some better examples, then.
    Mandy said, 'Where are you going?'
    The boy shouted, 'You've got my bag!'
    In both of these cases the first word spoken ('where', 'you') comes in the middle of the line but as it is the **first spoken** word. It must have a capital letter.

3   In a sentence involving speech, each part must have appropriate

punctuation at the end. It is here that many people make mistakes either because they don't know the rules or are careless.

Look at this sentence:

Peter said, 'He's in the Dog and Duck.'

Let's break this down into two parts: (a) Peter said, and (b) He's in the Dog and Duck

The first part of the sentence must have a comma before the spoken words: Peter said,

The second part must have a full stop to bring it to an end. Because what is said brings the sentence to an end, the punctuation mark is **inside** the inverted commas: 'He's in the Dog and Duck.'

If we put the sentence the other way round, this is what happens:

'He's in the Dog and Duck,' Peter said.

This time the sentence carries on **after** the speech, so we have only a comma, a temporary stop, after 'Duck', inside the inverted commas. The full stop comes at the end of the sentence which is now after 'said'.

There is **no** occasion when a part of a sentence involving speech would not have a punctuation mark ending it. When an exclamation is made or a question asked, an exclamation mark or question mark stands in for the comma within the SPOKEN part of the sentence.

Look at the following examples and note the punctuation used in each case.

Marcia said, 'Get me a coke.'

'What's going on?' said Andy.

'Don't tell me the bus has gone!' exclaimed Lisa.

He said quietly, 'Don't tell anyone I'm here.'

Make sure you notice everything we've looked at so far: the spoken words are enclosed in inverted commas, the first spoken word has a capital, each part of the sentence has the appropriate punctuation.

4   As we have seen, the first spoken word has a capital. If another part of the sentence follows a comma, it does not. In the examples shown above, 'said' in the second does not have a capital. It follows a comma and is not the first spoken word (it's not spoken at all, of course). The same is true of 'exclaimed' in the third. If you go back to an earlier example, you will see another illustration of this: 'Anyway,' she said brightly looking out of the window, 'it's going to be a lovely day.'

Here 'she' has no capital, following the comma and neither does 'it's'. This word is spoken but it is not the **first** spoken word – that's 'Anyway'. What is said is all one sentence, interrupted by the middle part, 'she said brightly looking out of the window'.

Here are another couple of examples of the same type of thing.

'It's Wednesday,' she said, 'so it must be market day.'

'Goodness me,' the woman said, 'is your name Angelica?'

In each of those cases a small (lower case) letter is used following the commas.

5   Things can get a little more complicated if the person speaking is using more than one sentence and these are interrupted by the 'he said' part. For example:

'I come here every week,' he said. 'Do you want to see the cathedral?'

In this case the speaker uses two separate sentences: 'I come here every week' and 'Do you want to see the cathedral?' There is no way two unconnected statements like this could be run together as one. Therefore, the 'he said' part will be attached to one of these statements with a full stop after it. Following the full stop, of course, you must start again with a capital letter. Look again at how it's written above. There is a comma after 'week' so 'he said' follows on after this without a capital letter. There is then a full stop and the first word of the **new sentence**, 'Do', starts with a capital.

It's really a matter of deciding whether what is interrupted is one continuing sentence or two separate ones. What would you decide about the sentences included in the exercise below?

Exercise

Put the correct punctuation into these sentences. Cover up the correct version while you do this then check to see if you were right.

a   At my time of life he said you don't want to work as hard
b   Pass the mayonnaise Helen said would you like something to drink
c   I'm hungry George complained where's the cat
d   You'll have to complete this assignment by Monday Jill said to Anita or you'll fail the course

Have you followed all the rules carefully? Have you missed anything out?

Correct Version

Cover what follows until you have punctuated the sentences.

a   'At my time of life,' he said, 'you don't want to work as hard.'
b   'Pass the mayonnaise,' Helen said. 'Would you like something to drink?'
c   'I'm hungry,' George complained. 'Where's the cat?'
d   'You'll have to complete this assignment by Monday,' Jill said to Anita, 'or you'll fail the course.'

In (**a**) and (**d**) what was said was one continuous sentence, interrupted by, 'he said' and 'Jill said to Anita'. In the other two, the speaker used two separate sentences, interrupted by, 'Helen said' and 'George complained'. 'Pass the mayonnaise' suggests that the setting is a meal but the second part, 'Would you like something to drink?' is clearly a different thought and therefore a different sentence. Similarly, in (**c**), unless George is very strange indeed his question about the location of the cat is entirely separate from his statement about being hungry! Did you miss out any of the necessary commas? If not, well done !

6   The final rule which you need to remember is that **every time a different person speaks you must start a new paragraph**.

It is quite possible, when writing speech, to leave out the 'he said', 'she said' parts altogether. If you have made it clear which two characters are having a conversation it is often unnecessary to identify the speaker each time. If you did not start on a new line, though, it would be impossible to follow what was happening. Look at these examples.

Version A

> 'Fred.'
> 'Yes, Vera?'
> 'Do you want to go to the cinema?'
> 'I don't mind.'
> 'What sort of answer is that?'
> 'Eh?'
> 'Well, shall we go then?'
> 'Where?'
> 'You're impossible! I'll go on my own then!'

Version B

> 'Fred,' said Vera.
> 'Yes, Vera?' said Fred.
> 'Do you want to go to the cinema?' said Vera.
> 'I don't mind,' said Fred.
> 'What sort of answer is that?' said Vera.
> 'Eh?' said Fred.
> 'Well, shall we go then?' said Vera.
> 'Where?' said Fred.
> 'You're impossible! I'll go on my own then!' said Vera.

The Version B is much slower moving and sounds far less realistic than the first. Version A has more pace and because each new speaker is indicated by a new paragraph, it is perfectly possible to work out who is speaking at all times. It's much more effective too. If it was all written as one paragraph it would be very confusing, though.

Version C

> 'Fred.' 'Yes, Vera?' 'Do you want to go to the cinema?' 'I don't mind.' 'What sort of answer is that?' 'Eh?' 'Well, shall we go then?' 'Where?' 'You're impossible! I'll go on my own then!'

If the same person carries on speaking for some time, using several sentences, uninterrupted by 'he said' or whatever, you just need to put inverted commas before the first word and again after the last, just as in the very first example.

Version D

> 'I'm tired of this, Fred. You never listen to what I say. How long is it since we last went out? I'll tell you. It was on my birthday and that was six months ago now. I sit here, night after night, watching the same stupid programmes on the television while you read that newspaper. This isn't what life is meant to be like. I'm thirty years old and I feel as if I'm a hundred. I'm wasting the best years of my life! What have you got to say to that?'

'Make us a cup of tea, love.'

As you can see, here the whole speech, starting with 'I' and ending with 'that' is enclosed in one set of inverted commas, despite the fact that there are ten sentences. It is all one speaker. When Fred speaks, thus changing the speaker, we start a new paragraph.

Exercise

Following the rules carefully, write a page of conversation between **three** speakers. Here are some suggestions of a situation which might appeal to you (you may invent your own situation if you prefer):

- three strangers at a bus stop;
- three friends having coffee in a cafe;
- three men in a bar;
- three young children in the school playground.

When you have written it, check and double check:

Are all the spoken words and nothing else, enclosed by inverted commas?

Does each word which is the first spoken in a sentence start with a capital?

Have you put in commas, full stops, question or exclamation marks wherever necessary leaving no part with no punctuation?

Have you put the capital and lower case letters in the right places?

Have you started a new paragraph for each new speaker?

If you can answer 'Yes' to all the above and your tutor agrees, award yourself a giant gold star.

You are ready now to write stories that include speech. Don't forget all this once you start writing your coursework!

Section B – Using Apostrophes Correctly

There are two uses for apostrophes:

1 indicating that a letter (or several letters) has been missed out of a word;
2 to show 'belonging' or ownership.

Apostrophes should never be used as a sort of decoration every time you write a letter 's'.

Missing Letters

Let's look at some illustrations of using an apostrophe to show a missing letter: don't is a shortened form of do not. The o is missed out and the apostrophe shows where it should have been.

There are plenty of similar examples: I'm; you'll; he's; ma'am; o'clock. In 'o'clock', there are four letters omitted as the full version is 'of the clock'.

Showing Possession

'Belonging' is a little more complicated. Originally it was probably derived from the usage shown above. Thus 'Peter his coat' in old-fashioned English becomes 'Peter's coat' in present usage. This means the coat **belonging to** Peter.

When the owner is **singular** (there is just one), you place the apostrophe after the word, followed by -s. This produces:

My lady's carriage; the boy's shoulder; Nelson's column; the dog's bone.

If there **is more than one** owner, and the plural of the word ends in -s, the apostrophe follows that -s. This time we have:

The lords' gowns; the students' files; the monkeys' cages; the fairies' wands.

The placing of the apostrophe can be the way of showing what you mean. For example a boy might own several items of clothing. Similarly several boys could also own several items. So you would write:

'the boy's clothes' if it was one boy
'the boys' clothes' . . . if you meant several boys

Don't be tempted to do something different if a word just happens to end with -s anyway. The rules still apply. If you only put an apostrophe, you would be changing the spelling of the word. Here are some examples:

Jesus's blessing; her mistress's dog; Frances's book; the duchess's portrait.

Exceptions

Plural words which **don't** end in -s **do** have to add -'s to show belonging. Here are some examples:

the children's toys; the mice's tails; the men's room; women's rights. Some words show belonging but DON'T have an apostrophe: yours, ours, theirs, hers (so do his and my/mine but you're less likely to be tempted to try and add an apostrophe into these words).

Its: When its is written without an apostrophe it means **belonging to it** just as 'yours' means belonging to you.

You only have an apostrophe in this word when it means it is – (or sometimes it has) the apostrophe indicates the missing -i.

> MEMORISE THIS:
> IT's = IT IS
> ITS = BELONGING TO IT

If you are unsure which is right in a sentence, see whether 'it is' would make sense. If it would, you need the apostrophe.

Exercise

Punctuate the following, putting the apostrophes in the right places. Cover the panel which gives the corrected version.

Im going to tell you a story. Its about a friend of ours who lives in another friends cottage. Hed been there for a week when he found animals droppings in his kitchen. Hed called out the pest control experts but the mans van broke down. Instead he called in his neighbour whos the owner of a bloodhound. Its nose is so sensitive it can sniff out an animals hiding place in seconds. Its been defeated by Toms case, though. Its been there for a week now but its found no trace of furry intruders. Toms decided to ignore the problem. Miless cottage is so attractive hes keen to stay. Ill tell you if anythings happened.

When you've finished this, check that you've made no errors. Make absolutely sure that you have **not** put apostrophes on words which are plurals and end in -s **unless** there is a **letter missed out** or it's a case of **ownership**. Check every time you see 'its' as to whether it means it is (or it has) or belonging to it.

Now look at the version below and see if yours agrees.

Correct Version

I'm going to tell you a story. **It's** about a friend of ours who lives in another **friend's** cottage. **He'd** been there for a week when he found **animals'** droppings in his kitchen. **He'd** called out the pest control experts but the **man's** van broke down. Instead he called in his neighbour **who's** the owner of a bloodhound. **Its** nose is so sensitive it can sniff out an **animal's** hiding place in seconds. **It's** been defeated by Tom's case, though. **It's** been there for a week now but **it's** found no trace of furry intruders. **Tom's** decided to ignore the problem. **Miles's** cottage is so attractive **he's** keen to stay. **I'll** tell you if **anything's** happened.

If you made no errors, award yourself a gold star. Check in all your written work from now on that you use the apostrophe correctly.

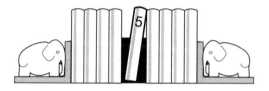

UNIT ⑤ *Choosing the Right Word*

When you communicate with other people, whether it's through speech or writing, you have to decide which are the right words to choose. In this unit there is some general advice about the decisions you must make, followed by a study of certain specific types of language. This is what you will be looking at:

1 choosing the right words;
2 informal language;
3 formal language;
4 jargon;
5 officialese;
6 the language of newspapers (journalese);
7 the language of advertising.

1. Choosing the Right Words

Three factors are likely to influence your decisions:

1 what the communication is about;
2 who you are communicating with;
3 what you are trying to achieve in this particular case.

Let's look at some examples.

Example A – Choosing Appropriate Language

A company is making substantial losses and has to make a percentage of its workforce redundant. The Personnel Manager writes to the staff whose jobs are to go.

1 The letter which is written will be about the current situation. It is very unlikely that comments about last year's staff party or plans for summer holidays would be included.
2 The same letter will be sent to the assistant storeman and the senior cost accountant. Because of this a vocabulary must be chosen which is suitable for both. It must be straightforward and easy to understand.
3 The purpose of this letter is to tell the employee the facts without any danger of misunderstanding. It is also to make the person feel that the firm appreciates the work which has been done and that the manager

is deeply sorry for the need to let staff go. Its tone must be tactful and reassuring. 'Dear Fred, You're fired!' would not be appropriate.

Example B – Choosing Appropriate Language

A drug company writes to GPs to tell them about a new wonder drug for asthma.

1   The letter will be about the drug and its wonderful properties.
2   The letter is to doctors who are highly educated so a certain of level of comprehension can be expected. A knowledge of medical terms can be assumed.
3   The writer must give facts but is also trying to persuade therefore the words will be chosen to try to achieve this.

Example C – Choosing Appropriate Language

A young man telephones his elderly grandmother to tell her that he has obtained a place at college to study on a highly technical computer course.

1   He will tell her his news.
2   She may not know very much about computers. In everyday conversation he may tend to use current slang which she may not understand. He will have to choose his words carefully because of the person he is speaking to.
3   He is informing her and trying to give her pleasure. He will probably not talk about how hard up he will be while living on his grant – unless, of course, his intention is for her to give him a contribution.

Often choices about appropriate language are made without conscious thought. When you are preparing for an assessed piece of work, whether as coursework or in the examination, you need to consider these aspects consciously in order to communicate as effectively as possible.

Let's look now at various forms of language (registers) which are customarily used in particular circumstances. You will learn to recognise them and to see in what circumstances they are appropriate.

2. Informal Language

What is informal language?

a   I think I'll have a cuppa before I get going.
b   It is my intention to consume a beverage before I begin.
c   The employee decided to take refreshment before starting work

The first is informal, the (**b**) and (**c**) are formal.

What is the difference?

Sentence (**a**) sounds like someone speaking. There is abbreviation (I'll) and colloquial or slang expressions are used (cuppa, get going). The words are very short and simple.

It is very unlikely that you would speak as in sentence (**b**). It sounds very stiff and awkward. More effort is needed by the reader to understand it as the words are longer and more complex (intention, consume, beverage). It sounds old fashioned.

Again sentence (**c**) does not sound at all like someone speaking. It is now impersonal – 'the employee' rather than 'I'. It is in the third person. The words are again longer than in sentence (**a**) but it does not sound awkward or difficult to understand. This sounds like written rather than spoken language.

Writing

Generally, when you produce work for assessment, you will write in a style more like (**c**) than (**a**). Exactly how formal you must be depends on the precise nature of the task. You will make a decision each time you start a piece of work. If you are writing in the same way as you would speak, then you are likely to find that your style is too informal.

Avoid slang or colloquialisms except in certain cases. Colloquialisms, such as *don't*, *let's*, or *I'll*, may be acceptable in some situations. For example, in this book I have tried to adopt a friendly, personal tone, and I have used these abbreviations to create this effect. Slang should normally be avoided. If you are writing a conversation, the characters may use slang (and even swear) in their speeches, for example:

'Get lost!' Harry shouted, standing up angrily.
'You what?' Mick sprang to his feet in astonishment.
'I've 'ad it, right up to 'ere!' Harry said.

In this example, Harry's speech is very informal and an attempt is make to suggest how his voice would sound by omitting 'h' from 'had' and 'here'. The description of the characters' behaviour is not written informally and correct punctuation is used.

Speaking

In spoken assessments, you can generally use more informal language. When you make a speech, give a talk or conduct an oral presentation you should adopt a fairly formal style. Certainly you should avoid using slang. However it is usually acceptable to abbreviate words as when you abbreviate 'I will' to 'I'll'. Indeed when you are speaking you will find it difficult to prevent yourself from doing this, and if you did, you would probably produce a stilted and over-formal effect.

In a discussion or role play, where you are expressing feelings and opinions, it is acceptable to use informal language but you should avoid the extremes of slang. Speak so that everyone involved can understand what you mean.

Exercise

1   Write down eight currently fashionable slang terms. Write beside each a formal 'translation'.
2   Referring to a dictionary if you like, think of (a) a less formal and (b) a colloquial way of saying:

The climatic conditions were inauspicious.

In the event of hostilities, immediate evacuation is advised.

At the location of our vacation, the recreational facilities were somewhat unsatisfactory.

3. Formal Language

We have already seen the difference between informal and formal language. For any particular task you will need to decide on the degree of formality required and use an appropriate tone.

To make your language sound more formal, choose longer words, usually with Latin origins. Shorter words with Old English roots are simpler and sound less formal. Here are some examples:

Latin	OE
employment	work
remuneration	pay
residence	house
conflagration	fire
terminate	end
merchandise	goods

Do not, however, choose longer words in order to make your work sound impressive while at the same time making it difficult to understand. Using a broad vocabulary is a good thing but not when a communication is addressed to someone who would not understand the words you are using.

Whenever you write, consider your audience and your purpose. When you read what you have written, decide whether the **tone** is appropriate. If you are writing a business letter, does it sound like one? If you are writing a factual report, does it sound like that? If it does not, you have probably used unsuitable words which may not be formal enough.

Exercise

a   You received a letter returning your money for a concert that was cancelled. It ended with these words: 'Sorry, mate. Here's the cash. Have a pint on me. Jason.' Rewrite this using formal business-like language.

b   Think of a formal way of saying:

She'd had a brilliant time and said it was just great.
This is the biggest dump I've ever had the bad luck to stay in.
She was in a right flap because of all the hassle the folks were giving her.

4. Jargon

The *Collins Paperback Dictionary* defines jargon as a specialised language concerned with a particular subject and familiar only to a specific group or profession.

It may be acceptable to use jargon if you are communicating with people who are familiar with it, as in example B (page 288) at the beginning of this unit where medical terminology could be used. Problems arise when people are faced with jargon which they do not understand.

For example, in the theatre, the curtains at the front of the stage are called 'tabs'. The word 'strike' is used to mean 'remove' when referring to a 'property'. A 'property' or 'prop' is an item used on the stage such as a piece of furniture, item of crockery or whatever. Someone who did not know these terms could be very confused if a command like this was shouted: 'Quickly, strike the armchair then drop the tabs!' It may be a sort of shorthand but it also may be a way of identifying fellow members of a select group. 'Remove the armchair and lower the curtains' doesn't seem any more long-winded!

Recently a law was introduced prohibiting estate agents from using misleading terms. In the past, their jargon had to be learnt if a buyer was going to interpret house adverts correctly. Here are some of the most frequently used phrases with a suggested translation:

- in need of a little attention – practically a ruin;
- ideal for the DIY enthusiast – it is a ruin;
- open aspect – overlooks the local tip;
- secluded – miles from anywhere;
- convenient-sized kitchen – all four walls can be reached by standing centrally;
- well ventilated – the window frames don't fit properly;
- sea view – you can see it provided you are not afraid to stand on the roof top.

Avoid using jargon unless you are deliberately putting it in a task where it would be appropriate.

Exercise

Identify two or three areas where jargon is frequently used, for example: in court, in wine tasting, in fashionable cookery. Collect examples of terms used (about twenty words) and write them down with a translation in simple English.

5. Officialese

This is a particularly dangerous type of jargon. Quite often in official documents – leaflets about tax, forms concerning grants, passports, rebates and benefits – a complex vocabulary is used which the average reader may not understand. This may be accidental – the writer is not considering the audience and purpose, or it may be deliberate – if the form is hard to understand, fewer people will bother to fill it in and claim money.

It is also a way of preventing strong reactions to unpleasant facts. When they are phrased in officialese they sound less serious. For example, 'There will be a substantial reorganisation of the company structure in order to effect increased efficiency.', means that a large number of workers will be sacked so that more profit can be made. 'Aerial targeting of subversive elements has led to a peaceful solution to the current crisis.' might mean that the rebels have all been shot so there is nothing left to fight about.

Avoid using this sort of language. Use familiar words with precise meanings and never use ten words where five will do.

Exercise

Rewrite the following in simple English:

a   All personnel are excluded from this area.
b   Vehicular access is permitted for bona fide inhabitants only.
c   Recreational facilities are not to be utilised by participants claiming state benefits.
d   The commencement of the constructional phase is subject to renegotiation.

6. The Language of Newspapers – Journalese

If you write newspaper articles you will want them to sound authentic. However, you must try to avoid the extreme form of journalese which exaggerates and overdramatises, unless, of course, a task requires you to copy this style deliberately.

There are two aspects which can usefully be considered: headlines and copy.

Headlines

An article needs an eye catching headline. Often the same first letter may be used for two or more of the words; there may be a play on words or pun; there may be an echo of a well-known phrase or saying.

When writing headlines, you do not have to write complete sentences. The smaller, less important words are often omitted. Often the words chosen are active and strong.

Here are some examples:

● council shocked by twin town tragedy;
● trivia teams top up hospital funds;
● frock horrors;
● Hope and Gloria;
● back him or sack him;
● dyslexia lad joins Mensa genius club.

Copy

When you are writing the article itself, you need to make it sound right. The best way of making sure that you do this is to read examples drawn from real newspapers. Here are a few tips.

First, mention the names of people involved, possibly their age, and if the article is for a local paper mention the area in which they live. For example:

> Amongst others involved was Brian King, 43, from the South Fields area of the city.
>
> The marathon was won by Jenny Redman, 27, who lives in Oakfield Drive.

Second, quote statements from participants, experts or witnesses. For example:

> Fred Haines, a local resident, said, 'It's a disgrace. The situation must be improved before any more lives are lost.'
>
> David Lyall, the Secretary for Heritage Conservation, said, 'We must fight to save this fine building.'

Third, use a lively tone so that the reader's interest is aroused. For example:

> Officials fear that materials are being over-extracted from local land to meet Government road-building targets.

The word 'fear' makes the situation sound serious; 'local' makes it sound relevant.

> The Tories suffered a devastating double blow yesterday.

The language here is dramatic – 'suffered' suggests severe pain. 'Devastating double blow' sounds like a physical fight rather than an election reverse. This sentence is an example of over-dramatisation or journalese.

Avoiding Journalese

You should avoid making a news item sound more sensational and dramatic than can be reasonably justified. To paraphrase an insurance advertisement, 'don't turn a drama into a crisis'. Avoid adding emotive words to create excitement. For example:

'Tragic tot Alan, three, was the only witness as his blonde mother was stabbed by a sex fiend. And his dad, Alex Hesham, fears for the boy's safety while the merciless killer is still on the loose.'

The piece starts with two words beginning with 't', 'tragic' and 'tot'. Can the child be described legitimately as 'tragic'? Look at the choice of the word 'tot' – it has lots of emotional overtones – the picture is of someone small, helpless and vulnerable. Why mention that the mother was 'blonde'? Describing the murderer as a 'sex fiend' adds extra drama. There is an avid, almost breathless tone created by starting the second sentence with 'And'. This time the killer is described as 'merciless' and 'on the loose'.

Exercise

Think of headlines for articles about:

a   an accident at a carnival;

    b   a pensioner winning a million pounds;

    c   a dangerous prisoner escaping from custody;

    d   the marriage of a pop star.

    e   Write the first 50 or so words of an article about a new firm starting in your area. The firm will create five hundred new jobs. Include at least one quoted statement from someone who knows the details.

    f   Rewrite the example of journalese about the 'tragic tot' in a less dramatic style.

7. Advertising

Advertisers tend to use romantic and poetic language to describe products which are anything but that. It may seem extraordinary today that an advertisement could describe a cigarette as 'cool as a mountain stream', but that is the sort of phrase which has been used in the past.

The effect of this is to devalue language. A word which conveys unimagined ecstasy may be applied to a furniture polish or shower gel. Here are some of the advertisers' favourites:

wonder; magic; cool; tingling; new; exciting; fantastic; delicious; tempting; fragrance.

The intention is to make a product sound irresistible by appealing to the imagination of the prospective buyer.

If you are not writing advertisements, you should not misapply language like this. It is not acceptable in descriptive or narrative writing to say that something is 'fantastic' unless you mean extraordinary, belonging to fantasy; only use the term 'magic' when referring to the effects produced by magicians or by magic spells. Use such words in their correct context.

Exercise

Find six to eight examples of 'romantic' language in current advertisements.

Think of an ordinary everyday way of describing each product and put it into the slogan. Your words probably wouldn't sell the goods but they are likely to be a lot more truthful. For example, 'Win a dream cottage' might be changed to read 'Win a small mock-Elizabethan cottage whose owners can't find a buyer'. 'Outspan – best under the sun!' could be rewritten as 'Outspan – pleasant grapefruit grown in the same climate as any other'.

Remember, then, whenever you are planning a piece of work, either for a spoken or a written assessment, choose your words carefully, remembering the following:

- What the communication is about.
- Who you are communicating with.
- What you are trying to achieve in this particular case.

If you do this every time, you can't go far wrong.

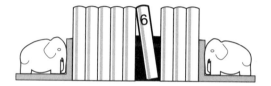

UNIT *Layout and Presentation*

In this unit you will be looking at various aspects of layout and presentation. First of all there is some general advice. Later there is information about how to set out particular sorts of writing. This is what the unit contains:

1 presentation of written work;
2 plays;
3 letters;
4 reports;
5 memos;
6 newspaper or magazine articles.

If you are looking for information on a particular sort of layout, turn to that section straight away.

1. Presentation of Written Work

Presentation is an important aspect of your written work, whether it is coursework or a question in the examination. Your work should be set out neatly and appropriately and your handwriting should be legible.

If you have untidy handwriting or if it is difficult to read, you will have to try to improve it during the course.

Coursework

If what you are writing may be included in your folder, you will have the opportunity to write more than one draft. Leave a margin at the left hand side of your paper. Your final draft should be neat and clear with no crossings out.

Should it have a Specific Layout?

You must decide, whatever the work is, whether it should be set out in a particular way. The correct layout of specific types of writing will be dealt with later in this unit.

What Headings Should be Used?

You should put the appropriate headings at the top. These are likely to be your name, the date on which the piece was completed and a title. Your centre may have a special front sheet for coursework where such details would be recorded. Use this if necessary.

Should it be Handwritten or Typed?

Syllabuses have rules about how much of a candidate's coursework may be typed. Normally it is about thirty per cent. If you are going to present some typed work, it is best to choose pieces which are particularly well suited for this type of presentation, for example, magazine articles or leaflets.

The presentation of your work will be assessed specifically so it is worth setting yourself a high standard. Think about this aspect of your work and take time over getting it right.

Examination

In the examination you are restricted by time. Probably you will only be able to write a single draft of a piece of work. You must therefore think about layout and presentation before you start to write. You must notice if you are being asked for a letter or a report so you can set it out correctly. You must try to write clearly and neatly from the beginning.

How Should you Make Corrections?

When you read your work through, if you notice mistakes in single words, you should draw a single neat line through those which are incorrect and write the new version above. If you need to cross out a longer section, rule a diagonal line neatly through it. Examination candidates are not normally permitted to use correcting fluid (because very often mistakes are painted out but then the new version is not written in). Examining boards often ask you to write in black ink.

2. Plays

In quite a lot of tasks you are either asked to write a short scene from a play or have the option of doing this rather than writing a conversation where direct speech must be punctuated using inverted commas.

How to Set Out a Play Scene

The characters' names should be written down the left-hand side of the page, possibly in the margin. You may wish to use block capitals. You should put a colon (:) after the name and before the speech. The speech starts with a capital letter. Normal punctuation rules apply in the speech. For example:

FRED: Are you going to the party?
BILL: Perhaps.

Descriptions of the setting, characters and actions have to be written so that they are clearly different or divided off from the speeches. You can use a different style of writing, italic for example, or a different colour of ink (for coursework). Alternatively you can separate this kind of material from the rest by using distinctive brackets, for example, square ones. You should use the present tense when writing this part. For example:

[*The scene is a crowded smoky public house, early on a Saturday evening. Fred and Bill are talking. Fred is a tall, lean man in his mid-twenties. Bill is older, possibly forty; he looks tired and ill at ease.*]

Fred: Are you going to the party?

Bill: Perhaps. [*He signals to the barman.*] Another pint in there, please.

Barman: [*wiping up some spilt beer*] Right away, sir.

The main mistake made by students when writing a play scene is to forget to put in all the punctuation which is necessary. In conversations where a few short statements are exchanged, normal punctuation **must** be included. Every line should end with a punctuation mark. You must decide which is appropriate.

John: Kate?

Kate: Yeah.

John: Em . . .

Kate: What?

John: Oh . . .

Kate: Look -

John: This is hopeless!

Kate: Are you kidding?

John: See you.

Kate: Okay.

Exercise

Punctuate the following extract:

Shop Assistant: Good afternoon. Can I help you

Customer: I am extremely angry about this clock which I bought on Monday

Shop Assistant: May I look at it

Customer: Here

Shop Assistant: But this seems to be working, sir

Customer: No it isn't

Shop Assistant: I'm sorry, but

Customer: Are you trying to tell me I'm wrong

Shop Assistant: Not at all, sir, it's just that

Customer: [*dropping the clock on the floor*] And I suppose you still think it's working

Shop Assistant: Not now, sir

Customer: Well then, I want a refund

Shop Assistant: Excuse me. I must find the manager

3. Letters

There are many different correct styles of setting out a letter. If you want to know all the variations, look at a textbook designed for business students. Here you are going to look at the traditional style and one other.

If you have been taught a different way, consult your tutor about its acceptability.

If you wish to check the layout of a particular type of letter, here is a list of what is covered:

a   informal letters;
b   formal letter from one person to another;
c   letters from a firm to a person (using headed paper);
d   letters from a person to a firm;
e   letters to a newspaper;
f   circular letters.

A. Informal Letters (Traditional Layout)

Here you are writing to a friend or relative. You are using an informal style so you only need the minimum in the way of headings. All letters must have at least this much. Here there is the sender's address, the date, the salutation or greeting ('Dear Jill') and a closing phrase, in this case 'With love'. The main body of the letter starts under the comma after the salutation. Notice the punctuation in the address. 'Hertfordshire' as the last line ends with a full stop. The post code never contains punctuation.

> 'The Cottage',
> 14 Mayfield Road,
> St Albans,
> Hertfordshire.
> AL2 5PG

12th April 1994

Dear Jill,
>> You'll be pleased to know that I passed my driving test . . .
>> With love,

Jack

B. Formal Letter from One Person to Another

This time the name and address of the person to receive the letter (recipient) is included also. As she is addressed as 'Dear Madam', the close is 'Yours faithfully,'. This would also be so with 'Dear Sir' or 'Dear Sirs'. Only if you start with 'Sir' or 'Madam' do you end 'Yours faithfully' – remember this!

'The Cottage',
14 Mayfield Road,
St Albans,
Herts.
AL2 5PG

Miss J. Bennett,
[this could be Ms or Mrs]
24 Hillside Close,
Harpenden,
Herts.
AL5 6TD

12th April 1994

Dear Madam,

Thank you for your letter of 9 April enquiring about . . .
Yours faithfully,

J. Spratt

This time, I did not start under the comma but left a line and started at the left margin. This is an acceptable alternative, particularly if the letter is typed.

Leave a space for the signature between the close and the name. A printed version of the name should be included so that it can be read – some signatures are totally illegible. In the case above, a reply would be sent to Mr J. Spratt. If the writer was Ms, Miss or Mrs, this would have to be stated in brackets after the name.

It would be acceptable to set the addresses out FULLY BLOCKED (i.e. with everything starting on the left) instead.

'The Cottage',
14 Mayfield Road,
St Albans,
Herts.
AL2 5PG

Mr J. Bennett,
24 Hillside Close,
Harpenden,
Herts.
AL5 6TD

12th April 1994

Dear Sir,

In this style everything starts at the left-hand margin. It is especially useful and easy if you are typing the letter.

If you are typing the letter it is also acceptable to leave out all the punctuation **except in the body of the letter** – i.e. in the addresses, the salutation and the close:

> The Cottage
> 14 Mayfield Road
> St Albans
> Herts
> AL2 5PG
>
> Mr J. Bennett
> 24 Hillside Close
> Harpenden
> Herts
> AL5 6TD
>
> 12th April 1994
>
> Dear Sir
>
> Thank you for your interest in . . .
>
> Yours faithfully
>
> J. Spratt

This is called 'open punctuation'. You must be consistent, though, putting it all in or leaving it all out.

If the name of the person to receive the letter (recipient) is used in the 'Dear. . . .', use sincerely in the close – like this:

'The Cottage',
14 Mayfield Road,
St. Albans,
Herts.
AL2 5PG

Mr J. Bennett,
24 Hillside Close,
Harpenden,
Herts.
AL5 6TD

12th April 1994

Dear Mr Bennett,

I am writing to you about. . .

Yours sincerely,

John Spratt

C. *Formal Letter from a Firm to a Person*

When a letter is written from a firm it is generally written on paper with the firm's address printed as a letter head. Find examples of this from your own mail. This printed stationery means that time does not have to be wasted in typing out the firm's name and address every time a letter is sent. Everything below the letterhead is exactly the same as in the previous type of letter except that the writer's status is mentioned below the name at the end. Here is an example:

British Bulldogs, PLC
40–43 Drummond Way, Homerton, Newshire,
Tel 0956 73415
Fax 0956 34211

Our ref:
Your ref:

18 May 1994

Mr J. Bennett
24 Hillside Close
Harpenden
Herts
AL5 6TD

Dear Sir

Thank you for your interest in . . .

Yours faithfully

R Barker
Marketing Manager

Sometimes a pictorial symbol is also used in the letter head. This is called a logo. Find examples from banks, water companies and so on.

D. Formal Letter to a Firm

If you are writing to a firm, this is exactly the same as writing a formal letter to a person. **Do not** put your name at the top above your address. Your name will be at the end. When you put in the address it's going to, include more detail if you have it. Look at the example which follows:

'The Cottage',
14 Mayfield Road,
St Albans,
Herts.
AL2 5PG

12th April 1994

Mr R. Walters,
Managing Director,
B. D. Products plc,
Top Way,
Bolton.
Greater Manchester.
BL4 6SD

Notice that the recipient's name is given, plus his position – Managing Director – followed by the company name and address. If you did not know the name of the person you would try to indicate the position or department – for example, The Personnel Manager, The Complaints Department, The Canteen Manager.

If you know the name you must decide whether you know the person sufficiently well to use it in the salutation, in which case you'll close 'Yours sincerely' or whether to be very formal, using 'Dear Sir (where you'd close 'Yours faithfully').

E. *Formal Letter to a Newspaper*

Use your own name and address as usual. This is the normal way of writing the recipient's name and address.

'The Cottage',
14 Mayfield Road,
St. Albans,
Herts.
AL2 5PG

The Editor,
The Staffordshire Herald,
Unit 7,
Industrial Park,
Stafford.
SF2 9ZX

12th April 1994

Dear Sir,

It has come to my attention that . . .
Yours faithfully,

F. Circular Letters

If a letter is going to many people rather than just to one, you can't include the recipient's address. You may wish to be less specific about the date – 'date as postmark' is sometimes seen. It may be written on stationery with a letter head or have an individual's address at the top.

MOOR LANE SOCIAL CLUB
115–117 Moor Lane, Chessingworth, Bucks. CS5 1YT.
Tel. 0834 765487

January 1993

Dear Members,

We are arranging a day out to . . .

Yours sincerely

Douglas Yellowlees
Social Secretary

This letter does not begin with 'Sir' or Madam', therefore it will close with 'Yours sincerely', not 'Yours faithfully'.

Exercise

a   You are writing to an aunt to thank her for a birthday present. What headings would you use? How might you sign off?

b   You are writing to an acquaintance who is the Purchasing Manager at Auto Electric, a company selling spare parts for cars. You hope to be able to get a temporary job with the firm. Write everything necessary up to the **end of the first sentence** in the body of the letter. Then write the close.

c   Your acquaintance passes your letter to the Personnel Department, who writes back to you. Write everything up to the **end of the first sentence** in the body of the letter. Then write the close.

d   Write the headings and the close of a letter to your local newspaper.

e   Write the headings and close for a circular letter written to everyone in your area about a Neighbourhood Watch scheme.

4. Reports

A formal report has certain standard sections. There is a very formal version which you probably do not need to use. This is really only required for a Business Communication course. Information about that can be found in a textbook written for that purpose. The layout and structure advised here is a simplified version.

1   Put a heading showing what the report is about, for example, 'A Report on the Staff Canteen at ABC Electronics'.

2   If it is for a particular person or purpose, state that next, for example: requested by the social committee so that standards can be improved.

3   State how you obtained the information e.g.- I personally have used the canteen daily for five years. I drew up a questionnaire which was filled in by all staff.

4   Information (the facts you have found): use sub-headings and number paragraphs for clarity. **Do not put opinions here**. For example do say that lunch is served from 12.30 to 1.00 p.m. as this is factual information. Do not say that this is an inadequate amount of time – this is an opinion.

   This will probably be the longest section. It may be acceptable to present some information as tables, graphs, etc.

5   Conclusions: what can you find out from these facts? For example, you might find that the canteen does not have sufficient staff or that the room itself is too small. Here you will present opinions **deduced from the facts** in (**4**). Here you will say that the serving period is too short.

   Use the same sub-headings and numbers as in (**4**).

6   Recommendations: if you are asked to say **what should be done**, i.e. what action should be taken, put that here; for example, that more staff should be employed; that an extension should be built. You will recommend that serving begins at 12.15 instead of 12.30 as this is **what should be done.**

   Again use the same sub-headings and numbers.

7   Finally, put your signature and the date. Do not put a 'close' like 'Yours faithfully'. This is not a letter.

5. Memos

A memo (short for 'memorandum') is a communication between people using an internal mail system. Probably, therefore, they work for the same organisation. A firm will have a standard version printed for use by the staff, possibly with the company logo at the top.

ABC
MEMORANDUM

To:
From:
Date:
Subject:

You do not need to put in any addresses. You do not need to sign it. All that information is presented at the beginning. Often A5 paper is used as the intention is quite often to present the necessary information as concisely as possible. Smaller paper encourages this.

6. Newspaper or Magazine Articles

To a certain extent the layout will vary according to the precise nature of the task you are working on.

It is not necessary to write in columns. Students who try to do this often put so few words in the line that the piece becomes very hard to follow.

Here is some advice on what you should do:

1   Use a catchy, large headline. You will find more about this in Chapter 5, Units 1 and 3 and also in Unit 5 of this chapter.
2   Follow this headline with your name – CATCHY HEADLINE by Celia Waters.
3   If appropriate, use sub-headings during your article.
4   If you are using illustrations, plan carefully where they should go and leave sufficient space. If your picture is in the middle, do not split the text so that it continues after a gap. This is very hard to read. In this case you might need to move the picture to one side and have a narrow column beside it.
5   Word processing or typing this sort of writing is often a good idea.

Remember – whether in coursework or the exam, decide about the appropriate layout **before** you start work. Every piece should be neatly written and easy to read.

Appendices

Appendix One: Index to Coursework and Tasks

Number of Activity	Date(s)	Title/Type of Activity Give source texts for written work and audience and whether Group, Pair or Individual for Oral work.	ATs covered

Number of Activity	Date(s)	Title/Type of Activity Give source texts for written work and audience and whether Group, Pair or Individual for Oral work.	ATs covered

Appendix Two: Coursework Checklist

Put a tick beside the Attainment Target (AT) which applies. If an activity is described as covering En 1, all four aspects have been covered so tick each of them.

En 1: SPEAKING AND LISTENING

1 Conveying and Understanding Information

☐ ☐ ☐ ☐ ☐ ☐ ☐ ☐ ☐ ☐

2 Expressing and Responding to Ideas and Feelings

☐ ☐ ☐ ☐ ☐ ☐ ☐ ☐ ☐ ☐

3 Group Discussion and Performance

☐ ☐ ☐ ☐ ☐ ☐ ☐ ☐ ☐ ☐

4 Knowledge about Language

☐ ☐ ☐ ☐ ☐ ☐ ☐ ☐ ☐ ☐

ASSESSMENT MADE:

Individual ☐ ☐ ☐ ☐ ☐ ☐ ☐

Pair ☐ ☐ ☐ ☐ ☐ ☐ ☐

Group ☐ ☐ ☐ ☐ ☐ ☐ ☐

En 2: READING

1 Response to Literature

☐ ☐ ☐ ☐ ☐ ☐ ☐ ☐ ☐ ☐

whole work by Shakespeare

☐ ☐ ☐ ☐ ☐ ☐ ☐ ☐ ☐ ☐

pre-twentieth century literature

☐ ☐ ☐ ☐ ☐ ☐ ☐ ☐ ☐ ☐

2 Response to Non-Literary and Media Texts

☐ ☐ ☐ ☐ ☐ ☐ ☐ ☐ ☐ ☐

3 Research and Information Retrieval

☐ ☐ ☐ ☐ ☐ ☐ ☐ ☐ ☐ ☐

4 Knowledge about Language

☐ ☐ ☐ ☐ ☐ ☐ ☐ ☐ ☐ ☐

En 3: WRITING

1   Production and Variety of Writing

☐ ☐ ☐ ☐ ☐ ☐ ☐ ☐ ☐ ☐

2   Style

☐ ☐ ☐ ☐ ☐ ☐ ☐ ☐ ☐ ☐

3   Drafting and Revising

☐ ☐ ☐ ☐ ☐ ☐ ☐ ☐ ☐ ☐

4   Knowledge about Language

☐ ☐ ☐ ☐ ☐ ☐ ☐ ☐ ☐ ☐

5   Spelling and Presentation

☐ ☐ ☐ ☐ ☐ ☐ ☐ ☐ ☐ ☐

Appendix Three: Activity List

COURSEWORK

The following activities give you the opportunity to produce coursework. Check the exact requirements for your folder with your tutor. Most syllabuses ask you to select your four or five best pieces.

Please note, coursework may require that you do earlier preparatory activities in that unit. Look carefully in the unit to see what is necessary for each activity listed there.

Speaking and Listening: En 1

Chapter	Unit/ Activity	Page	Description of Activity	ATs Covered
1	1e	10	describing a person (group)	1, 4
1	2d	15	describing a room (pair)	1, 2
1	3e	26	reading aloud or improvising (individual)	all
1	4e	32	presenting information about Christmas (individual)	1, 2
1	5e	39	finding out about dialect (individual)	1, 4
1	6g	47	talking about a place (individual)	1, 2, 4
2	1c	54	talking about an embarrassing incident (individual)	1, 2, 3
2	2c	62	discussing a family situation (group)	1, 2, 3
2	3e	77	reading aloud (individual)	2, 3
2	4d	84	reading or improvising a scene (group)	2, 3
2	5c	94	telling a traditional tale (individual)	all
3	1c	107	discussion of a story (group)	all
3	2b	114	reading and discussion of a poem (individual/group)	all
3	2d	116	discussion of material about love (group)	all
3	2e	118	discussion of a story (group)	all
3	3c	127	oral book review (individual)	all
3	3e	129	oral film review (individual)	all
3	4b	140	discussion of war poems (group)	all
3	5b	152	discussion of poems about childhood (group)	all
4	1d	160	giving directions (pair)	1, 4
4	2b	168	discussion of letters (group)	2, 3, 4
4	2d	169	simulating a telephone call (individual)	1, 4
4	3b	178	simulating a telephone call (individual/pair)	1, 4
4	3g	185	discussion about job interview and role play (group or pair)	1, 3, 4
4	4b	189	recording a timetable (individual)	1, 4
4	4g	194	interviewing an expert (individual/pair)	1, 2, 4
4	5b	197	discussion of consumer rights (group)	all
4	5e	200	role play of complaint (pair)	all
5	1c	208	discussion of newspaper contents (group)	all

5	1e	211	discussion of newspaper front pages (group)	all
5	1g	214	reading and discussion of newspaper article (individual or group)	all
5	2b	218	collecting information then discussion (individual or group)	all
5	3(Part 1)d	237	role play of a meeting (individual/group)	all
5	3(Part 2)c	238	presenting an argument (individual)	1, 2, 4
5	4c	244	discussion of case studies (pair)	1,2
5	4f	247	presentation of information/discussion (individual or group)	all
5	5(Part 1)b	252	role play of meeting (individual/group)	all
5	5(Part 2)c	255	presenting an argument (individual)	all

Reading – Response to Literature: En 2.1

Chapter	Unit/ Activity	Page	Works Studied
1	4h	33	*A Christmas Carol* – Charles Dickens, pre-twentieth century
2	2f	66	*Romeo and Juliet* – Shakespeare pre-twentieth century
2	5d	95	'Tam Lin' – traditional, pre-twentieth century
3	1d	107	'Insert Knob A into Hole B' – Asimov
3	2c	115	Four sonnets – Shakespeare pre-twentieth century
3	2d	116	'Love is...' – Adrian Henri
3	2e	118	'Eveline' – James Joyce
3	3b	125	own choice for review
3	4c	141	several poems from the First World War
3	5c	152	several poems about babies/childhood, some pre-twentieth century
4	2j	174	'Our Day Out' – Willy Russell
5	2h	225	'The Ram' – Selima Hill
5	2i, j	227, 228	*Jane Eyre* – Charlotte Bronte, pre-twentieth century

Reading – Non-Literary/Media Texts: En 2.2

Chapter	Unit/ Activity	Page	Description of Activity
3	3d	128	film review (own choice)
3	3f	129	TV programme review (own choice)
3	3g	129	writing about soap operas
3	4d	142	writing about the First World War as seen in *Blackadder*
5	1c, e, g	208, 211, 214	oral assessments on newspapers
5	1h, i	215	written assessments on newspapers
5	2f	224	writing about *Thelma and Louise*

5	3(Part 1)e*	234	information and letters about Denholm House
5	3(Part 2)d*	238	information and letter about war in Croatia
5	4c, d	244, 245	oral assessment and writing about case studies
5	5(Part 1)c*	252	information about Piggotts Wood
5	5(Part 2)c*	256	oral assessment and writing about whale hunting

Activities marked * can be done either as coursework **or** for examination practice.

Reading – Research and Information Retrieval: En 2.3

Chapter	Unit/ Activity	Page	Description of Activity
1	4a, b	28, 29	finding out about the origins of festivals
1	6e, e, f	46	finding out about far away places
2	2d	63	finding out about love
2	5e	99	finding out about traditional stories
3	4e	143	finding out more about the First World War
4	2c	168	planning a day out
4	4f, h	193, 194	finding material for a factual article
4	5a, b, i	196, 197, 204	reading about consumer rights
5	1a	207	finding out about British newspapers
5	2k	229	finding out about women's roles
5	4e	246	finding out about marriage
5	5d	257	finding out about an environmental issue

Writing: En 3

Chap	Unit/ Activity	Page	Description of Activity
1	1d	8	describing people
1	2b, e	14, 16	describing a room
1	3c	24	describing a place in summer and in winter
1	4b	29	writing a magazine article about a festival
1	4f	32	describing a wedding
1	5c	37	describing a crowd scene
1	5g	40	describing a 'science fiction' crowd
1	6f	46	writing a travel article for a women's magazine
2	1e	56	writing a story
2	1f	57	writing a story given the opening paragraphs
2	2d	63	writing a story in letters
2	2e	65	writing a story inspired by a letter
2	3d	76	writing a mystery story
2	4b	81	writing a story as a play and vice versa
2	4c	84	writing a scene in a play
2	4e	85	writing a scene exploring a controversial issue

2	5b	93	writing a traditional story
2	5d	95	writing in response to a traditional ballad
3	1d	107	writing in response to a short story
3	2c	115	work in response to Shakespeare sonnets
3	2d, e, f	128, 129	work in response to literature about love
3	3b	125	book review
3	4c	141	work in response to poems about the First World War
3	5c	152	work in response to poems about babies or childhood
4	1f	163	writing a guide to a hobby or activity
4	2e–i	170–4	writing letters and a report about a day trip
4	3c–f	189–94	applying for a job
4	4h	194	writing an article using material researched
4	5f, g	201, 202	letters of complaint
4	5h	202	report on shops
5	1h, i	215	writing about and for newspapers
5	2f	224	work on *Thelma and Louise*
5	2h	225	work in response to 'The Ram', Selima Hill
5	2i, j	227, 228	work in response to *Jane Eyre*, Charlotte Bronte
5	3(Part 1)e*	234	writing about Denholm House
5	3(Part 2)d	238	writing about Radica's dilemma
5	3e	239	writing about a worthwhile cause
5	4d*	245	writing letters in response to a case study
5	4g	247	writing about what makes a marriage successful
5	4h	248	writing about finding a partner
5	5(Part 1)c	252	writing about a threatened stretch of woodland
5	5(Part 2)c	256	writing about whale hunting
5	5(Part 2)d	257	writing about an environmental issue

Activities marked * can be done either as coursework **or** for examination practice.

Knowledge about Language: En 1, En 2, En 3

Chapter	Unit/ Activity	Page	Description of Activity	ATs covered
1	5e	39	study of dialect words	En 1
1	5f	40	study of place names/etymology	En 2
2	3c	73	analysis of techniques used to build suspense	En 2
2	4a	78	study of language used in play scripts	En 2
2	5 all*	90	study of language used in traditional tales	all
3	1b, c	104, 107	study of techniques used in a short story	En 2
3	2a, b	111–115	study of the language of a Shakespeare sonnet	En 2
4	3a	176	study of job adverts	En 2
4	3g	185	discussion of job interviews	En 1
5	1 all*	207–215	study of newspapers	all

Activities marked * would be suitable for the 'language based unit' required for the LEAG syllabuses.

Examination Practice

The following activities are similar to those you are likely to meet in the written examination at the end of the course. You will find it useful to practise these, particularly once you have completed your coursework.

Chapter	Unit/ Activity	Page	Description of Activity	Recommended time
1	2f	17	reading and response	unlimited
1	3d	24	reading and response	one hour 30 mins
1	4c	30	reading and response	one hour 30 mins
1	5d	38	reading and response	one hour 30 mins
2	3c	73	reading and analysis	unlimited
2	4a	78	reading and analysis	unlimited
4	5e	200	writing instructions	one hour
5	2c	219	writing an article or dialogue	one hour
5	2e	221	reading, understanding and response	one hour 30 mins
5	3(Part 1)e	234	writing a letter and article	one hour
5	3(Part 2)a	236	reading and understanding	45 minutes
5	3(Part 1)e	239	writing a report and a letter	one hour
5	4a	242	reading and understanding	45 minutes
5	4d	245	letter writing from material read	one hour
5	5(Part 2)c	256	writing a letter and article	one hour